Mrs. Myers

Act II

Mrs. Myers

Act II

Jeannette Murray

Rev. date: 03/15/2019

To order additional copies of this book, contact:
Xlibris
1-888-795-4274
www.Xlibris.com
Orders@Xlibris.com
792009

Dedication

To all who bravely step out of their comfort
zone to defy oppression, refuse to settle, and dare to
rewrite the script of their lives, and all who
contemplate doing such, this book is for you.

Chapter 1

The Adirondack Mountains moved closer as the car sped past an ever-changing diorama of freshly budding trees and amber fields, setting the stage for the blue foothills and violet mountains that lay ahead. The Northway was busy today, but when wasn't it? The weather was sunny and chillier than usual for late spring; but, all in all, it was a perfect day for a getaway.

So far nothing had stood in her way. Nothing except her husband who tried, but failed, to force her to stay and admit her folly. Lydia thought about the events of the past weeks. At times her emotions sent signals to her right foot that made her stomp on the accelerator, making the car leap ahead. She switched to cruise control to avoid the ever-vigilant officers of the law lying in wait for hapless daydreamers like her whose minds were on other things than their driving.

This wasn't a vacation or weekend sojourn to the mountains. She wasn't on a lark or pretending to be free as she used to when the kids went to school and she took a short drive after grocery shopping. It was a real getaway. All the way up I-87, along the Hudson River, past Albany and Saratoga Springs, she thought about the times she'd made this trip with her family, each one marked by excitement and anticipation of happy times at Lake George. This time would be no exception. There'd be happy times, yet it would be different in every other way. There'd be no children with her, and no husband, thankfully. Just her. She'd be completely on her own with no plan to return. Her one and only plan was to escape and it was

1

underway. Her next plan would be to work on her divorce. The idea sent shivers up and down her spine. The thought struck her as funny. *Work on a divorce?* How much work could there be? And who would be supervising, or, at best, advising her? Her attorney, of course, but where were all the divorced people she knew who could be giving her some pointers? Teaching her the steps? She wondered why someone hadn't put together a manual or something like a cookbook. *How to make a proper divorce. First, start with...*

The thought of divorcing should have made her depressed. Her divorced friends all had been, at least at the beginning. Why, then, was she drumming the steering wheel and singing, *"I'm free, I-I'm free-ee,"* at the top of her lungs?

Was it because of what she left behind in New York City? A fetid pile of rotting hopes and disillusionments? She wasn't simply driving away from her home and spouse, she was leaving behind something that no longer held any worth to her, no longer had a reason for existing. Of course, in her mother's eyes, in Mary Anne O'Connor's Catholic Guide to Ruining Your Life, one did not divorce. One did not break the covenant of marriage. You stayed married no matter how broken or toxic or depressing it was. *Well, ma, I got news for you,* she thought. *Your son-in-law not only broke the covenant but pissed all over it when he fucked his mistress.* Naturally, she would never utter such words. They'd give Mary Anne O'Connor a stroke. But, it was delightful thinking them.

The whole thought of being free of Jack was exhilarating. She gave her shoulder length russet hair a shake as she pounded out another beat on the steering wheel recalling the words of an old favorite sung by Linda Ronstadt. She saw her live at the Saratoga Performing Arts Center years ago when she was in college. The words meant nothing at the time. They were just lyrics that belonged to someone else whose attitude about love differed so much from hers. Now they felt like gospel and she belted them out with gusto.

All I'm sayin' is I'm not ready
for any person, place or thing
to try and pull the reins in on me.

Drivers passing by no doubt questioned the sanity of the woman behind the wheel of the Subaru Forester, her arms and head flailing in a way that suggested psychosis or some type of seizure activity was taking place. Was she having a psychotic episode? If she was, it felt great. Besides, she didn't care what anyone thought. Jack would have told her she was acting crazy again. He was always trying to get her to believe it, concerned and supportive as he always was. He even tried to get her to see a shrink to put a label on it and prove, once and for all, his wife had a screw loose. Why else would a wife act depressed while her husband was working so hard to support her and cheating rampantly on her the entire time?

Sure, she was probably having some kind of episode, and it felt good. She felt high, intoxicated, out of control and having the time of her life. The echoes of her husband's voice tried to drown out the music, but she refused to listen. A new song came into her head. This one by Janis Joplin.

Take another little piece of my heart now, baby.

Oh, she could relate to this one, too. Jack took quite a sizeable chunk of hers, ripped it out and ran roughshod over it. But he didn't manage to break it. She would have had to care too much for that to happen. Forget about him, just for now, she reminded herself. There'll be plenty of time in the days to come to deal with all the accusations, protestations and contestations the divorce proceeding promised to bring.

Right now there were better things to think about. The scenery, for one, was compelling. Hills, valleys, expanses of forest, cobalt blue waters, and early spring blossoms screaming for attention. It seemed spring was desperately trying to liberate the landscape from the ravages of a long, hard New York winter. Lydia felt sorry for those who never got out of the city—the big tarnished apple that had so many blemishes and bruises on its skin. They were missing so much. Upstate was where the state strutted its best stuff, its peacock feathers, at least in her opinion.

She zoomed past the historic landmarks, thinking she should stop but not wanting to take the time. The Catskill Mountains, Olana—home of one of her favorite American artists, Frederic Edwin Church. Sleepy Hollow and Woodstock, where she once pretended to be the prototypical hippy flower child in her peasant blouse, broomstick skirt and love beads. It was where she learned the slogan "make love, not war," only to find out later it was just an excuse for hedonistic spoiled rich kids to indulge themselves when they were away from their parents.

Still, it had a big impact on her life. Smoking pot with friends, drinking Night Train because it was the only wine they could afford, disgusting as it was, and spending hard-earned money on concert tickets and clothes she could never wear at home. It all made sense back then. Life revolved around friends, weed, dating, music, and when there was time, college and homework.

She cruised by the capitol city of Albany and glanced over at the spectacular Delaware and Hudson Railroad Building with its eight-foot weathervane replica of Henry Hudson's ship, the Half Moon. The kids used to have a game of seeing who could spot the ship first.

Trailing the scenic Hudson River, she passed by its picturesque banks bordered with trees and hedges and three-story homes with boat landings, followed by gnarled and blackened railroad tracks and ruins of abandoned brick buildings. Along the way were signs for Troy, where her mother had been born and lived until she met Liam O'Connor and he moved the family consisting of her, her brother Tom and her sister Theresa, and the family cat to Poughkeepsie. Troy, her mother told her, was once known as the "collar city" because it was where Arrow shirts were made in the Cluett-Peabody factory. Some of her relatives had worked there. As a child, Lydia thought the name was elegantly impressive, like a name in a fairy tale book. She imagined it a castle with gilded staircases where all the happy workers wore starched white lab coats and sang as they stitched collars on broadcloth shirts.

After Troy came Saratoga Springs—a place rife with memories where she'd spent many a lovely evening under the stars on the lawn of the Saratoga Performing Arts Center, indulging in wine drunk straight from the bottle as she and her friends passed around a joint. Her tension began to melt away as she let her shoulders droop and her hands loosen their grip on the steering wheel. She was glad of these memories, even as she thought she wouldn't want her children to follow in her footsteps, at least where the pot and alcohol were concerned, knowing full well they would.

She'd made it through youth relatively unscathed. They would, too.

After several minutes of dipping into the Elysian pools of nostalgia, she reminded herself this was not a trip down memory lane. She was leaving her home, her city life, her friends and social contacts to live alone in a cabin on Lake George. She was going to a private, serene sanctuary where she'd have time to sort things out and find her way out of the forest of marital entanglement and back to the land of singlehood—a place she hadn't visited for twenty-two years. It was not a rash or impulsive move on her part, regardless of what Jack thought. She knew what she was doing. There was no point in brooding and, if she could figure out how, she'd put all of that part of her past in a closet and lock it so it couldn't come out and invade her mind. As much as she tried, though, she couldn't even force the door shut, let alone lock it. It kept opening of its own accord, perhaps because it was overflowing with memories, some of which were precious to her. Some of which were nightmares.

Jack said she was being selfish, irrational and irresponsible, as always. She'd just returned from a month in Paris and was already taking off again, escaping reality. She was incorrigible. Spoiled. As for the divorce, she didn't have a leg to stand on. She stood to lose everything, including her children. She had to laugh at that one. She reminded him they weren't going to be fighting for custody of their nineteen and twenty-one year old kids, but if he really wanted to press the case, she'd allow him full parental rights as long as she had visitation. Life would go on just as usual. They would have sided with her anyway, so it was a moot point.

Nature. Beauty. Concentrate on that, she reminded herself, taking slow, deep breaths. All around her was perfection not marred by human interference or industrial blighting. Each lovely scene melted into the next, each foothill and mountain called for her attention as she struggled to keep her eyes and her mind focused on the road.

She took a sip of the green tea sweetened with honey she'd put in her Camelbak thermos. It had a warm, soothing effect. Was she escaping? Of course she was. She had a right to. But it wasn't altogether a vacation trip. The cabin needed tending to, cleaning and probably some long overdue repairs. The shed and the rowboat and kayaks needed some attention, too. The whole place teetered on the brink of neglect and in time would fall to ruin if she didn't keep it up. Now that both kids were in college and they weren't taking family vacations with her brother, Tom, and his family, it was virtually abandoned. They would have sold it only the price for sentimentality was too high. So, there was a practical purpose to her flight. The cabin needed her care.

Though she didn't want to, she thought about the kids and what they would think when she told them the news. Victoria, who preferred to be called Tori, and Carl, who went by Leo, couldn't care less about spending their summers there anymore. In time, they might appreciate the cabin and the lake again, but right now friends, college activities and social media were all that mattered. The cell phone was their golden idol and WiFi receptivity didn't have much of a chance of survival in the lake area. Yes, she'd miss them, but right now she was glad they were there, in college, and she was here. Besides, she'd be busy preparing for their visit.

There was much to be done, most of which could all be handled via computer and phone. She planned to complete her master's program in counseling, then work on her résumé. As for what to put on it in terms of years of experience, she'd have to be creative. She read somewhere that one could stretch it if they had little or no relevant work experience. A "functional" resume, as it was called, would highlight her skills rather than career she never had. As much as she believed waitressing had been her best training in dealing with difficult people and practicing counseling skills, those jobs were in the distant past before she became a mother, a wife and a household manager. The skills she learned there were innumerable, yet she didn't think they belonged on a résumé.

Then there was the divorce. She could deal with that online and over the phone, as well. If something necessitated a trip to the city, she could be there in five hours. It was possible to do. She had to contact her attorney first. That would be the first course of action. One could initiate a divorce from a distance and many other women probably had to do it that way. Besides, it wasn't like she was overseas or in some third world country.

She wished she had stayed longer in Paris. She could have, except that the overpowering urge to come home and carry out her objective took precedence over the desire to continue enjoying the unparalleled experience of being an artist, free to paint and sketch people's portraits on the banks of the Seine. She came back early to confront her husband in person. Whether it was the wise thing to do, she couldn't say. The effect of her words were nothing short of a shot over the bow.

The look on Jack's face when she said she wanted a divorce would be forever etched in her mind. It wasn't a look of surprise, or shock, or even sadness. It was a look of pure outrage. The kind of outrage he felt when a subordinate did something incredibly stupid or bold enough to threaten his authority. The fact that she accomplished both in one brief moment was enough to convince her she needed to take immediate action. She had no choice but to get away.

Chapter 2

Paris had initially been an escape for her, a way to "find herself" as much as she found that cliché contrived and overused. It did, in fact, help to rediscover herself. She'd gone with the intention of rewriting the script of her life and she did.

She enjoyed a brief stint as a fake psychiatrist, almost four weeks as an artist, and she even did some detective work, fully disguised as a man. In the course of her time in Paris, she also found out about certain of her husband's activities that she'd intentionally overlooked. Well, to be perfectly honest, she'd denied and refused to believe, even though the proof was as evident as a dog barking in her face. She found out about at least one current affair that was in full swing and had been going on for two years. She assumed there were others, such as the brief overnighter with the woman he met in Paris—the woman she got to see up close when she took pictures of the two of them without their knowledge. There were probably several others over the course of their marriage she didn't need or want to know about.

The question at hand was, what she was going to do now? Where would her new script be now that she was back in the states and ready to resume life as a divorced woman? She'd still keep her minor role as mother of two college students and then there was her obligatory, self-imposed role of college student in pursuit of another master's degree, this time in counseling. Was she still going to continue as artist? And would she find fulfillment as a counselor, not to mention work? Would there ever be another person in her life who completely and unequivocally loved her? Someone as far on the opposite end of the narcissism spectrum as her husband? Was it possible? Probably not.

Not knowing any of the answers made her feel all the more adventurous.

Lydia looked up to see a pair of red tail hawks floating on air currents, engaged in an aerial ballet that mesmerized her and caused her to almost ram the bumper of the truck ahead. Good thing she had the brakes checked not too long before she'd left for Paris.

Jack told her she was a dreamer. She needed to wake up to reality. She agreed with him about the dreamer part. As for needing to wake up, she wasn't buying it. All she really needed to do was write Jack out of the script. If she had her way, he wouldn't have any part to play in her life, outside of his connection to their children, which, at best, was a frayed bond. As far as her children needing her, she doubted they'd appreciate her dropping by their dorm rooms and tucking them in at night. She'd be as 'in touch' with them as they'd allow her to be.

Leaving the house this morning wasn't something she ever wanted to experience again. Not that it was hard not fighting with Jack who left work to come home and talk her out of it. He never left work during the day unless it was for a business lunch, a meeting with a client, or a tryst with a woman that he could excuse as work-related. He did it solely to tell her what he thought of her running away.

He thought he could change her mind, make her feel guilty, remind her of her duties as his wife and the mother of his children. She also knew he did it because he knew he was losing control over her. That was something Jack Myers couldn't live with. Losing anything, but especially control.

Jack was good with words. She used to think he was brilliant in his artful way of manipulating and swaying people to see things his way, no matter how much it clashed with their own beliefs and values. He used it oftentimes to get the kids to take his side. He wielded this power every day in his work, which was why he was such a valued member of the law firm of Parker, Cross, Epstein, and Myers. It was only natural he'd attempt to use the same strategy with her, knowing how well it worked in the past.

The past. So strange to think of a marriage of twenty-two years as "the past." So often during their marriage she'd listened to Jack reduce people to rubble in his clever and sarcastic manner. He was a master of intellectual jousting and scathing criticism, first making a person feel small and uninformed, then breaking them down with objections that sounded reasonable, then knocking them flat to the mat only to raise them up, bloodied and spent, with words of encouragement that there was still hope they could do better. She'd been on that mat more than she cared to think.

"Lydia, be reasonable. You just got back from Paris. The cabin isn't even ready. The water and electricity aren't turned on. You don't know how to work the furnace and you probably don't even remember the alarm code," he said.

"Yes. I do. It's 109B56."

Jack hadn't been expecting her to resist. She could tell by the flushed look on his face he hadn't prepared his offense and was resorting to improvisation.

"You can't keep doing this. You have a home and children. You have responsibilities. It's not like you're some teenager having nothing to do but indulge your whims."

He was fuming and pacing as he spoke. She hadn't seen him that way in a long time. In fact, the only other time was when he'd lost a big case because of the "lame-brained judge who didn't know his ass from an affidavit." Jack had a way with insults.

"You're my wife. You took a vow. You're a Catholic, after all. Isn't marriage supposed to be sacred? You have to own up to that responsibility."

"You broke that vow. You have a mistress."

Lydia had kept on packing, knowing there was no point in arguing with a man who was always right, never sorry and unable to see his own flaws. In his mind, they didn't exist. He probably already had a completely plausible reason why he'd had a mistress for the past two years. Jack was a man who went after what he wanted and did whatever he pleased because, in his mind, he earned the right. Well, it was high time she did what she pleased. He was, after all, her best teacher.

"I've kept you up all these years. I've shared my life with you. God knows, I've paid all the bills and provided a good home. I'm paying for the kids' colleges. I haven't heard you complain about that."

He touched on the nerve she knew he would and it stung, but only for a moment. He was right. She had been supported by him and had lived very well off his income. "You're right, Jack. I am your wife and the mother of your children and you have kept us up very nicely. You've been a good provider. For that I am grateful." It irked him even more when she was calm and rational. She could see veins on his forehead that normally weren't there.

"What about Tori and Leo? How do you think this will affect them, or haven't you thought about that? Are you going to divorce them, too?"

Lydia looked him in the eyes. "Of course not, Jack. This isn't about them. They're my children and not the reason I'm leaving. I don't think they're going to be neglected either. After all, it's been quite some time since I changed their diapers and wiped their noses. You know they frown on that in college. And just so you'll know, they're coming to spend the weekend with me. I'm going to tell them then."

"Sweet. One big happy family gathering, so you can give them your side of the story and paint me as the villain."

"I certainly don't want to give them your side of it. And as for painting you as the villain, I'll let them decide for themselves how they want to feel about you."

She hadn't let him get the upper hand, although she'd been trembling inside. The thought of it made her feel free. Free of home, free of husband, and soon to be free of marriage. She wouldn't add the kids to the list because that would mean she'd be a terrible mother, but deep down she was glad to be free of them, too, for just a brief while. They hadn't missed her during their first semesters in college and now they were becoming more independent, rarely even talking to her unless they needed something. Usually money, or her intercession to get it from their dad.

She shuddered when Jack slammed his fist on the bedroom doorframe. Would he have harmed her physically? She didn't think so, but even if he did, she hadn't been afraid. He was angry enough to hurt her, but the man had restraint. Besides, he was well aware of the legal ramifications of spousal abuse. It wouldn't go over well in divorce court if he gave her a black eye or knocked her to the floor. She certainly wasn't the type to provoke an attack, although she understood why some women did. If he did attack her, she knew what to do. Being afraid and cowering would not be part of her modus operandi.

Jack had stood at the door as she tried to make her way out of the bedroom. She hadn't expected him to help with the two suitcases and the overstuffed tote she carried and he didn't. She realized she'd have to come back for other things at some future date, but for now, she had all that she needed for the summer. When the weather cooled, if she still wanted to stay and possibly winter over at the cabin, she'd have to come back for her winter clothes and more blankets. She'd get an electric blanket for those bitterly cold nights.

Perhaps it was a snide remark, but she preferred to think she was justified when her last words to her husband as she walked out were, "You can feel free to have Serena come and stay. But do tell her she has to get her own bathrobe. I packed mine." This was in reference to finding his mistress in her home, in her bathrobe and turban when she returned from Paris earlier than either of them had expected.

Jack's last words to her fell from his lips like caustic acid.

"You're making a big mistake, Lydia. You'll regret this."

Chapter 3

The afternoon sun pierced through the skylights casting golden rays on the burnished hardwood floors. Fresh picked wildflowers adorned the French country kitchen table. Mason jars with smaller bouquets decorated both end tables, the coffee table and the mantel above the fieldstone fireplace in the living room.

"Mom, the cabin looks fabulous." Tori twirled around the kitchen with her arms outstretched. "I see you've been busy putting all your little touches everywhere. I love it!"

Lydia smiled. Tori, christened Victoria Anne, her nineteen year old, rarely complimented anything she did, so it was especially gratifying to hear such praise coming from her lips.

"I'm glad you like it. I thought it would be nice to cut some wild flowers and use grandma's lace tablecloth for a change."

"It's so *Martha*, as in Martha Stewart, in case you didn't know," Tori exclaimed. "You never did aspire to be like her, I know, but you're so meticulous and perfect about everything. It's enough to piss off most normal women. Not that you're not normal, but, you know what I mean. You never miss a beat."

Now she was back to sounding like the usual Tori. The one who inherited her father's ability to couch insults inside compliments.

Lydia shrugged. She never thought of herself as an accomplished homemaker and never aspired to impress her friends with crocheted blankets, handmade doilies, flower arrangements, and perfect table settings. Picking the flowers had come naturally as she loved their fresh, simplistic beauty. Also, it was something fun and soothing to do. Once having amassed an armful, she had to do something with them.

"It's no big deal, really. Just flowers and a tablecloth." She really was pleased with her flower arrangements. It gave the cabin a cheerful look and gave the impression that it was a cared-for home.

"Just mom, doing her artistic thing easily and perfectly, as usual." Tori dropped into a Morris chair and dangled her legs over the side.

A sound of stomping and huffing at the door caught their attention.

"Don't have to worry about staying warm tonight. I got it covered." Leo walked in carrying an armload of wood and began to stack the wood in the iron wood holder next to the fireplace.

Lydia walked over and gave him a kiss on the cheek. "Thanks, honey. Maybe we can roast some marshmallows later on. I got some at the store. Graham crackers and chocolate bars, too. You used to love s'mores."

"Still do." Leo opened a bag of apples and washed one at the sink. In a twangy voice he said, "Any ideas for victuals? I'm pert near ready to gun me down a rabbit or a squirrel."

Tori raised her eyebrows. "Don't forget, mountain man, we're dining with Miss Vegan America. No flesh and blood on this table, Jethro."

Leo walked over and messed up Tori's hair. Though just a year and a couple months older, he'd liked playing the role of older brother which, in his estimation, gave him license to tease, torment and mock his little sister.

"Since when did you start eating the flesh of innocent creatures, pajama pants? I thought you went vegeterrible last Christmas after the turkducken disaster grandma tried to pass off as dinner." Leo poured himself a glass of soymilk and turned to his mother. "Hey mom, did you hear about this new drink called cow's milk? It's really good and has lots of calcium and protein in it."

"And cholesterol and hormones, not mention it's meant for baby cows, not humans." Lydia stuck her tongue out at her son. Leo turned back to Tori.

"So what's with the butch haircut and the flannel shirt? I'm not saying I don't like it, but did you decide to take a walk on the Lesbo side in your freshman year or are you hoping to pick up a lumberjack while you're here?"

"Bug off, dipwad. It's my new style."

"Oh, sorry. I missed the latest Teen Girl Magazine coverage of the ultra-grunge look. Or is it the 'don't-associate-me-with-New York-even-though-I-live-there look?'"

"Up yours, egghead. Your fly's open, by the way. Or is it customary for the mountain man to leave the barn door open?"

Lydia busied herself making a salad in the kitchen. The banter had all the potential of crossing the line and ending up in a screaming match that would leave both of her children sullen and not speaking for the duration of their stay. She'd been the referee throughout many of their skirmishes and knew just how much each could take before the explosion occurred. She had her plan of intervention already in place.

"Cookies, anyone?" She went to Tori first with the plate of freshly baked chocolate chip cookies. Tori wrinkled her nose, hesitated, and gingerly picked up one cookie.

"Oh my god, you *have* gone Martha!" She was ever on the patrol for excess calories that threatened to push her weight up to normal limits. She bit into the cookie. "Wrong. You've outdone her. Shit, mom." She took another.

Leo scooped up a handful and crammed a whole one in his mouth. "Mmm" was the only sound he could produce.

Lydia hoped that bringing both kids to the cabin to break the news was a good idea. She thought it would give them quality time to talk with her and among themselves and come to terms with what was sure to be an unexpected and shocking turn of events in their heretofore stable home life. Perhaps it would give them a chance to vent and reconcile some of the feelings that were sure to arise in such a peaceful setting. There was also the possibility that they'd blame her for shattering their memory of the cabin as a happy place.

When the salad was done, she chopped vegetables for a stir-fry and put water on to boil for the noodles. The kids always liked a pasta primavera. She'd even let them each have a glass of wine, the intention being to help them mellow a little and hopefully be more amenable to what she was about to tell them.

Brilliant golden and mauve-pink light pierced the trees surrounding the cabin sending rays across the white china plates and polished wooden table as they sat down to eat. Lydia poured the wine and passed the salad to Leo. He heaped a man-sized portion on his plate, drenched it in the balsamic vinaigrette, and passed the bowl to Tori.

"Sure you got enough there, Jethro?" She gave her brother a look of disgust. "It sucks that guys' metabolisms are so grossly efficient they can scarf down bushels of food and never gain an ounce."

Leo didn't wait to swallow and said with his mouth full, "Maybe if you got off your lazy ass once in a while and chopped some wood, you'd drop a few pounds."

"Maybe you could learn some manners while you're in college. Oh, I forgot, you eat with knuckle walkers. Wouldn't be advisable to get above yourself. They might kick you out of the gorilla bachelor group."

"Up yours with a salad fork sideways, little sister." To his mother, he said, "This sure beats the food in the cafeteria. I think they have a contract with the local hospital to see how many students they can send their way with ptomaine poisoning."

As they were finishing eating, Lydia noticed how little food Tori had put on her plate and how much of it still remained. She hoped the anorexia they'd spent years battling hadn't returned. They'd have to have a private talk later on. Leo ate with his usual gusto. In between mouthfuls he talked about his classes and some of the clubs he'd joined and the "dudes" he'd met.

"Leave it to you to join the chess club." Tori nibbled on a piece of celery. "So, are there any normal people in your program or are they all super-nerds like you?"

"I wouldn't talk if I were you," Leo said, now filling his mouth with a forkful of pasta wound several times around till it formed a meatball sized wad. "You're into what, your fourth major now? Can they award a degree to someone who tries all the majors at NYU?"

"Bite me, meathead."

Lydia could feel the tension rising. It didn't bode well for what was coming. Neither the food nor the wine was having the palliative effect she intended. "Okay, I think that's a good place to call a truce." She decided to try a different strategy.

"I suggest we all sit and relax in the living room and have our dessert there. Leo, could you make a fire? Maybe we could talk about things that aren't so emotionally charged."

As soon as she said it, the irony struck her. She was about to tell them she was leaving their father. Had already left him, for all intents and purposes. It might be better to bring out dessert, eat it, and then have the discussion later.

"Good idea, mom, but I'm not done yet." Leo reached for the pasta bowl and helped himself to another serving. "Let's talk about what we're going to do tomorrow. I suppose Dad isn't coming up, is he? Always too busy. I called him to see if he could advance me my allowance and he said something about being tied up all weekend."

Tori pushed her plate away. "Well I don't know about you, but I want to take the canoe out in the morning and go skinny dipping later on, if the water's warm enough."

Leo shot her a look of surprise. "You? Go skinny dipping? Aren't you afraid you'll get a little bitty titty bitten off by some fish? You always hated the water."

"Leo," Lydia warned as she reached for dishes and began clearing the table. "Why don't you start the fire while we clean the table?"

Tori stood up. "I didn't hate the water. I just never liked the feeling of slime between my toes. Besides, I don't like swimming where you can't see the bottom, or where hungry fish could be looming nearby."

Leo chuckled as he brought an armful of wood to the fireplace. "I'm sure the fish don't get much of a thrill seeing you in the water either. They probably think somebody dropped a skeleton out of a boat."

Lydia stood up. "Okay, guys. That's really enough. We don't need to have a bloodbath on our first night together. Let's have dessert. Tori, you can carry the coffee. Leo, you have fireplace duty. I'll bring in the homemade strawberry shortcake."

Leo clapped his hands and did an imitation slam-dunk. "Woo-hoo!"

Tori groaned and muttered under breath, "F"ing Martha! Trying to kill me."

Lydia drained her glass of wine and poured herself another.

A crackling fire was soon casting showers of sparks against the screen from the moist wood that had been left outside all year. Aside from the fire noises and Leo's moans of pleasure, there was silence for a few minutes. Tori picked at her dessert working to extricate the strawberries from the biscuit. Leo devoured his first serving and handed his plate to his mother. "Can you make the next one just a little bigger, with more strawberries and whipped cream?"

Tori rolled her eyes. "Yeah, super-size it for him, mom. He wants to look like Uncle Tommy."

"Hey? What's wrong with Uncle Tommy? I love Uncle Tommy. He's leaving a bigger carbon footprint than most, that's all."

"A megalodon footprint, you mean. He eats enough for a small village."

Lydia went to the kitchen and brought back another dessert for Leo. It pleased her to see him enjoying her cooking. Though it had been years in coming, her little boy had somehow been resurrected after years of sullen teenage enmity.

"You're the best, mom. This is awesome to the tenth power. No, to pi. To infinity."

"Thank you, Leo. Tori, how is yours?"

"Fattening. Good."

It was time. Clearing her throat, Lydia said, "There's something I was hoping we could talk about tonight. Something important that, well, I wanted to talk to you about in person, not in a text message or on email."

Tori arched her shoulders, eyes widening. Leo looked up from his dessert with eyebrows raised.

"It's about your father and me." Lydia stopped. A thousand thoughts came cascading down in an avalanche in her forebrain. How to sort them was the problem. "Well, I…what I wanted to tell you…what I think you should know is…"

Tori interrupted. "We already know, mom. We already talked about it. I told Leo I saw Dad downtown a few weeks ago with that woman. They were having lunch together. She was a total bimbo. I mean a capitol B-Bimbo. Her chest alone was enough to make me nauseous. I wanted to puke my guts out right there on Thirty-Second." Tori stood up and pantomimed getting sick. "She looked like she was capable of producing calves for offspring. And the way they were acting together, ugh. Disgusting." She put two fingers into her mouth and made a retching sound. "It was, like, abundantly clear they weren't having a business meeting. Duh. Didn't take a genius to figure that out. That's when I sent you a text message in Paris, but you didn't answer. I was kind of glad because I didn't want to blow your whole trip."

Leo swallowed his last mouthful and swiped the napkin across his mouth. "I saw her, too. They were leaving the apartment one day when I went to get my scientific calculator I forgot to pack. Dad looked like he was seeing a ghost when I walked in. He told me she was his colleague and they were having a business meeting. Yeah, like right. Sure dad. Like I was born yesterday. Thanks for giving me credit for being such a cretin. Shit. I mean, he acts like I'm still a toddler with snot in my nose."

"Nothing's changed there," Tori said, getting up to return her plate to the kitchen, ignoring the raised middle finger he waved at her.

From the kitchen, she shouted, "So what's the plan, mom? Are you two getting divorced?"

Lydia had the sensation of a billowing sail that suddenly went limp in the doldrums.

"I, well, yes. We are. I mean, we decided, maybe not we, but I decided it would be a good idea to end the marriage and go our separate ways." She swept her eyes around the room as if trying to get her bearings. "I thought it would come as a shock to you both, but…Wow. I really underestimated you two."

Leo got up and put his arm around her shoulders. "Look, Mom, you don't have to protect us anymore. We're not frickin' babies, after all. Well, at least one of us isn't. We saw this coming for a long time. We knew Dad wasn't working all those long hours at the office. I mean, for shit's sake, even a douche bag would know he was screwing around, coming home after midnight, hardly ever around in the evenings. I asked all my friends if their dads worked such long hours. They all said, 'hell no.' They wished they did."

Lydia wondered when her son started talking like this. Outside of one time when a friend broke his bike, she had never heard him say anything worse than "damn." She reminded herself he was a teenager in college, getting a well-rounded education in every sense of the word.

Tori wasn't about to be outdone. "Yeah. So I, being the more enterprising child, confirmed it after I saw him with that big brunette with the humongous ass wearing some kind of knit dress she poured herself into. I mean, literally, it was, like, congealed on her." She ran her fingers through her short hair. "After they parted with a kiss, I followed her into a store and walked right up to her. I looked her right in the eye and said, 'You're Celeste, aren't you? I met you at a party last year.' To which Miss Rhino-hips replied, 'Oh, I'm sorry, you must have the wrong person. My name is Serena.'"

"Did you tell her to stop fucking your father?" Leo poked his sister in the arm.

"No, I'm more subtle than that. That would be more your style, dipwad." To her mother, she said, "For god's sake, is he that desperate he'd go for someone like her?"

Leo pounded his chest. "I would have seized tit-woman by the strands of her hair and mopped the floor with her." Leo pantomimed what he was describing, causing both Lydia and Tori to break out laughing.

"Like hell you would. You would have been drooling over her bazookas. Oh, and she had an accent too, like that actress, what's her name, Charissa Pallino, from Brazil. Not that she looked like her. Oh god, no. Serena's a whole lot meatier. A real heifer."

"I like 'em meaty, but not heifer-like," Leo said, pounding his chest.

Lydia sat stunned. Was this a dream or were her kids handling the news of what should have been a traumatizing, emotionally shattering event as if it were some kind of comedy? Should she be laughing along with them or hoping they'd start crying? What kind of role model would she be if she laughed? On the other hand, what would she do if they started weeping and wailing and cursing their father?

She cleared her throat, swallowed hard and poured herself another glass of wine.

"So, this isn't really a surprise to either of you?"

Tori jumped up from her chair and wrapped her arms around her, saying, "Oh mom, this is the worst thing that could ever happen. Can I please have another glass of wine...just to calm me down? My nerves... you know how it is."

"Me, too," Leo said. "I'm definitely going to have some posttraumatic stress from this."

Lydia shook her head. "I'd normally say, absolutely not, but go get the bottle. You're not going out after this, either of you, unless it's down to the lake. You're both of legal age, at least what it was in New York for me when I started drinking at 18. Let's overrule the great State of New York just this once."

They held out their glasses and Lydia filled them half full. "Don't you dare say a word to your father about this, understand?"

"Promise," Leo said, taking a sip. "I promised dad once that I wouldn't tell you about the time we smoked weed together. Oops. Forget I just said that."

Lydia's sat bolt upright. "You did what?"

Leo put another log on the fire. "Only joking. You know dad, the total killjoy when it comes to drugs. Remind me never to follow in his footsteps and become an asshole, okay? Correction. I meant to say attorney."

Lydia didn't know what else to say. Neither child showed any of the emotions she'd been expecting. Had she raised them to be insensitive and incapable of normal emotions? Or had she done well, having two mature children who were able to take bad news in stride and show admirable resilience? She looked over at Tori who was now silently sipping her wine and stirring it with her finger.

"Tori, are you okay? I mean, is there anything you want to say?"

"Yeah. I was just wondering if I brought my blue bikini or my red tankini. I hope I brought the red. If I didn't, can we go shopping tomorrow?"

Chapter 4

The cabin was eerily quiet after Tori and Leo left to return to the city. Lydia found herself alone for the first time in a long while. As she stood on the shore looking out over the lake, watching a kayak gliding along, she felt a mixture of relief and intense loneliness. A mist was still rising from the water in the early morning chill. It was still too cold to swim, otherwise she'd have thrown off her shoes and plunged in. She thought about doing it just to shock her system and snap her out of the mood she was in, but decided not to.

The surroundings were too beautiful to let herself sink into the mire of self-pity. She had so much to do, but lacked the motivation to do more than just stare at the water. A couple seagulls flew overhead, one of them diving down to snare some tidbit it saw on the surface. Seagulls in upstate New York? They must have missed a turn somewhere in Massachusetts and ended up inland. She thought about when the kids were little, splashing in the water, catching frogs and salamanders, shrieking at the top of their lungs just because they could and catching fireflies at night. They would put them in jars, bring them inside and peer at them under the covers until it was time to set them free.

Leo, who'd been a picky eater most of his life, had devoured everything in the refrigerator and managed to consume everything in the pantry, including every last cookie she made. Tori kept to her usual restrictive diet, though she did eat a halfway decent breakfast before they headed back to the city.

She needed to get to a grocery store. She also needed to gas up the car, renew her library card, go to the bank and get some cash, call her attorney and get started on her divorce. The thought brought on a smile that became a laugh. Her checklist went something like this: grocery shopping, library, bank, gas, divorce. Something about the last agenda item made her stomach twist into a knot.

The hamlet of Stephentown was closer to the cabin, so she decided to get gas first, then head on to the village of Lake George. It would be busy already with the start of the summer season, but at least it'd be nothing like the months of July and August when one could scarcely find a parking place or walk along Main Street without bumping into scores of tourists.

It was no wonder. Lake George was the jewel of the upstate. Thirty-two miles of pristine natural beauty, which only got better the farther north you headed into the Adirondacks, up to Whiteface Mountain, Saranac Lake, and beyond.

She decided she would take a day to drive up to Whiteface Mountain and Lake Placid and visit some of the old places she used to frequent years ago. There were so many memories of joyful times spent there, and not so joyful, but triumphant ones, such as when she scaled Whiteface on her own, reached the summit and was barely able to walk for three days after. Even the thought of that gave her stomach a twinge. Jack had dropped her off at the bottom and told her if she was pigheaded enough to hike the mountain, she could do it alone. He agreed to meet her at the top in six hours. She'd made the ascent in five and a half hours, just to prove a point.

Suddenly, she caught herself dissolving in a mixture of regret and sadness. Had she actually reached the time in her life when all she had left were memories of happier days gone by? Words that she always hated hearing, mostly from her parents, came to mind. Over-the-hill. Past your prime. Let out to pasture. Was this where she was in her life? Had the best part of her life already happened and the rest was downhill from here? Was she finished, her youth spent, not just relationship-wise, but with her life in general? She made a note to buy a couple bottles of Prosecco, not that she planned to get drunk, but she needed to celebrate her newfound freedom and hopefully get her mind off the track to doom city.

Dammit if she wasn't going to feel happy one way or another.

The Sunoco station wasn't busy, which was another thing that would change soon as the season got underway. She pulled up to the pump, inserted her Sunoco credit card, and waited. An error message appeared on the screen. *Invalid card.* She took out her MasterCard and inserted it. The same message flashed. It was one of those petty annoyances of small town service stations. Things just had a way of going awry in the boondocks. The townsfolk found it enormously entertaining when the tourists would get all riled up and incensed over things being the way they were. It was status quo. The way they liked it.

She walked inside the store, seeing the usual array of junk food and hot dogs sizzling on the rolling bars of a grill. The intense aroma of meat cooking for what probably had been hours, maybe days, permeated the store. A country music station was playing on the radio. For a moment she thought she'd taken a wrong turn and ended up somewhere far south of New York.

A couple of men in hunting jackets were buying a fair supply of six-packs. As she glanced around, she noticed that the bulk of the store's inventory was beer. It must have been a hunter's necessity. She spied a few dusty bottles of wine on a bottom shelf, but decided to wait. It probably wasn't a good idea to indulge her needs here.

"So, what can I do for you, ma'am?" A corpulent man wearing overalls and a stained Grateful Dead t-shirt, with a thick white beard that reached the middle of his chest smiled at her. She winced at the sight of a few teeth badly in need of attention, or extraction. He looked her up and down as if appraising a steer at an auction.

"My credit card's not working. I wanted to fill up on Number 4." The man stopped to think for a moment, then replied, "Hand me your card. I'll try it here." He swiped the card once, then twice, and tossed it back on the counter. "Sorry, not working here neither. Gotta use cash."

"You can't take another credit card?"

"Nope. Not here."

This was going to be a problem. Lydia had given all her spare cash to Tori and Leo before they left. She wanted to be sure they had enough gas and food money to get them back to the city. Now what?

"I'm afraid I don't have any cash, just a handful of change. Is there an ATM around here?"

The man shifted his weight to his other leg, extended his arm out to the side as if he had to warm it up before he could lift it, and pointed out the door. "Down the street, oh, say two blocks, on the left. Past the Jiffy

Lube and the apple stand, although you won't find any apples this time of year, there's a branch of Wells Fargo. I think they have an ATM but I won't swear to it, though, on account of I never use those things."

Lydia thanked him, left the store, and moved her car off to the side. She could have driven, but it was such a brilliant day and just slightly chilly enough to make a sweater necessary. She decided to walk. Her five mile run around the lake this morning had been refreshing, but she needed to get in more exercise before the day was over. The cabin had been toasty warm that morning when she got back from her run. Leo had taken great pride in keeping the blaze going as he finished the bag of marshmallows before he left.

To Lydia's relief, there was a walk-up ATM at the bank. She waited till the person ahead of her completed his transaction, then stepped up and inserted her VISA card. The machine flashed the same message. *Invalid card.* She pulled out her MasterCard. Same. Capitol One. *Invalid.* American Express. *Invalid.* What on earth was going on today? Was the entire town of Stephentown gearing up for a mass attack on tourism? This was unprecedented. It was one of the reasons Jack complained incessantly whenever they went into the village to stock up on necessities. He detested small town inconveniences.

Lydia went inside and waited for an available teller.

"How ya doing, ma'am? What can I do for ya?" The teller looked about sixteen. Her hair was a combination of orange and purple with black roots. She had a small tattoo on her forearm, nothing elaborate, but it made her think of Nicole, in Paris. Nicole Dubois had a body that served as a canvas for her many and varied tattoos. She also wore her hair in dreadlocks. She wondered how her friend was doing. Only last week she'd learned she was pregnant, by a New Yorker, no less.

"Hi. I tried to withdraw money outside at the ATM, but it doesn't seem to be working. I'd like to get cash from a credit card."

"Sure thing. Let's have your card." The teller went to work tapping numbers on her keyboard, chewing gum and producing small pink bubbles with it, then snapping them loudly. She stopped chewing and wrinkled her nose. "Got another card, ma'am? This one ain't working."

Lydia handed her a second card.

"Whoops-a-daisy, this account's closed too."

"Closed? What do you mean closed? I used both these cards over the past three days."

The girl squinted at the computer screen. "Looks like the accounts were closed this morning at around 8:30 AM. Does anybody share these accounts with you? It's possible they might have closed them."

Lydia caught her breath. The accounts were in Jack's name. In fact, all her credit cards, including the Sunoco, were in his name.

"I suppose my husband could have closed them. Could you check into this and see if I can withdraw from my checking account." Lydia handed the teller her checkbook.

The young woman busied herself at the computer, continuing to make popping sounds with her gum and periodically leaning forward to squint at the monitor.

"Well I hate to tell you this, ma'am, but it looks like that account's been closed out, too. Again, it was this morning, at 8:45."

All of a sudden Lydia felt dizzy, her knees became shaky and almost unable to support her as the world shifted on its axis. Everything seemed momentarily unreal and unfamiliar. She looked at the teller, but couldn't see her. She knew she was standing at the counter, but couldn't feel the floor beneath her feet. The next sensation she had was that of falling headlong into a dark, bottomless abyss.

"Ma'am? Are you okay?"

The teller's voice brought her back. She felt her cheeks burning. "Yes. I mean, no. I don't have any money. I don't have any way of getting money."

"Well now, I think you probably do. Maybe you could call your husband and tell him what's going on. Maybe he didn't know you were using these accounts. It wouldn't take anything for him to re-open them. Why don't you try that?"

The words fell on Lydia's ears with the sound of screaming hyenas, with Jack leading the pack. He was on the warpath. This was the first gauntlet dropped. She imagined him sitting in the chariot seat, lashing the horses, relishing every minute. She could see him leaning forward at his computer, a sinister grin plastered across his face, cackling as he closed each account.

The teller was waiting to serve the next customer. "Is there anything else I can do for you today, ma'am?"

Lydia thanked her and left the bank. It was as though her mind was caught in the eye of a tornado. She had to get some money. She could call her mother. No. Horrible idea. There was no way Mary Anne O'Connor was going to help her without first aiming the hot lights at her and putting her through an interrogation that would have rendered Lydia babbling and bordering on suicidal.

She couldn't ask the kids for help because they probably would have spent everything she gave them by the time they made contact. Her sister, Theresa, was in no position to help her. Theresa always came to Lydia for help. Besides, they hadn't spoken in about six months after their last falling out over the phone. Theresa always held a grudge against her, believing she was privileged and had so much more than she. Part of it was true, but the rivalry had started early in their life. No matter what Lydia's achievements, they were always an affront to Theresa. Wouldn't she be thrilled to know Lydia was strapped for money and not doing so well. She decided it would be best not to feed her sister's neurosis by involving her in this debacle.

Her brother, Tom, was now in Beijing teaching a class for graduate students at Fudan University. He would have helped her at a moment's notice, but not now, at such a great distance. Perhaps she should call Becky, his wife. She knew Becky wouldn't hesitate to loan her some cash. She hated to trouble them with her problems, though. Still, this was an emergency. Unusual circumstances. She knew they'd both be offended if she hadn't at least asked.

Back at the car, she stood outside it, pulled out her cell phone and called Becky's number. Instead of reaching Becky or her voicemail, a recorded message answered the call. *"We're sorry, your call cannot be completed. This is an invalid account. If you believe you have received this message in error..."*

Lydia stood stock still, then leaned against the car as her knees weakened again. He'd done it. He'd effectively cut her off from all resources in one morning. She could hear a hundred female voices—voices of friends, relatives, mentors—all echoing in her ears. *"You never should allow a man to have control over all the money. You need to have things put in your name. You never should share accounts with your spouse, even if the money is his. You should always have your own...you should never... never...never..."*

But she had. She'd committed the mortal sin of feminism. She'd violated the prime directive of all liberated women and allowed her husband to control the purse strings. She'd always trusted him to take care of her and, until now, he had. Begrudgingly, yes, but still, he paid for everything even if he did grouse and admonish her for what he considered frivolous and needless expenditures. Paris had been the final straw. She saw that now. The charge of nine-hundred twenty dollars at Maxim's had surely been the coup de grâce. How could she not have seen this coming? How could she have been so gullible and trusting? So damned naïve?

She got back in the car and started the engine. The fuel indicator bordered on empty. She could go back inside and beg for a free gallon or two, but judging by the way the man had looked her over, not to mention the fact that begging and groveling were not in her repertoire of survival skills, she pulled out and started the drive home. Fortunately, she just reached the entrance to the driveway when the engine died.

It was minutes before she lifted her head from the steering wheel. The need to cry was there, only the tears wouldn't come. The thought of beating her head against the steering wheel passed. Self-harming wasn't the solution, either. She went inside the cabin only to discover the lights did not turn on when she flicked the switch. There was no electricity.

As startling as it was to realize she was penniless, another thought came. This was just another development in her script. A mere twist in the plot. Granted, it was an unexpected one and quite a bit more frightening than she would have written, but it was just that. A development. She was going to work through it. She was going to adapt herself to the role and do her best to play it out. It was time to suit up, pull on her big girl pants and forge ahead into the unknown.

After an hour by the lakeside and a great deal of thought, she stood up. It was time for action. *Jack Myers, damn you, you're not getting away with this.* Had he known what was going through her mind as that moment, he might have had cause to be afraid. He'd taunted, criticized and dominated her for so many years. He'd poked and prodded her, wanting to see if there was a tiger within. Until now, he'd found only a kitten.

Little did he know that the kitten was now full-grown. The tiger had awoken and was free. But it was not only free. It was hungry…and very angry.

Chapter 5

The stretch of highway between Lake George and Stephentown was a favorite of Officer Paul Mancini. There was always a lot of action starting in spring and going all the way through to Thanksgiving. Never was there a month when he didn't meet his quota for speeding tickets, DUI's, and just routine citations awarded to assholes who thought they could forget the rules of driving because they were in the country.

He liked nothing more than to pull over those cocky pricks from the city who liked to wind out their Ferraris and Lamborghinis. And their wives who partook a little too heavily of the sauce and tried to argue their way out of a ticket by telling him who they were married to and how he'd better be careful. What a joke. He once told a particularly belligerent woman that he didn't care if she was married to the King of Persia, she was driving under the influence and he could have her license. He usually never pressed more than a ticket on them, but every once in a while... That one he brought kicking and screaming to the station. She cursed him the whole time till her husband came and got her. Real lady-like.

The crazies were the ones that caused him the most concern. It wasn't all that often, but there were times he had to take someone to the hospital in Glens Falls, or Saratoga, for a psychiatric assessment. Sometimes he had to break up a fight when things got hot and heavy among the wannabe gang members. Or when a homeless person went too far with the drugs and had to get to the nearest hospital. It wasn't that he had anything against them, it was just that they were unpredictable. He had a buddy in the force who got stabbed by a homeless guy he was trying to resuscitate after an overdose. Sometimes it just didn't pay to be a Good Samaritan.

It seemed to him the homeless numbers were on the increase in the Lake George area. But then, his brother, Gino, who was a cop in Albany, said it was pretty much the same there. Drugs, alcohol, overcrowded prisons and very few psychiatric facilities made for an interesting array of problems for law enforcers. Still, he wouldn't give up the job for love or money.

Tonight was a new and different experience altogether. He was making his usual rounds when he saw a lady hitchhiking on 9 North, just past Stephentown. She was dressed okay, even looked sort of upscale, carrying a large tote bag and a handbag he knew was expensive because he and his brothers went in on one for his mother last Christmas. The thing cost a small fortune and didn't strike him as being anything more special than what he saw in K-mart. In fact, nothing about her looked funny except for the fact that she was trying to hitch a ride. So weird. Maybe her car broke down.

She wasn't bad looking either. In fact, he thought of an old actress she reminded him of. Grace Kelly. Or was it Maureen O'Hara? He never could get them straight. He pulled over and got out of the car. To his surprise, before he could stop her, she ran toward him. For a moment he thought she was going to hug him, or attack him, so he had his hand already on his holster. Instead, she opened the back door to his patrol car and got in.

"Uh, ma'am. Can I ask what you think you're doing?"

"Officer, please. You have to take me to a shelter or someplace for the homeless. A church, maybe."

Okay. This was going to be interesting. Mancini wanted to give her the benefit of a doubt, so he used his training that came in real handy when dealing with the whack jobs. He spoke in a calm, soothing tone.

"Ma'am, I'm here to help you, but you have to know that it's illegal to hitchhike. I have to give you a ticket. Tell me your name, please, and your address."

"I'm Lydia Myers and yes, I'm well aware that it's illegal to hitchhike. I'm not hitchhiking. I wanted you to pick me up. I'll be happy to accept the ticket, as long as you can take me somewhere where I can spend the night. I need a place to stay."

This was a live one, only she didn't look dangerous, or even high. Was she a hooker running from her pimp, or just someone looking for excitement? What better way to find it than to accompany a cop on his beat? Something about her told him she wasn't a hooker. She didn't look the part, or even sound it. In fact, she spoke the way his English teacher in high school did, in a cultured kind of way.

"Mrs. Myers, why don't you just tell me what's going on and I'll see if I can help you get to wherever it is you need to go."

She proceeded to give him a detailed account of the events that had transpired since this morning when she went to fill her car up at the gas station. Mancini listened, nodded and watched her from his rear view mirror as she talked rapidly behind the cage. She didn't look like she was going psychotic on him, but you never could tell. Sometimes the delusional ones could fake it until the last minute, then go explosive. So far, this one may have had a few screws loose, but she was keeping her cool and telling her story like she really believed it. He decided to see if the story was consistent.

"So you're saying you have a cabin by the lake and up till this morning, after your kids went back to New York City, you found out your husband closed out your bank accounts and cut off your utilities, and...what? You have no money and all your credit cards are gone? Stolen? Or what?"

Lydia shook her head. "No. All the accounts were closed. The credit cards are defunct. I couldn't even get gas. Not even make a phone call. I have no money, no phone, no car. Nothing at all."

Defunct? He had to look that one up. He never heard of a credit card going defunct.

"And you think your husband had something to do with it? Like he closed all the accounts on you?" She had to be stretching it because no man in his right mind would be that big of an asshole. Well, maybe a few. Around here, with all the richies from the city, that would be cause for homicide. Maybe the husband wasn't in his right mind and she was the normal one. At any rate, it would be a story to tell around the precinct.

"Yes, I know he did. It's something Jack Myers would do."

The woman stopped talking and looked out the window. She didn't seem to be in great distress. Maybe she took something for her nerves. She was nice looking. Probably in her forties, possibly older only because she said her kids were in college. She didn't look like she had kids in college. She could have passed for late thirties.

Mancini had to do some figuring. If she was really crazy, he'd have to take her to the hospital for an evaluation. After that, they'd call to have him escort her to the Adirondack District State Hospital. If that was full, he'd have to take her all the way to Albany, to the Capital District Psychiatric Center. He could call his brother if he was working the night shift. Get him to meet him halfway. Gino might not be working tonight. The other possibility was the hospital. They'd keep her in the ER for observation, then call for someone to take her to the Lake View Rescue Ministry if she checked out normal. It wasn't a place he liked to see her going to, but what was the alternative? He couldn't drive her back to the city. He thought it would be a good idea to find out where she lived.

"You said you lived in New York City. What part?"

"East Manhattan, on Central Park."

It didn't take much to figure this lady's story was getting more blown out of proportion by the minute. Next thing you knew, she'd be telling him she and her husband were millionaires.

"My husband is a prominent New York attorney. Do you remember the big court case that made the news last year when several people sued MegaBurger for discrimination? He represented MegaBurger. You can look it up."

Paul Mancini had heard of the case. A friend of a friend of his was one of the people involved in what he said was a class action lawsuit. He was a black brother who claimed the restaurant refused to serve him and kicked him out on the basis of his color and for no other reason. Mancini and his brother never ate a burger there since.

"So what kind of place do you live in? A house? Apartment?"

"A brownstone walk-up. I can give you the address if you want to check."

Okay, now he really was losing his trust in this woman's story. Wife of a prominent attorney. Lives in a brownstone. He knew what those places cost. His cousin used to clean windows in the city. Five years ago you couldn't touch one of those places for under two million, maybe even more today.

"Mrs. Myers, can I ask you one question? Are you bullshitting me or is this story for real?"

"What would it take for me to prove it to you?"

Now that was a good question. Usually he never got this far with a crazy person. They would get to babbling and saying ridiculous things and then start hallucinating. Those were the scarier ones.

"I suppose we could call your home phone number and see who answers."

"Yes, that might be a good idea. My husband may be home with his mistress. He might answer the phone, but I highly doubt it. Maybe she will, thinking it might be him calling. You'll have to call, though. I no longer have any cell phone service."

Officer Mancini punched in the number Lydia gave him. The phone rang twice and a female voice answered. She had an accent that sounded Latino.

"Hello, this is Officer Paul Mancini calling from Lake George district. I'm looking for a Mrs. Lydia Myers. Could you put her on the phone, please, or tell me how I can reach her."

There was a pause, then the woman said, "I'm afraid you have the wrong number. There's no Lydia Myers here." She hung up before he could say anything else.

From the back seat, Lydia heard the reply and did something she was working very hard not to do. "Why you lying, sneaky, low-down, conniving bitch!" she hissed, slamming the cage with her hand.

Mancini looked back to be sure she wasn't about to bolt from the car or start banging her head against the cage.

"Ma'am. Just sit tight. I'll get you to a shelter in just a few minutes."

The patrol car pulled up alongside the curb of the Lake View Rescue Ministry.

"Wait here, please, Mrs. Myers. I want to be sure they can take you." He walked in, noticing several of the man standing outside giving him looks as he passed. Some looked scared, some had that look of a really bad attitude toward cops, and some just looked completely out of it. He personally knew the director, Ron Davis, and walked up to the reception desk.

"Ron, my man, how's it going? Family all good?"

"Paul, hey, everything's great. Busier than ever around here. I hope you don't have anybody for me tonight."

Mancini pulled Ron to the side. "Look man, I got this woman out in the car. I swear she isn't nuts and she doesn't look like she's homeless, but I gotta put her somewhere. She doesn't have a dime on her and claims her husband froze her out of every penny, even though he's a rich dude, some big time attorney in New York. I can't say I buy her story, but she really believes what she's saying, and from what I can see, she could use a safe place to stay for the night."

"She can't stay in a hotel?"

"No money."

"At the station?"

"Nope, no cause to lock her up."

"Hospital?"

"She'd end up here when they finished the eval."

Ron pondered the request, trying to figure out how to make this work for all concerned. He was running at maximum occupancy and even turned away a vagrant couple, a guy and a girl, who were hitchhiking their way to California and staying at homeless shelters along the way. Officer Mancini had been good to his people and genuinely seemed concerned about them. Not like the other cops who seemed to think they were either shiftless bums or criminals just by virtue of being homeless. Some were, but the majority weren't.

"Look, man. I owe you. Send her in. I'll find a place for her to sleep."

As Mancini was leaving, Ron called after him, "No more, tonight, hear? I'll be sending them to your place to sleep."

Ron checked in the newcomer and jotted some notes in his daily log. He liked to keep an account of all the people he sheltered, things like names and addresses, even cell phone numbers, if they had one. Many did. He always thought it would be important to have an address and phone number for several reasons. Some of the homeless were runaways whose parents were sick with worry and trying desperately to find them. Some were running from the law and he was sure as hell not wasting his precious few resources on providing a safe haven for fugitives. Besides, it wouldn't be safe for the rest.

Then there were the ones he really felt sorry for. The ones who ended up in his shelter because their lives had been taken over by alcohol and drugs. They were from all walks of life. Right now he had a former priest, a doctor who lost his license due to "misdirection of pharmaceuticals," namely pain medications, and a single mother who couldn't take care of her three kids and hold down a job, so her landlord evicted them from their apartment. Homelessness was a whole different world from what most people thought.

Now, standing before his desk, was an attractive, healthy-looking and obviously well-off lady who had no place to stay because she'd run out of money. Go figure. Maybe she was a gambler or a raging alcoholic. Or something else. He'd keep an eye on her. She had all the signs of being an actress rehearsing a role. He had one once before—a guy, in fact, doing off-Broadway plays who needed to experience what it was like being a homeless person. He wasn't very talented because Ron saw through him right away and kicked him out. Not that he faulted him for trying. There just wasn't room enough in the shelter for aspiring actors, unless they were truly homeless and it was pretty easy to tell the difference.

Chapter 6

Lydia followed the volunteer down the hallway, through a dining room, down another hallway and up a flight of stairs. They passed a room filled with double bunk beds each topped with a gray blanket and thin pillow. This must be the woman's sleeping area. Though she didn't have time to count, Lydia figured it held at least twenty bunks. There were that many homeless women needing shelter?

"This used to be a glove factory," the volunteer named Lunetta said. "They gave it to the city for a dollar. Can you imagine that? Prime real estate and all they paid was a dollar. Wish I could find me a small house for a dollar. Right now I'm living with my sister and her husband and two kids. Don't get me wrong, I'm not complaining, but it's pretty tight in a two-bedroom apartment. But hey, I thank the Lord Jesus I'm not out on the streets like I used to be. It ain't pretty out there. Not that I have to tell you. How long you been on the streets, honey?"

Reflecting a moment on whether it was better go along with Lunetta's assessment or tell the truth, Lydia opted for the former.

"Not too long, actually. It just sort of happened all of a sudden. One minute I was doing fine, the next I was out of a home with nothing but the clothes I'd packed for...well, I mean, the clothes I carried with me. You know, for quick changes."

"Oh, I know it, baby. How I know it. It's a hard life. It surely is. A girl has to do what a girl has to do. But let me tell you something. The good Lord knows what He's doing and He's looking out for you. He sure reached out a long arm when He came to rescue me. That's why I'm a volunteer now. You might want to be one someday, too, when you feel better about yourself, I mean. It takes a lot out of a woman, being on the streets. I was lucky my pimp knocked me out cold right there in broad daylight. The cops arrested him and brought me here. Then they locked him up and he got out in a day. Why they even bothered to put him in the hold is just plain stupid. Only made him madder than a rattlesnake. After that he stalked me. He even threatened to kill me when I wouldn't come back. I told him the Lord saw fit to save me and I wasn't never going back. Oh, that got him going. He kept it up until he found himself some other poor thing to do his dirty work. They're devils, those pimps. Every last one of them. Possessed by demons. That's why I pray for them every day. I pray for their filthy, rotten, decaying souls, hoping God will turn them around. Do you pray, Miss Lydia?"

Lydia thought of her mother's pre-bedtime inquiry, "Did you say your prayers?" and later, the nuns' dictum, "Say your prayers every day, or else." She stifled a grin and nodded her head gravely.

"Why, yes. I do, sometimes. I was brought up Catholic. We learned how to pray early on. I went to a Catholic school, too. I prayed a lot when I was younger. Guess I should pray more often now."

"Especially now," Lunetta said, pushing open a door that had *Chapel* written in black magic marker on a piece of loose-leaf paper taped to it. "Time's a wasting. Even pray for your pimp, if you have one, on account of he's a child of God, too. Even his lousy, stinking turd of a heart needs to be healed."

"My pimp? Yeah, I have one. I should pray for him, but I don't want to. At least not right now." Lydia thought about Jack and how he'd feel being called a pimp. He was one, actually. And she was, or had been, his high-priced hooker. She'd slept with him. She'd given him children. She served as his escort. In return, he kept her up. When he wasn't happy with her, he threw her out and cut her off from all means of survival. The filthy, poison-minded pimp that he was. She liked Lunetta's phrasing better. Stinking turd of a heart.

Lunetta put down the blanket and pillow she was carrying and swept her hand across the top of the bench, removing a layer of dust.

"Here it is, Miss Lydia. It ain't much, but it's a bed and someplace to lay your head. Besides, you'll be safe here. And look up there. You got Jesus looking over you. What more could you want?"

Lunetta pointed to the crucifix above the altar. She leaned closer and whispered in Lydia's ear as if someone might be listening in. "Besides, you'll probably like it here better here than in the bunk room. Let me tell you. Ooh, wee, sister. Things can get heated up there real quick."

Before she left, Lunetta informed Lydia of the rules. She could not stay in the chapel during the day, when everyone had to vacate the shelter by 9:00 AM. All except for the pregnant moms and ones with babies. There were also hours of religious service which she was welcome to attend but she had to leave her stuff somewhere where no one could take it.

Her last and most important disclosure was that of the small bathroom at the back of the room, not typically used by the general public and only in emergency situations, that is, when the other bathrooms were unavailable due to plumbing malfunctions or prime time traffic.

Lydia knew by the way Lunetta told her about the bathroom that this was a special privilege and one she'd better appreciate. After she left, she looked around the small chapel. It was simple in décor. A wooden altar with a torn lace tablecloth, a bible, and a wooden bench for the priest or minister to sit on. About twenty rickety pews, ten on each side, and a bare wooden floor that smelled of old wood and disinfectant cleaner. That, and the mustiness of age, blended into a scent she'd noticed only once before in her life, in her grandmother's dirt-floor cellar.

She imagined the chapel had to be non-denominational, as the residents were probably from different faiths, yet there was only the crucifix behind the altar serving as the sole religious symbol on the cracked plaster walls. The shelter was called a rescue ministry, after all, so the denominational side had to lean somewhere. She wondered what the Muslim, Jewish, agnostic and atheistic homeless thought about it. Then she chided herself. It was a shelter, after all. There probably wasn't much attention paid to such details. The walls were sorely in need of paint and it was evident no major modifications had been made since the days the place was a factory, other than that the sewing machines had been replaced by an altar and pews.

The bathroom was a real plus. She gave herself a sponge bath at the sink, trying not to notice the black mold growing from the baseboard and halfway up the walls. At least the water was hot and there was a bar of Ivory soap. She used her body wash instead, brushed her teeth, ran a brush through her hair and returned to her sleeping bench.

The clothes she wore all day would have to serve as pajamas. It just didn't seem like a good idea to change into a semi-transparent nightie in a chapel. Although she tried to plump up the pillow, there wasn't enough substance to it to make a difference. The pillow case smelled of bleach that tried to mask the smell of mildew on the inside, but didn't succeed. It reminded her of summer camp and damp sleeping bags. She tried to push thoughts of the day out of her mind and focus on tomorrow as she wrapped herself cocoon-like in the pilled, threadbare blanket.

She was grateful. It was just an adventure. Instead of focusing on where she was and how she got there, she decided instead to imagine herself sleeping outdoors on the ground at the cabin. She'd be back there soon. This was just a temporary side trip.

Sleep came fast. Even the noises of men arguing out in front of the building and a few sharp cracking noises that might have been gunshots awakened her only momentarily. She fell right back to sleep and returned to her dreams.

She saw herself flying over the Seine River in Paris with her friends, Nicole DuBois and Ellsworth Witherspoon beside her. All three were laughing as they sailed over dark waters that splashed and danced in the city lights. There was Notre Dame in the distance and the shimmering Eiffel Tower. She looked down to see her husband in a sailboat with a dark-headed woman. She had a long nose with a wart on the end of it. The boat overturned and she heard a piercing scream and a sound of something knocking. Knocking.

What seemed like only a couple hours had been a full night of sleep. There was someone knocking at the door of the chapel. It opened and a woman poked her head inside.

"Rise and shine, sunshine. It's time to get up and get yourself to the dining room. Breakfast's only till nine, then everybody's out."

The voice was female, only it didn't sound like Lunetta's. Lydia hoped she'd see her at breakfast so she could thank her again for her kindness. She roused herself, sniffed her armpits, and realized she was badly in need of a shower and deodorant. Even though homeless, there was no excuse for poor hygiene, especially when she had soap and running water.

A bird bath at the sink would have to suffice. She did her best, noticing as she was drying off that she wasn't alone. A mouse was watching her from a shelf above her head. She wondered if the shelter had a laundry service but thought it best not to ask.

When she found her way to the dining room, there was already a line.

"Hurry it up, already," the man behind the cafeteria counter yelled. "We ain't got all day here. I gotta close up shop at nine. That's the rules. Take it or leave it."

Lydia stood in line with a tray, wondering what, if anything, there would be to eat. Some words of her mother came to mind. She hadn't thought of them for years. *Beggars can't be choosers.* Somehow she never thought they would apply to her. She was relieved to see Lunetta bustling about the dining room, throwing napkins and plastic forks on the tables.

"Good morning Miss Lydia," she called out. "How did it go last night?"

Lydia told her it went just fine and she slept well. She was about to ask about a shower when Lunetta grabbed her by the hand and pulled her out of the line.

"I want to introduce you to some people you need to know. That short girl over there with the black tights and the white blouse is Miss Jessica. She's the assistant director. You already met Ron, our director."

A young man who looked to be about sixteen walked up and extended his hand. "I'm Diego. And that guy over there with the beard who can't take his eyes off you is Simon Simple, or Simple Simon, however you like. But don't let him fool you. He ain't simple, not one bit."

Lunetta interrupted. "Hush now! I'm doing the introductions, Diego Do-Gooder. Let me finish." She turned back to Lydia with a big smile on her face. "He's my baby. I love him like my own son. Now where was I? Oh yeah, going down the line, that is Miss Janice Jewel, DeShaun the Shark, Gabriel Archangel, Antoinette Hollywood, and you just met Diego Do-Gooder. That one leaning on the wall is Cody Code-Blue. Don't even ask."

Turning to the line, Lunetta announced. "Everybody, I want you to welcome Miss Lydia. I don't have her last name yet." Turning back to Lydia, she said, "We don't use our last names here. We make up a name for ourselves. Something we like or we think describes us. Mine is Lunetta

Loves the Lord, but most everybody calls me Mama. So, what would you like to be, Miss Lydia? I was thinking Lydia Morningstar. It seems to fit you."

Lydia thought for a moment. A number of possible names came to her, but they all sounded pretentious. Lydia Lightworker. Lydia l'Artiste. Lydia Mankiller? Uh, best not to go there with Lunetta censoring. Then it came to her.

"Call me Lydia Chapel, because that's where I'm sleeping."

Everybody clapped and Lunetta gave her a hug. "That's just perfect. Now Miss Lydia Chapel, you get back in line and get you some breakfast. Eat up 'cause it's gonna be a long time till supper."

Simon Simple offered her a place front of him. "When's the last time you ate?"

Lydia had to stop and think. "I guess it was breakfast yesterday. I didn't realize how hungry I am."

Simon chuckled. "Well, don't get too excited. The coffee is decaf and the sausages and bacon are stuff that falls off the truck on the way to the grocery stores. The bread's okay, usually only one or two days old. Sometimes there's cereal. That's Irving Glock behind the counter, by the way. Watch out for him. Don't let the fact that he's working here fool you."

When they got up to the counter where Irving was serving food on paper plates, Lydia saw that the toast was already buttered and there was no fruit or yogurt. To her relief, there was a large pot of what looked like oatmeal.

"May I have some of that? And would you happen to have any almond or soy milk?"

Irving scooped a generous portion of the oatmeal into a paper bowl and handed it to her. His deadpan response to her question was, "Milk's down there. Cow's milk. It's good for you. Lots of calcium. Take it or leave it."

Lydia looked down at her bowl. It did resemble oatmeal, not the whole oats or steel cut oats that she preferred, but the kind of instant oatmeal her mother used to make.

"Actually cow's milk has been proven not to be good for human consumption and, as for calcium…"

Irving shouted, "Next!"

Lydia found an empty seat and sat down with her bowl of plain oatmeal and cup of decaf coffee.

Simon pulled out a chair and sat down. "Like I said, this isn't the Waldorf Astoria, but at least it fills you up till supper."

"I'm hungry. It's fine."

"So, are you vegan?"

"Yes."

"No eggs? Fish? Cheese?"

"No. Only plant-based. Whole grains, vegetables, legumes, fruits, nuts."

"Sorry. You're going to starve here."

They ate in silence. Lydia tried not to stare at the people around her, but it was almost impossible not to. The varying degrees of poverty were reflected in the clothing, state of health, condition of teeth, or lack thereof, and the general demeanor of the residents. Homelessness had a more devastating effect on some. They looked like they'd be better off in a hospital or a psychiatric ward. One gentleman was carrying on a conversation with himself, gesturing and shaking his finger at whomever he was addressing. A couple of women who looked to be in their late fifties or sixties, one obese, the other weighing in at about ninety pounds, were engaged in a lively discussion about welfare benefits. Lydia listened.

"You know you just can't get ahead on welfare," said the heavier woman. "I wanted to buy myself a flat screen TV last week and my worker said I couldn't use the money for that. Can you believe that?"

"Tell me about it," the other woman replied. "I wanted to take the bus to Orlando to see my kids. They told me I couldn't. You'd think they owned you. Of course, there's still that restraining order, so maybe she was right. They could have arrested me."

"You got that right."

Simon was eating his sausages and eggs without looking up. Lydia desperately wanted to ask him what brought him here, but something told her there was an unspoken code not to ask others about their personal situations. She tried to think of anything that might be appropriate in the way of breakfast conversation. She couldn't exactly ask about his work, which he obviously didn't have, or his goals, which may have been too painful to discuss, or even what his plans for the day were. It was best to keep silent and just listen.

Lunetta came over to the table.

"Now, Miss Lydia Chapel. You being new here, I just wanted to let you know some more of our rules. We don't let people hang around inside here during the day. Too many fights break out. Also, there's no place to store your stuff so you gotta take it all with you. We don't allow drugs or alcohol inside here, but if you come back high or drunk, we won't turn you away, unless you're a problem, that is. You can come back inside at 5:00 when the first supper hour is, then there's a second one at 6. If you don't eat here, curfew is 9:00. Think you got all that?"

Lydia affirmed that she got it. It was almost 9:00. She had to leave the dining room quickly to get her belongings. The volunteers were now ushering everyone out the door. She hurried back to the chapel, gathered up her tote bag and stuffed all her belongings inside, including her sketch book. Then she remembered her towel, toothbrush, and toiletries from the toilet tank cover and threw them in. Last was her handbag that she grabbed running out the door.

Outside, several of the residents were standing around smoking cigarettes. Some were just staring while others walked away from the shelter as though they had someplace to be. She had no idea what to do now or where to go. With no money, there weren't many options. If she were at the cabin, she'd be putting on her running clothes and doing her morning run around the lake or taking the kayak out to explore the endless inlets and coves.

Simon must have noticed her predicament and walked up to her. "You can hang with me, if you want. That is, if you don't have any big plans. I just gotta warn you. I'll be looking for balloons today."

Lydia was curious. "Are you going to a birthday party?"

Simon chuckled. "Oh, you are so naïve. I love it. Let's get going."

Along the way to the park, Simon talked about how he liked to watch the ducks swimming in the pond and other people wiling their time away. Sometimes he made up stories about them and wrote them down in a notebook he carried. When they reached the park, he led her to one of his favorite benches. It was a lovely, sunny morning. Tulips and daffodils were blooming in the surrounding garden beds and the azalea bushes were covered in pink and white blossoms. The pond was edged in cattails and balancing precariously on them were several red-winged blackbirds. She saw a yellow bellied sap sucker and three ducks gliding across the pond, making ripples that flashed rays of the morning light.

Simon took off one of his shoes exposing a torn sock and set to work folding it over to hide the hole. Lydia took out her sketch book.

"Do you mind if I draw you?"

"Mind? Heck no. I don't get offers like that very often. Sketch away." He resumed working on his sock. "So, if you don't mind me being nosey, what's a nice girl like you doing in a place like this? The shelter, I mean."

"How much do you want to know?"

"All of it, I guess. I like to hear people's stories. Someday I may write a book."

Lydia studied Simon's face. It was a good, strong face, with sensitive eyes, even if they did seemed somewhat puffy and hazed over from whatever he must been doing, or using, the night before. His clothes were shabby and he looked to be badly in need of a shower, but the way he spoke told her he had an education beyond high school. She felt she could confide in him. Also, after she told him her story, perhaps he'd tell her his own.

Simon looked up at the tree casting shadows on their bench. "Everybody has a story. I like to hear them. Sometimes I think about all the people I've met and all the interesting lives people lead. It's better than going to the movies, really. Living out on the street is good. Ha. I'm bullshitting you now. But, in a way, it is. It's good to know other people have it tough."

Lydia talked as she sketched, occasionally telling him to hold a certain pose and not move. She told him the story of her sudden transition to homelessness, finding it almost unbelievable as she put it into words.

Simon listened intently, but said nothing. He'd taken out a small notepad from his jacket pocket and was jotting things down as she talked.

"What are you doing? Taking notes?"

He laughed. "For that future book, remember?"

When Lydia was done with her story, she stopped sketching and looked away toward the pond. Some of the other homeless people were on the other side.

Simon stared at her. "I've heard a lot of stories from homeless people, but I have to say yours surpasses them all. So, let me see if I got this right.

Effectively, you have no money, your old man is some hotshot attorney in New York City, you have no cell phone because he cut that off, you had to leave your cabin on Lake George because there's no power, and you hitchhiked and got picked up by the police so you could get to the shelter. Jesus Christ on a bicycle, this is some story. You're not making any of this up, are you?"

Lydia shook her head. "I wish I was. Even I'm having trouble believing it. It seems like someone else's story. I have two kids in college. I live in a brownstone in New York. Now I'm living in a shelter. The craziest part is, for the first time in my life, I have no idea what to do next. I can't call home or my kids, or my relatives, or anybody because I don't have a phone. I can't get a phone card because I don't have money. Do people ever stop to think what it's like to have absolutely no money, not even a dime? Well, that's not completely true. I do have a little bit of change in my wallet. Maybe enough for a cheap cup of coffee."

Simon frowned. "Well, I guess I won't hit you up for a loan, then." He sat silent for a moment, then said, "Can I at least buy you a coffee?"

"If you can afford it, yes. I'd love one."

They left the park and walked down the main street, passed a Starbuck's, and went farther down two more blocks to a McDonald's. *Beggars can't be choosers* echoed in her mind. Seated at a booth next to a window, she looked at the tourists walking by. They looked very much like she and her family looked when they used to stroll the streets of the village. It was interesting being on the other side. Not alarming, but vastly different. It was as though she'd stepped out of her life into some parallel universe where she wasn't sure exactly who she was or what role she was supposed to play. Her new script was that of a homeless person and she had to learn her part quickly.

Suddenly the thought of it made her sad, not because her plight was dire at the moment, but because she knew her situation was only temporary. That wasn't the case with the sweet young man seated across from her who bought her a coffee with probably all the money he had to get him through the day.

Simon noticed the change that came over her. "What's wrong? You look like your pet pooch just got nailed by a truck."

Lydia wiped away a tear. "I'm just feeling sad because I'm so fortunate. That's all I want to say about myself. Tell me about you. What's your story?"

Simon looked down at his cup of coffee. "I'll give you the condensed Reader's Digest version. I was in college, had a promising future ahead of me, majoring in journalism, working on my master's. Then I did the ultimate stupidest thing a person can do."

Lydia clutched her coffee cup in both hands. "What?"

"I went to a party and got hooked on heroin."

She sat back, finding it difficult to fathom what she was hearing. This couldn't be a heroin addict she was talking to. Although she'd taken a course on addictions in her counseling program, she never got any real sense of what addiction was like. In her mind, heroin addicts were old men in filthy clothes lying in gutters, drooling, covered in newspapers, who people stepped over. This was a fine looking, healthy young man who'd fallen on hard times. He had an education and was carrying on an intelligent conversation with her. How could this be?

"I don't understand. Please forgive me, but how could someone like you become a heroin addict?"

Simon grimaced. "Oh, it's not all that hard at all. You go out to a party. You have a group of friends who give you something to try. You think, oh, this is cool. Harmless. Why not? One time can't hurt. Then before you know it, you're hooked and every cell in your body is jonesin' for your next fix."

Lydia sat stunned for a moment. She thought of Tori and Leo. Could such a thing happen to them? Could addiction be that fast and overpowering? They were always taking risks and doing things she didn't approve of. What if...? Maybe she shouldn't have allowed them to drink wine.

"But Simon, are there no treatment programs? No therapy you could get to help you get over this?"

Simon smiled at her over his cup of coffee. "Yeah, sure. I've tried several. I stayed clean once for a whole year. I thought that chapter was over, but it wasn't. A series of events in my life, which I don't care to talk about, sent me right back. There's no such thing as 'take only when needed' with horse. It takes you for a ride and makes it impossible to dismount."

"I'm so sorry. I hope you don't mind if I ask you more about it. I'm going back to school for my master's in counseling and I need to know about these things."

"I don't mind. I'll be your tutor. Ha! Your heroin tutor. Drugs 101. Straight from the horse's mouth, no pun intended. Maybe you can use me as an example to warn other people." He set down his coffee and leaned forward. "You'll make a good counselor, Lydia Chapel. You're a good listener."

Lydia and Simon spent the rest of the day walking around the village, returning to the park and feeding the ducks some crumbs of a bagel Simon bought. She was hungry, but didn't want to ask him to buy her food. At one point he left her on the bench and she watched him approach a man in the park. They looked like two college boys chatting about something interesting, laughing at a joke. She saw Simon hand the man some money. He returned to the bench carrying something in his hand.

"I told you I was looking for balloons. Well, this is a balloon."

Lydia looked at the round, lime green object in his hand. It was no bigger than a dime in diameter.

"Is that what I think it is?"

"Yep. Lesson number one, counselor. This is how they package it. In these tiny little balloons people never buy. I think they're made solely for this purpose."

Lydia shuddered to think what just took place. Never in her life would she have imagined it, had the proof not been flashed before her eyes like a neon sign. She'd witnessed her very first drug deal and it looked no different from two friends meeting in the park. Two college kids sharing a laugh on a beautiful spring day.

Chapter 7

The clock on the Town Hall tower struck 5:00 as Lydia and Simon began heading back to the Lake View Rescue Ministry. Limping along on worn out feet that had covered the distance of the village at least four times gave her a whole new appreciation of what it meant to be homeless. Living on the streets was arduous enough, but it took a great deal of stamina to walk eight hours a day, with occasional rest stops on available benches before getting frowned on or asked to leave. The shop owners and police weren't exactly unkind, but the implication was obvious. Homeless people were not helping business and were not wanted.

Simon had been cheerful for the most part, although as the day wore on, he seemed increasingly nervous and fidgety. She wondered if it had anything to do with the little package he'd bought in the park. Perhaps he was getting closer to the time he needed to use it. She didn't want to know how or when he would, and she certainly didn't want to be around to see it, except for the fact that he might need her help in case things didn't go as well as expected. The thought crossed her mind she could be charged with being an accomplice to an illegal act if she went with him and waited while he shot up. Judging by his behavior, she guessed it would be soon.

As they neared the shelter, she saw a small crowd gathering out front, waiting for the door to open. Simon put his hand on her arm to stop her.

"Hold up, Lydia. You go on ahead. I'll catch up with you later." He took a few steps away, then turned back. "Save me a seat in the dining room, okay? And don't finish all the caviar before I get there, hear?"

Lydia wanted to reach out to him, pull him back, hug him and try to talk him out of doing what he was about to do. Of course, she knew it wouldn't have any bearing on his actions and would only cause a scene. He was an addict, after all. She knew what it felt like to crave a glass of wine in the evening. This had to be a hundred times worse.

Instead, she gave him a broad grin and said, "Be careful. Hurry back." It was so lame, but the best she could offer someone who was going off to shoot heroin into his veins. At least she let him know she was there and would be waiting for him when he accomplished the deed. She caught him rolling his eyes as he turned to walk away. Her heart suddenly felt weighty in her chest.

She approached a group of three women standing in a huddle outside the door. Two of them she'd met that morning at breakfast—Janice Jewel and Antoinette Hollywood. The third she didn't recall meeting. They waved to her as she approached.

"Hey there, Lydia Chapel. Come on over here. We were just talking about you." Antoinette put a hand on her shoulder. She was a pretty girl, probably no more than twenty-five, with long cornrows that cascaded halfway down her back. "I was just telling the others what nice clothes you had. Expensive looking, too. You haven't been living free for long, by the looks of it."

Living free. She hadn't thought of it that way. It certainly had a more positive ring than walking the streets, selling her body, or hooking Johns.

"Thank you. About the clothes, I mean. And to answer your question, no. It hasn't been too long. I'm just getting my sea legs."

The remark had all three women laughing uproariously. Antoinette spoke up first. "Sea legs! I knew there was more to you than just a pretty face. You got a killer sense of humor, girl. You got it going on. I like a sailor every now and then, myself. They're usually some kid with pimples from the Midwest, away from home for the first time. Pitiful, really."

"Oh yeah," Janice joined in. "Virgins, too. Most don't even know where to put it. Shit!"

Lydia smiled as if she knew exactly what they meant. She hadn't been trying to be funny. Once again, she was at a loss for words. The topic of conversation was outside her range and she didn't want to pretend she knew her way around that particular block. Fortunately, Janice Jewel spoke up.

"That jacket you're wearing, girl? My, oh my. It sure does look expensive. I bet you got it at the mall. Am I right?"

She actually had gotten it at Saks Fifth Avenue.

"Uh, yes, I did. At Penney's. On sale. Great sale. Black Friday. Everything half off and reduced even more, if you applied for a credit card."

She noted by Janice's reaction that she should have left the last part off.

The woman whom she hadn't met spoke up. "I'm Cynthia, by the way. Cindy Sinful. Lunetta tried to talk me out of that name, but I said, hell no. I like it. I'm not no Jesus-freak like her. I'm a sinner and I plan to stay that way. As a matter of fact, I love sinnin'!"

The other two women laughed again with gusto and Lydia joined in. That she could agree with, somewhat. When she was in grammar school, she and her best friend, Suzanne, would set up and take down the altar for mass in the school chapel. Occasionally they 'sinned' when they dared to drain the last drop of wine left in the chalice. She always made sure she confessed it, because to go to hell over a drop of wine just didn't seem right.

Cindy eyes rolled over Lydia's handbag, then locked onto hers. The steely look of greed sent chills up her spine as she moved in closer, giving Lydia the impression she might rip the bag off her shoulder by the strap. "How much you want for that bag? I can give you ten, cash, right now."

Antoinette stepped in. "Hold on, girl. Are you high or what? That bag goes for over a hundred dollars. I know because I saw one in Macy's last year. Shit. Ten dollars. That's chicken feed. I'll give you twenty."

Janice pushed the other two aside. "Honey, forget these two losers. That bag is mine. I'll give you thirty five and that's my final offer."

Under any other circumstances, Lydia would have said casually the handbag wasn't for sale. To let a Pierre Cardin that cost three hundred dollars on sale go for thirty-five would have been ludicrous. It was an anniversary gift from Jack. He'd told her how much he paid for it. No. This bag was definitely going on the auction block. It probably wasn't advisable, but given that there was no reason to hold onto such a token of his generosity, and the fact that she had nothing to lose and everything to gain, she took a chance.

"Tell you what. I'll sell it to the highest bidder. I can promise you, you'll be getting a very expensive handbag and you won't regret it when you see how envious everybody will be. And I mean green with envy. This bag sells for over three hundred dollars."

The bidding war started and continued as the door to the ministry opened and everyone began shuffling inside. By the time they got to the dining room, Antoinette was ahead at fifty-five dollars. Cindy had dropped out.

Janice was seething. "You know I'll have to turn a few more tricks to get that kind of money. Sixty-five, then. That's it. Beat that, why don't you, Miss Hollywood." She reached into her bag and fished out three twenty dollar bills. She rummaged for more, but came up with only two single dollars. Lydia said it was fine and took the money.

Antoinette folded her arms and muttered something under her breath. Before they sat down at a table, Janice exchanged bags with Lydia, giving her the cloth bag that held most of her possessions. "So you'll have something to put your stuff in," she said. "I won't even charge you for it."

The bag was more like a canvas sack. It probably had been blue at one time, but now it had a dark, grease-stained gray look that spoke of years of dedicated service and avoiding any type of laundering. Were those jagged patterns on one side tire tracks? She must have dropped it in the road and someone ran over it. It was better not to ask.

"Give it a wash and it'll look just like new," Janice said as she began filling her new bag, all the while humming to herself.

A whistle sounded and they all fell into place in the line leading to the cafeteria. Janice kept stroking her new bag and talking to it as if it were a pet. Antoinette was pouting and Cynthia was busy conversing with an older man who was bent over and leaning on a cane. She wondered if he might be her father, or perhaps an uncle.

A different worker was serving the food tonight. What a relief. He looked friendlier than Irving Glock. When he saw Lydia, his smile broadened and he flashed brilliant white teeth as his eyes crinkled.

"I haven't met you yet. I'm Benny. Benny Blessed. Welcome to the ministry."

"I'm Lydia Chapel. Thank you. It's nice to be here. I feel blessed." She could tell she said the right thing by the look on Benny's face. There was an angelic glow about him. Perhaps he was an angel.

"Everyone comes here by the grace of God, and you, Lydia Chapel, you've been given a double blessing."

"How so?"

"You get to stay in the Lord's house." Benny put his hands together in a prayerful pose. "So, Miss Chapel. What's your pleasure?"

The dinner tonight consisted of chili, cornbread, a small saucer of salad with Thousand Island dressing, and a piece of yellow cake with white icing for dessert. She was afraid to ask for a large bowl of salad, so when she put only a small saucer of salad on her tray, Benny's eyebrows went up.

"Not a chili eater, huh? Me neither. It tears my stomach up. Here, let me get you something else." He went to the refrigerator behind him and came back with a baked potato and two containers of sour cream. "I'll just heat this up for you and then I'll fill up the rest of the plate with salad. Any particular kind of dressing you like?"

She was about to say oil-free balsamic vinaigrette and hold the sour cream, but she stopped herself. "Anything would be fine. Thank you, Benny."

He served a few more people as she waited for her potato, then he presented her with a huge portion of iceberg lettuce salad and a steaming baked potato. "How about some margarine to go with that sour cream?"

"No. No thank you. This is fine just as it is. Perfect. Thank you so much."

"That's what I like to hear. Somebody who appreciates my cooking." Benny let out a belly laugh and continued scooping chili into bowls for the next in line.

Back at the table, the three women were huddled again. For some reason Lydia had a feeling it was about her. She looked around for Simon, but didn't see him. Now she was beginning to worry. Why hadn't she tried to stop him? She should have, even though she knew it would have been futile. She could have at least tried, or done something. Maybe offered to go with him. Ridiculous. He would have had to revive her after she passed out.

"Now, Miss Lydia Chapel," Antoinette said. "I was wondering just what you might want for that jacket of yours. I've been admiring it ever since this morning. It sure would look good with my complexion, don't you think? You're a little pale for it, in my opinion. Of course, who cares about what I think. What do you say?"

Lydia's jacket was an *Artistico* original, hand-painted silk with gold embroidery, lined with sateen. She'd bought it in Greenwich Village last year in a funky boutique that specialized in one-of-a-kind wearable art. She was embarrassed to admit, or even hint at, how much she paid for it.

They negotiated for a while. The bidding was tense. She ended up pocketing forty-five dollars only because she felt bad Antoinette hadn't gotten the handbag. If her math served her well, she'd just lost three hundred seventy-five dollars on the deal. Janice was now back in Antoinette's good graces and they chatted about their day throughout the meal. She ate her potato in silence, hoping no one would question her about it. They didn't. Antoinette gave a lengthy and harrowing description of her latest narrow escape from a meth head.

"I swear there isn't a man in this town who isn't on something," she said. "Alphonso, that's my brother, he got busted a few months ago for possession and paraphernalia. He's doing time at Otisville, now. Last time it was Coxsackie. That boy can't keep his nose clean to save his life. But they're all like that."

Janice nodded enthusiastically. "You don't have to tell me." She looked across the table. "You ever been to the big house, Lydia Chapel?"

Lydia chewed the mouthful she had, wondering how best to answer the question. She knew the reference was to prison, having heard it from a fellow student in her substance abuse class. Going out on a limb, she said, "I almost got arrested in a protest march when I was in college."

Janice and Antoinette exchanged glances, their eyes widening simultaneously. Janice went first. "What were you protesting? The food in the school cafeteria?" Antoinette stepped in. "Or the professors who didn't kiss your ass and give you all A's?"

"Actually, it was a civil rights protest. We were protesting the fact that the university wasn't hiring enough people of color." Now there was a foot-in-the-mouth moment, she realized too late.

"People of color?" Janice shrieked. "What kind of color? Purple? Green? Maybe pink and white polka dots?" That sent the two women into spasms of laughter. Lydia suspected they either had something to drink, or maybe smoke, before she met up with them outside.

Antoinette got up from the table and strutted around it with her thumbs tucked under the bra straps beneath her sweater. "I'm a person of color in my new colorful jacket. Uh-huh. Look at me. I said, *look* at me! I say, I'm of color."

Janice waved her down, saying, "Get your colored butt back in that seat and finish your chili, bitch. We got a long night ahead of us. I'm tellin' you I gotta show off this new bag of mine. Say what?"

By the end of the meal, Lydia had given her dessert to Janice, sold her watch—another anniversary gift—to Cindy, who said she always wanted a nice one like that and would pay anything Lydia wanted. When she threw a fifty dollar bill on the table, Lydia realized there would be no bargaining on the Rolex. All things considered, her earnings weren't bad. She now had one-hundred fifty-eight dollars. Not many could boast of those earnings even on a good day at the homeless shelter.

Janice got up to leave, announcing it was time she made some more money so she could buy up the rest of Lydia's clothes. Fortunately, their shoes size didn't match, otherwise Lydia would have been wearing rubber flip flops instead of her *Impressions Organic.*

She wished the three women good night, bussed the table, and went back to the chapel. Piling her belongings on the bench, she had a quick wash up at the sink, overseen by the voyeuristic mouse. Teeth brushed, sweat pants and shirt put on for bed clothes, she went to her bench and sat down. Suddenly she remembered something else Lunetta had told her. She got up, went back to the bathroom, pulled one of the already loose tiles from the wall, and stashed her money behind it. A shiver of excitement coursed through her and bubbled up into a giggle. Her life was now a spy novel. She was engaged in espionage, rubbing shoulders with addicts and prostitutes, plotting ways to stay alive and protect her assets.

Back on the bench, she lay her head back on the pillow and thought about Simon. If anyone needed prayer, that poor soul did. She looked at the crucifix and made a special petition that he be guarded over by angels who specialized in addiction. She said prayers for all the others in the shelter, too, especially Ron. He was practically running the place single-handedly, with the help of the volunteers, of course, but many of them required a fair amount of supervision. She would pay him back someday, hopefully soon. She would possibly even become a volunteer. A disciple, as they called them. Yes, that would be a good way to pay him and the others back. Lydia Chapel, a disciple. Wouldn't that be something her brother, Tom, would love to add to his repertoire of family stories? She shuddered to think how he'd never let her live it down.

As her eyelids drooped, she thought about tomorrow. She had to plan her strategy. Now that she had cash, the possibilities were endless. First, she'd have to get a phone card and start making some calls. She had no idea how the cards worked or where she'd get one. She fell asleep wondering if Simon would accompany her, or if she'd ever see him again.

The next morning, she awoke refreshed after a surprisingly good night's sleep, even though parts of her were impossibly stiff from remaining unmovable on the hard wooden bench. After washing and getting dressed, she went directly to the cafeteria line, greeted the others she'd met yesterday, and was introduced by Lunetta to some new faces. Sebastian Cruiser was a young man with a scruffy beard and torn jeans, which, in his case, were not meant to be in keeping with fashion. Freddie Fandango had the look and moves of a flamenco dancer, while Laura Luscious Lips looked exactly as her name described. It was yet another name Lunetta frowned on, Laura told her.

This time the menu included French toast which, at first, was a total disappointment until Lydia heard one of the residents complaining it wasn't made with real eggs, but egg substitute. She asked for three slices and poured a generous amount of the imitation maple syrup over them.

As she was eating, Simon came over to her table and set his tray down. "May I?"

She nodded with her mouth full and pointed to the empty chair.

"Are you okay? I was worried about you last night. You didn't come back for supper."

Simon studied her face for a few moments, then tilted his head and gave her a quizzical grin. "You really were worried, weren't you? It's been a long time since anyone was worried about my whereabouts."

"I was. Not so much your whereabouts, but your…well-being. I didn't know if I'd ever see you again."

Simon shrugged his shoulders. "I'm here."

Just then Janice Jewel came over to the table and set her tray down.

"Hey Simple. I hope you're being good to my friend Lydia here." She pulled out a chair. "Lydia. I hate to do this, but I am really hard up for cash right now. I don't need a lot, just fifty or so, and I know you're the kind of person who likes to help out a friend in a pinch."

At that moment Lunetta happened to be walking by. She stopped, put her hands on her hips, and glared at Janice. "Now you listen up, sister. You know we got rules about that kind of thing. You leave Miss Lydia in peace and no more asking her for anything. It's a wonder she got a stitch of clothes on her back." To Lydia, she said, "You pay her no mind, and don't you dare give her anything else of yours, you hear?"

Janice looked at Lydia, then back at Lunetta, and shrugged her shoulders. "Okay, Mama. Can't blame a girl for trying."

After Lunetta went over to another table to intervene in an argument between a man and a women over whose plastic fork was whose, Janice resumed the conversation. She had a wary look about her, as if she expected Lunetta to descend on her at any moment.

"Hey, Lydia. Seriously, I need your help. I got a question about money. Not yours, but mine. About making it, is what I mean. You obviously have found the secret charm and I wanna learn from you. I can see you got it going on and I'm not dumb enough to think there aren't some tricks of the trade I don't know yet. You know what I mean. I'm pretty new at the game, so I decided I'm gonna let you be my teacher. How's that for starters?"

Lydia stopped eating and put down her fork. "I...well, I'm flattered. But, I'm not sure how much help I can be. What exactly do you want to know?"

Janice raised her eyes to the ceiling. "Come on, girl. Don't mess with me. How do you do it? How do you get so much money you can go out and buy those expensive things you have, like you stepped out of a, well shit, a damn Vogue magazine? I mean, you got the look and we all know it's the look that makes the money and it's the money that makes the look. Are you getting my meaning?"

Lydia paused for a moment. "I think so. I guess I never thought about it that way, but I can see your point. Let me think. For starters, you have to believe you have the look. You have to think you're worth it. You have to convince others you're worth it. That way they'll treat you as if you're worth it, and they'll pay you more."

"No, no, girl. That's not it at all. That's just bullshit. I mean, I think I deserve more. Hell, I know I deserve more, but they won't pay me more.

They just say, "Hey honey, I can get it a lot cheaper just down the street, so get off your high horse and let's get it on."

Lydia could see her point. It took more than just confidence. The venue had to be a factor as well. "Okay, I think I know what's happening. For one, location is important. You have to be in a good location where the big spenders are. You have to look like someone who only takes on the big spenders, who only goes with the, well, the high-paying johns. The doctors, the bankers...the lawyers." She thought about Jack. "You need some bling, and some killer shoes. You need some really good make-up and nice clothes, too. Not too whorish looking, but clothes that say, 'Hey, look at me. Want a piece of this? You pay for what you get.' You know, that kind of thing."

What else could she tell her? Counseling prostitutes on their career plan had never been covered in any of her courses. She was pretty sure coaching them on how to bring in the bucks would never enter the curriculum. "You have to look like a movie star. Yes, that's it. A movie star. Someone the world wants to be associated with. Someone special and charming. Someone irresistible."

"Well hell, sister, are you saying I don't look good? Shit. You think you're some movie star, huh? Well I got news for you..."

Janice folded her arms across her chest and looked away.

"No, Janice, hear me out. That's not at all what I mean. You're a beautiful woman. I'm plain and I dress simply most of the time. But, when I do dress up, it's to make a statement. You have to make a statement."

"What are you talkin' about? What kind of statement?"

Lydia was pulling from a role she played once in her Drama class in college. What was the advice her professor had once given her? Oh yeah. "It's like this. You have to make the audience think you're the most desirable, most delicious, most alluring, and most fuckable woman on the planet. But you can't come across as easy. You have to play hard to get, like they're lucky if they can have you. But you have to be choosy. You don't want to settle for anything but the best."

She could tell by the way Janice closed her eyes as if viewing a scene of herself in action that she was getting her point across. Janice confirmed it when she burst out, "I get it. I really get it. You gotta play the part, whether you feel it or not. You gotta convince them and don't sell yourself short. You gotta be the lady who gets the rich johns all the time. I see it."

Janice stood up and put her hands on her hips and took long strides around the table, arching her back, jutting her chest out, and wiggling her hips. To the entire room, she shouted, "Hey baby. You want the best there is? Huh? You want the queen? You want a movie star? You want the jewel of the town? Well you found her. Janice Jewel. That's me. Uh huh. Come on now, baby. I'll take real good care of you. Just whip out that hundred and we'll have a good ol' time."

A couple guys in the back of the dining room made wolf whistles, while others clapped. One man called out, "I'm here baby. Any time you have the time."

Janice stuck her chin out. "I got no time for you, sweetheart. I'm going for the big fish. I'm going for the biggest fish. Hell, I'm going for the whales. The whales with the big wallets."

When she sat back down, satisfied with her performance, Lydia decided it would be best to change the conversation.

"You know, Janice, there are other ways to make money, and I mean good money. Better ways where you'd feel good about yourself all the time."

"I feel good about myself most of the time. I feel better about myself when I buy myself nice stuff." Janice flounced back her hair and folded her arms.

"You're smart, you're enterprising, and you're young. You could go back to college. I'm sure there's a community college near here where you could get training in something and become a professional."

"Sister, you still don't get it. I *am* a professional."

"I know, I know, but a different kind of professional. Someone who wouldn't have to work so hard and so late at night. Someone she wouldn't be putting herself at risk all the time. It's not safe being on the streets."

Janice looked concerned now and put her hand on Lydia's. "Anything bad ever happen to you?"

Lydia looked down. She hated to lie, but, in certain situations, it was the only appropriate thing to do. She decided not to tell a total lie, but to stretch the truth a little.

"Yes. I don't usually talk about it, but I once had a customer who really abused me. I thought I'd never go back to work. It took all I had to go back, but I was always cautious after that. Always on my guard."

She was recalling an incident when she worked at a sales clerk in a linen shop during her undergraduate years. A women yelled at her for giving her the wrong change.

"Did he beat you up bad?"

"Pretty bad. I wasn't the same after."

"And you still went back?"

"No. I went to college."

Janice slammed her hand on the table. "And now you're sittin' here tellin' me to go back to college. So, what? I'll end up homeless and on the streets again, like you? No, thank you, ma'am!"

Lydia realized her mistake. She should have left her college experience out. Thank goodness she didn't mention her marriage.

"What I'm trying to say is, you're young and you can do it. I dropped out. I made some bad choices. You can do better. I know you can."

Part of it was true. She did drop out of her master's program in counseling to get her daughter settled in college. She supposed some of her choices, like marrying Jack and ignoring his extramarital affairs, could be construed as bad choices. Janice didn't need to know all the details.

It was time to clear the dining room. People were gathering up their belongings and heading out the door.

"Just think about it, okay? You deserve better. I think you'd do great in college. Better than I did." Lydia paused, wondering if she should ask the question she'd had on her mind ever since entering the shelter. "Janice, I like to sketch people's faces. Would you mind sitting for me sometime so I could do your portrait?"

Janice's eyes doubled in size. "Are you serious? You're an artist? You wanna draw my portrait? Hell yes, let's do it. Come on girl, I got places to be. Let's go find us a place to sit and you can draw away. Heck, if it's good, I might even be able to sell it."

They walked out the door together. As they were leaving, Janice yelled to the others outside, "Hey, y'all. I'm gonna get my portrait drawn today."

Chapter 8

Simon was waiting outside the building. When he saw Lydia struggling through the door with her belongings, he walked up and took her tote bag. Lydia thought he looked surprisingly fresh this morning, red-cheeked, as if he'd had a shower or just come from a brisk run. His eyes were bright. It wasn't at all what she expected.

"Janice is coming with us. I'm going to sketch her portrait."

"Cool. Come on then. We'll go to the park."

Lydia first wanted to know if he'd help her after the sketching session was over. "I was wondering. After we're done, depending on how much walking you want to do, maybe you could show me where I can get a phone card. I have some money now and I need to make some calls. If you have other things to do, I understand." She had absolutely no experience with phone cards and was going to have to rely completely on his, or someone else's, knowledge.

Simon shrugged. "Yeah, my calendar's pretty full. Massage at 10, mani-pedi at 12, meeting with my broker at 1. Yeah, I think I can fit that in."

They headed down the street as Janice sang in a powerful soprano voice, "This is the dawning of the Age of Aquarius, Age of Aquarius..."

"So, you came by some money," he said. "Not the way the others do, I take it."

Janice stopped singing long enough to say, "Hey, Simple, you know Miss Lydia Chapel ain't some two-bit hooker. She's a high-priced escort, like I'm gonna be."

"I heard you bought her handbag. It looks good. Antoinette wasn't real happy about it, I gather."

"Oh, that Antoinette Hollywood can go screw herself. She's always jealous of me on account of I get better business than her. She's got no style. Seriously. I tried to help her, but the girl is stubborn. Thinks she knows it all. I ain't got time for that crap."

Lydia found herself enjoying the conversation. She was happy to be with her new friends. They were so much more brassy and interesting than some of her acquaintances in the city. It seemed that homelessness came with certain benefits. Lack of pretense, for one. Fewer attachments. No need to prove anything to anyone. Some of them, the younger ones, had a certain boldness that laughed in the face of adversity. They were genuine. Not quite what the textbooks might say, but so real and endearing. The bulk of them were worn down and polished to a sheen by suffering, not dulled by defeat.

When they arrived at the park, Simon led them to same bench where she'd sketched his portrait the day before. She positioned Janice where the sunlight best illuminated her face.

"Now just sit still and feel free to talk, but try not to move."

"Oh, honey, I can do this all day. I can sit still and not even move a muscle. I am good at that." She said this turning her head, looking up and pointing at a bird overhead, then smoothing back her thick hair. "Try not to draw that mole by my left ear, if that's okay. I want a little cosmetic surgery thrown into this deal."

Simon sat on a bench opposite them and occupied himself with his notebook.

When the sketch was done and Lydia felt she'd conquered the challenge of drawing a very restless subject, she tore off the page and handed it to Janice.

"What do you think?"

Janice held the drawing and studied it, frowning for an entire minute. She murmured, "Mmm, mm-hm." Then she stood up, raised it above her head, and shouted to the entire park. "I just had my portrait done by a famous artist and it is good. I mean real good. I love it."

Grabbing Lydia by the shoulders, she planted a kiss on her cheek and slapped her hard on the back. "You are one good artist, Lydia Chapel. I gotta show this one around. And I ain't selling this, no way. I'm going to Woolworth's right this minute and gettin' me a frame."

Janice waved to Simon and headed off to do her shopping.

Simon rejoined Lydia on the bench. "You know you just opened yourself up to a whole lot of requests. Watch out tonight. You'll have them all lining up."

Lydia smiled. "I'd love that."

He shook his head. "You're nuts. Come on, let's go get you that link to the civilized world. Phone card, here we come."

They walked several blocks to a store Simon knew carried phone cards. Lydia suggested stopping along the way at Starbuck's and insisted on treating him to anything he wanted. They walked away with mocha lattés and scones, sipping their drinks along the way. After purchasing the card, she suggested they head back to the park where she could begin making her calls in the peaceful setting.

Simon was agreeable. He seemed more subdued today. Perhaps it was the aftermath of his indulgence yesterday. He didn't seem to be hung over or even having a headache. She was surprised he actually seemed contented, albeit pensive. She didn't want to question him about it, figuring that heroin must have different effects than alcohol. It only proved to her how little she knew, even after completing her Substance Abuse class with an A. So much for a master's level education. All book learning, no real-life experience.

Her first call was to her sister-in-law, Becky. The call went immediately to a full and unreceptive voice mailbox. She tried Tori's number, wanting to be sure her daughter hadn't been trying to reach her and was becoming panicked when she couldn't. Tori had a tendency to be histrionic. As much as she wanted to tell her what was happening, she had to be careful to couch it in a way that wouldn't set her off, or pit her against her father. Tori had little enough respect for him as it was.

The same applied to Leo who said to her over the weekend he hoped he'd never turn out like his dad. It wasn't a healthy attitude for children to have about a parent, but at least she gave them credit for having minds of their own. She had never tried to sway their opinions and probably defended more of Jack's behavior than she should have. Still, they didn't miss much.

Tori's voicemail picked up. "It's me. You know what to do." That was just like Tori. Terse and to the point.

"Tori, it's me. Mom. I wanted to let you know I'm not at the cabin and my phone isn't working so I had to get a phone card, which is why I'm calling you from another number. You can reach me at this one." She recited the card number. "Also, something came up and I'm in a bit of a predicament. I need some money. Would you do me a huge favor? Would you call Aunt Becky and have her call me at this number. I tried to leave her a message but her voice mailbox is full. That's all for now. I love…"

Tori picked up the phone. "Mom? What on earth is going on? I've been trying to reach you for two days. Did you drop your phone in the lake? And what's this about needing money? Don't they have ATM's up there in the boonies?"

Lydia explained as gently as she could what had transpired since Tori was last at the cabin.

Tori was silent for several moments, then the explosion came.

"What the hell kind of fucked up thing is this? What the hell is dad thinking? How dare he cut you off? How dare he put you in danger alone up there without any money or a phone? How can you even stay at the cabin without money, or food, or anything? God, I don't believe this. This so seriously sucks the big one. This is insane, mom. Are you okay? Should I come up? Should I ask dad for more money—he just paid my allowance— but I could say something else came up and I need more. He'll probably say no because, well, he always says no. Or he'll think it's for you. What the fuck? I hate him. I hate him. I hate him. I hate him. I hate him…"

Lydia felt compelled to interrupt the tirade. "Tori, no, please don't say that. He is your father. You owe him some respect."

Tori exploded again. "Are you serious? How can you say that? How can I respect someone who isn't respectful? How can I respect such a…a dipshit? A monster? How can he do this to you? I have half a mind to go to the office and raise holy hell. Tell him to go fuck himself. Yes, I think I will."

As much as Lydia found it amusing to think of her daughter disrupting the sacrosanct atmosphere of the firm, she knew it would be grave mistake that wouldn't serve her best interests in any way. She knew what would happen if Tori fell out of grace with her father. It could spell the end of her college career and cause irreparable damage to her future. Jack wouldn't react as Tori might expect, so it was imperative she protect her daughter.

"Tori, listen. You don't want to get on your father's bad side. In fact, it's better if you pretend you don't know anything about this. I wouldn't have told you all this if I didn't need your help. Will you do that for me, please? Call Aunt Becky?" She wouldn't let her off the phone until she promised not to go to the office or say anything, except to Leo.

After they hung up, she called her son and left a message, knowing his reaction would be entirely different from Tori's. In fact, he might find the whole story amusing. She saw a lot of her brother in Leo.

Her next call was to attorney, Shawn O'Malley. Shawn had been a classmate of Jack's in law school, who later became an arch enemy by virtue of making Jack look bad during a high profile trial in which Jack lost the case. He never stopped holding a grudge against Shawn.

Lydia had known Shawn since high school and later, at Columbia, where they rekindled their friendship and became inseparable for a time, but only platonically. They probably would have dated had Jack not asked her out first. From then on, she and Jack were exclusive and her friendship with Shawn was, at best, strained. She still had a tender spot in her heart for him and sometimes wondered what would have happened had he asked her out first.

She even felt a little twinge of regret when, years later, she heard he'd gotten married. It was long after she and Jack exchanged vows and her reaction surprised her. Somewhere deep down inside she'd kept an ember of hope alive that she and Shawn might regain the friendship they once enjoyed in college. Although they kept in touch via Christmas cards, she wasn't invited to his wedding, which she knew was because of Jack. It bothered her that Jack's enmity prevented them from staying in touch. The very mention of Shawn's name around Jack evoked expletives.

Now, there was nothing preventing them from having a professional relationship. If their friendship renewed itself, so much the better. She needed Shawn for his legal expertise. He'd made a name for himself and was a sought-after divorce attorney, according to several of her friends.

Simon busied himself with his tiny notebook as Lydia called Shawn. He answered right away. Simon stopped writing to listen to her side of the conversation.

"Shawn, this is Lydia Myers. Yes, I know, long time, no see. Look, I need your help. I want you to handle my divorce. (Pause.) Uh huh, that's right. (Pause.) Yes, I can hardly believe it, myself."

Shawn talked for a while. Then Lydia resumed the conversation. "It's a long story, but I'm now living at the behest of the Lake View Rescue Ministry. (Pause.) Yes, great people. It's very safe. I'm with a friend I met there right now."

There was no point in going into more detail. By the sound of alarm in Shawn's voice, she had to play it down, as she'd done for Tori. "I'm okay for now. I left a message for my sister-in-law to send me some money. (Pause.) Thank you. I really do appreciate that. I promise I'll make it up to you. I'm sorry, but I have nothing for a retainer, but don't worry. You will be compensated later."

Lydia paused and let Shawn talk for a while. Simon wished he could listen in to both sides of the conversation, but he was getting the gist.

"Yes, that sounds great. Shawn, I'd like an uncontested divorce, but we both know that probably won't happen. Yes, I agree. If that happens, we'll do that. No holds barred. In any case, he's been cheating on me and I have proof. (Long pause.) Photos. Even a DVD. (Pause.) Long story. Let's talk about that another time. Also, his mistress is probably living at the house as we speak. At least she was there the last time I dropped by when I got back from Paris."

Lydia spent the next couple minutes listening and nodding her head. "Got it. I'm so grateful to you. I'll look forward to seeing you. Here's my phone card number. I'm not sure how phone cards work, but if I get a new one with a different number, I'll let you know. Shawn, it's been great talking to you. (Pause.) I know. Too long. I'll be in touch. Thank you. Take care. Talk soon."

Shawn hadn't changed. He insisted on sending her an advance on the divorce settlement. She knew it was so out of the realm of standard procedure, but she accepted it gratefully. He told her his secretary would wire two thousand dollars to Western Union within the hour.

Lydia hung up the phone, took a deep breath, looked up at the tree overshadowing the bench and burst into tears. Simon cocked his head, taken aback by the sudden change of mood.

"What happened? It sounded like everything was cool and he was going to help you. What's wrong?"

She took a few moments to compose herself, dabbing at her eyes and blowing her nose. "He is going to help. I'm not homeless anymore."

Simon shook his head and leaned closer. "Okay? So, where's the shit end of the stick? I'm confused."

Lydia looked at him through misted eyes. "I'll have to leave the shelter. I won't be Lydia Chapel anymore. I wanted to do more sketching...and..." She was about to say, "and help you," but decided not to.

Simon lowered his gaze and looked at her under a furrowed brow. "Okay. So, come back and visit us, silly. It's not like you're banned from the club, enviable as it is, just because you have a home. We'll try not to treat you like a pariah. You can sketch all you want and even sell more of your clothes, if that turns you on."

She put her hand on his and gave it a squeeze.

Shawn O'Malley had been organizing his notes for a trial that afternoon when the call from Lydia Myers came in. For a moment he wondered if it could it be his old high school friend, Lydia O'Connor, who he'd rekindled a friendship with at Columbia until she met that jackass, Jack Myers, and married him. After that, he'd lost touch with her. He'd thought of her often over the years, especially when he had to deal with her arrogant asshole of a husband in the course of his work. He thought about her more after his marriage dissolved and wondered how hers was going. He always found it hard to imagine her married to Jack.

What on earth would Lydia O'Connor be calling him about? They hadn't seen each other or spoken to each other in, what, twenty years? He'd wanted to keep in touch and occasionally get together with her, given they both lived in the city, but then, there was that small matter of her husband. Not that her marital status should have precluded a friendship, but it was who she married. Jack Myers, hotshot attorney by reputation, certified prick by all who really knew him. It certainly wouldn't have done Lydia any good if he tried to keep up a friendship with her. Jack hated his guts, poor loser that he was, and the feeling was mutual.

"Put it through," he told his secretary.

"Shawn? This is Lydia Myers, formerly O'Connor. Remember me?"

"Of course I do. How are you, Lydia?"

"I'm fine. I'm sorry it's been such a long time. I've thought of calling you over the years but, well, you know how it is."

Shawn knew all too well how it was and how it would have been had her husband gotten wind of it. Much more grief and trouble than she needed.

"Lydia, it's great to hear your voice. I thought the same thing, about calling you, I mean, but, same reasons, I guess. Time just has a way of slipping by. We all know about that."

"I do. And I appreciate that you didn't."

It was clear Lydia knew any contact with him would have been ill-advised, given that Jack, in his egotism, took the loss of a significant case as a personal affront. Jack Myers took to losing like a cat takes to water. He never wasted time on professional courtesy and couldn't tax himself to handle defeat with even a modicum of grace.

Shawn would never forget the look on Jack's face when he threw down his papers and stormed out of the courtroom after the verdict was announced. His company got slapped with a three million dollar fine in addition to jail time for some of its senior executives. Jack walked away with not only egg on his face, but the whole dozen smeared all over him. It was a big win for the other side and pure satisfaction for Shawn.

"Shawn, as much as I wish this was just a friendly call," Lydia said, "I need to enlist your services. Jack and I are getting a divorce and I would like you to represent me, if you're available. Would you be my attorney?"

Shawn hesitated. This was completely unexpected. Not only receiving a phone call from Lydia, but hearing she and Jack were splitting up. For just an instant, his heart leapt. He gathered it back under the cloak of professionalism and said, "Of course. I'd be more than willing to represent you, Lydia. I have to ask first, though. Does Jack know about this?"

Lydia took a deep breath. "About the divorce, yes. About hiring you, no. I thought that might come as a nice surprise. I don't mean to put you in any awkward position, but I really think it has to be you."

Shawn wanted to believe she meant that she preferred him over any other attorney because of his reputation, and because she still considered him a friend. If there was the ulterior motive of getting back at Jack, so be it. It didn't matter. He had no intention of refusing this case. It was the kind of challenge he liked, and he had a personal interest in helping an old friend. Also, it would give him another chance to take a crack at exposing Jack Myers for the unethical attorney and rampant egotist he was. Jack would never accept that he lost the People vs. Boyd Enterprises case. It wasn't that he'd done a poor job of representing his client, but that the plaintiffs had an airtight case of discrimination in hiring. They also had irrefutable evidence that anyone who spoke out against the company was let go without cause.

Yes, this would be a divorce case he'd be happy to take. Others he was more discriminating about, and some he refused just on principle. Not this one, though.

As much as he liked doing divorce cases, he still smarted from his own and probably always would. It had been neither congenial nor fair. He'd given in to all his wife's demands mainly to get rid of her and her interfering family. In comparison with other divorces, his was relatively straightforward and simple, mainly because he refused to fight.

It wasn't worth it. His wife, Stephynia, wasn't the most balanced individual she so convincingly portrayed herself to be. She was largely influenced by her holy roller fundamentalist Christian family who never wanted her to marry a Catholic, lapsed though he was, in the first place. Her holier-than-thou attitude became the catalyst to many arguments and nights when he left the house and stayed away all night just to avoid her preaching. Her parents were even worse. They convinced her he was putting her salvation at risk by not becoming "saved," as they called it. When he remarked jokingly that his interpretation of being "saved" was like buying an insurance policy that guaranteed passage into heaven, the rift between them became a chasm.

One thing he always marveled at was how couples who joined together in love and holy matrimony could turn into the most vicious and vindictive of enemies. Stephynia's family led their own personal crusade against him. She carried the banner.

This case of Lydia and Jack Myers would likely be different, but maybe not. One thing was for sure, the added enticement of dealing with someone who already considered him an arch enemy would add spice to the proceedings. While it was not in his nature to poke the lion, in this case he was ready to get a knife and start sharpening the stick. If there was one objective to accomplish, it would be that Lydia was assured a fair settlement, because he already knew that would not be Jack's objective.

"I'll be happy to take your case, Lydia. It's been too long. We need to catch up on the years gone by. Let me give you back to my secretary and she'll make an appointment."

The next part was a little unexpected.

"Wait, Shawn, there's something else," Lydia said. "I don't have any money to pay you right now. In fact I..." She paused. It sounded like she was a bit choked up. "Let me just say, I will be able to pay you in the future, just not right now. Also, I'm not living in the city. I'm at Lake George, in our cabin, so I'll do my best to get there on time. It's a good five hour drive in the best of traffic."

Shawn reflected for a moment. Money wasn't the issue for him. He knew if he did his job right, and he had every intention of doing so, Lydia would be collecting a sizeable share of her husband's assets. There was no fear of not getting paid for his work, even though he required a retainer of all other clients. It was the drive to the city that concerned him. That was a strenuous trek for anyone, let alone a woman doing it by herself.

An idea came that he thought might resolve the situation and be mutually agreeable.

"Well, it just so happens I have a free weekend coming up and was going to take a drive up to Saratoga and points beyond. I haven't been to Whiteface Mountain in a long time and it's been on my agenda to get there sometime this year. Suppose I drive up and meet you somewhere for lunch? Would that be acceptable to you?"

"That would be more than acceptable. It's a fantastic idea. Tell you what. You can come to the cabin and I'll make lunch. Then I can show you the lake and we'll have plenty of time to talk."

Before hanging up, they made plans for a meeting time. As much as he tried to suppress the excitement he was feeling about seeing Lydia O'Connor again, he couldn't stop smiling when he put the phone down. She'd been more than just a friend. She'd been the reason he finished high school and gone on to college. He'd been a shy kid, totally lacking in confidence, and a real dud with the ladies back then. Lydia had made him feel important, like he had something to offer the world. He'd been in love with her ever since high school, but never told her. Then Jack came along and ruined everything.

It was going to be an interesting reunion, not that he had any intention of making it more than a professional meeting. If it worked out, and he hoped it would, it might be a rekindling of an old friendship. She was his client and that was the long and short of it. If anything more came of it, which was highly unlikely, he'd welcome an occasional contact to reminisce about old times.

Ever since his divorce, the idea of another committed relationship had been out of the question. Completely absurd. Not happening. Marriage was a minefield. It was one of the riskiest propositions that existed on the planet. His divorce had left permanent scars, convincing him that one was much better off single and only dating women who weren't interested in commitment, but not necessarily in it just for the sex. That didn't appeal to him, either. There were prostitutes for that kind of thing. To him, sex wasn't reason enough to build a relationship, and friendship was preferable to just meeting one's animal needs.

Yes, it would be interesting to see how the years had treated Lydia Myers. There was a time he thought her the most beautiful girl in the universe, both inside and out. The trouble was, he'd always been too shy, too reticent. Damn him, if that cocky bastard Jack Myers hadn't come along. He and Lydia might have explored a serious relationship together.

This wasn't the time to speculate on how things might have been, but it was difficult not to let his mind drift there. Lydia O'Connor certainly would have been a different kind of partner from Stephynia. Ironically, after they divorced and she moved to Hoboken, he heard she married a stock broker. A Christian, of course. Nothing but the God-approved best. At least that wasn't as surprising as Lydia's choice. She married the last man on earth Shawn would have approved of. Jack might as well have been the devil incarnate.

He couldn't wait to sink his teeth into this case.

Chapter 9

They found the Western Union office at the far side of Main Street. The wire transfer was already awaiting her. Next stop was the Wells Fargo bank where she opened a debit account, deposited twelve hundred, and pocketed eight-hundred dollars. Simon found it amusing how methodically she went about her work. When she was done and they were outside the bank, she took out the wad of hundreds.

"How much do you need?" she asked Simon.

"Put that away. Geez. They'll think we're making a deal." He pushed her hand away, taking a quick scan around. "I need the whole eight hundred, if you really want to know, but I'll take fifty, when we're back in the park. Only if you can spare it. Twenty-five would be cool, too."

Lydia handed him a hundred dollar bill which he grabbed and thrust in his jacket pocket.

"Don't do that again, okay? We could both end up cooling our heels in the local slammer."

Something about that made her laugh. "Going from homeless to jail. Not bad for a morning's work." She suddenly became serious. "I know I shouldn't say this, but I will. Please don't spend this on you-know-what."

Simon found that enormously amusing and burst out laughing. "You-know-what? No, I don't know what, but if I could get some of you-know-what, you know what I'd do with you-know-what."

He began making up rhymes as they walked along the street.

Lydia Chapel married a louse.
Lydia Chapel had a house.
Lydia Chapel lost it all.
Then Lydia Chapel got rich and had a ball.

"Don't push me. I may take that hundred back." She gave him a shove, then stopped abruptly and looked across the street. "Listen, I want to do something for the others. Maybe get them a gift card of some kind. Food, perhaps. What would you suggest? There's that nice restaurant over there—the Village Tavern. They could enjoy a nice meal and have a glass of wine there.

Simon grabbed her by the arm. "You are by far, without a doubt, the most feckless woman I've ever known. Your heart's in the right place, that's for sure, but, Holy Sweet Jesus, you're quite the act. If you really want to help them, give them a ten dollar gift card for McDonald's. It'll buy coffee for a week. They'll go ape shit over it."

Lydia pondered for a moment. "No, it has to be more special than that. I want them to have a nice sit-down dinner."

"Well, it sure as hell isn't going to be at the Village Tavern. That place caters to the Saratoga crowd. They'd take one look at them and out the door they'd go. I know because I went in there once to use their restroom and they threw me out unceremoniously, as if I was dropping cooties on their Sicilian tile. Seriously, Lydia, don't do it. Get them a gift card for somewhere else. Taco Bell or Burger King, if you don't like golden arches."

They continued walking down the street. "I want them to eat something they don't ordinarily get. How about that one there? The Lobster Trap. It's rustic and within walking distance of the shelter. Surely they can get a good meal there and not get thrown out. Is that better?"

"Yep. That one's better. I ate there once. It's good and reasonably priced. Their wait help all look druggy and homeless themselves. They can sit outside, too. That would work better for the odor factor. Not too hoity-toity for the gang and they'd feel more at ease."

They crossed the street and Lydia went inside, leaving Simon on the sidewalk at his request. "I don't want them to think I'm your pimp or anything," he joked. After a few minutes she came out smiling, holding ten thirty-dollar gift cards. She handed them to Simon. You give them out, okay? Just tell them it's from a friend. And keep one for yourself."

"What's this for? You don't have to give me one. I just nailed you for a hundred cool ones."

Lydia took Simon's hand that was holding the cards, pulled one out, and tucked it in his jacket pocket.

"Take it. I also want to have you over to the cabin for supper some night. Just give me a couple days to settle back in and get supplies and have all the utilities back on line. I'll probably have to clean out the fridge, too, since the power's been off."

"Well, sure. I think I can handle that. I'll just have to check my social calendar first and see when I can spare you the time."

Back at the shelter, Lydia told the staff she was leaving and thanked them for their hospitality. She took Ron aside to speak privately.

"I'm afraid I don't have the money now, but please take this and just know that in the future, your ministry will be one of my top charities." She handed him a hundred dollar bill. "You're doing wonderful work here. It's so important, but you already know that."

Ron took the bill and peered at her with a look of distrust. "So you *are* an actress studying a part. I was right again."

Lydia burst out laughing. "Seriously? Is that what you thought? No, I really am, or was, a homeless person without money. I told you the truth."

Ron was still shaking his head as Lydia walked out the door.

Outside, she called a taxi. While waiting, she made plans with Simon to meet for supper over the weekend.

"Be careful," Lydia said in parting. "I don't want to lose you as a friend."

"I don't either."

She watched as Simon trudged down the street, the soles of his shoes having separated from the rest, slapping the sidewalk. Maybe he would use the money for new shoes, or a better windbreaker. His was full of holes. She didn't think so, but she could only hope. When they met again, she'd tell him what she was planning. One way or another, she was going to help him. She just counted on him staying alive long enough for it to happen.

Simon walked about six blocks and sat on a bench overlooking the lake. It was his favorite spot to make phone calls. He felt a little guilty about taking the money from Lydia Myers and not letting on that he had a phone she could have used. He couldn't risk blowing his cover. She totally believed him, and even though it felt shitty to be so deceptive, he had no choice. He'd make it up to her later.

He punched in the number and waited for his boss, Donnie Maslowski, to answer.

"Maz? It's me, Simon. Listen. I got way more than a piece about homelessness. I got something that will end up on the front page if we play it right. I've been hanging out with this newcomer to the shelter and it turns out she's the wife of Jack Myers. Remember, attorney Jack Myers? The one you interviewed last year about the Carlisle and Maddigan case? Also, we covered the People vs. Boyd Enterprises, the case Myers lost."

His senior editor thought he was putting him on. "Okay, so what's the punch line?"

"No, I'm not shitting you. It's really Jack Myer's wife and she's homeless, or was until this morning, because he kicked her out and cut off all her money."

"Unbelievable. He's an even bigger bastard than I thought."

"I know, right? He closed all the credit card and bank accounts, cut off her cell phone, took away everything. She couldn't even put gas in her car."

"I can see there might be some possibilities here. Go on."

"Yeah, for real. But, there's more. They're getting a divorce and Shawn O'Malley's representing her."

"The same Shawn O'Malley who trounced Myers in the Boyd Enterprises case?"

"You got it."

"We'll have to talk to him, once they get the divorce ball rolling."

"Oh, and get this. She caught good ol' Jack in the act, or at least her detective did. There're even photos and a DVD.

"No fucking way."

"Fuck, yes!"

A grin spread across his face as he listened to his boss's string of expletives. It was always a good sign when Maz used a lot of profanity. It meant he really had his attention.

"It's crazy, I know, but what a story."

He paused as Maz talked to someone else in the office and heard the same reaction, more curses, coming from one of the other reporters. Maz came back on line and he listened for instructions.

"Got it. No, I won't be at the shelter too much longer. I still have a few more stories to get. They're rich, let me tell you. And just so you know, I'm having dinner with Mrs. Myers day after tomorrow. I'll get more on the family and kids. You get whatever you can on Jack Myers and Shawn O'Malley, okay? If we do this right, this'll be the story of the summer. I'll be back in the city in a couple days but I want to get things wrapped up here. I want this article to be good and I know it will be. Talk soon."

Simon sat for over an hour, looking out across the lake that, today, seemed larger and more impressive than ever before. It was good to be here, but it'd be better to be back in the city in his own apartment. He wanted to be Simon Vanderlaan again, not Simon Simple, the down-and-out heroin addict. Still, the experience taught him a lot about homelessness and even more about the problem of drug addiction. It was too easy, too unavoidable for young, disenfranchised youth, and the older, not so lucky disenfranchised. He'd met several people from affluent families—kids who'd been born with the proverbial silver spoon that morphed into a heroin spoon. They were no different from the skid row bums pumping pleasure into their veins. All were on a lethal trajectory.

What it came down to, he wrote in his notepad, was that heroin was an equal opportunity addiction. Anybody could get hooked under the right circumstances. Sometimes it took only one use. One stupid move. One peer-supported lark encouraged by friends. Once you were hooked, you were alone, invisible, a non-entity. You had no identity other than as an addict. You become the drug and the drug became you. It lived and crawled under your skin. This is what the others told him. It was the filter through which you made choices and governed everything you said and did. Drug addicts loved to tell their story. It was about all they had.

It was ironic that most people assumed that once a person was addicted, it was the final chapter of their life. There was nothing beyond. Even the well-meaning staff of the shelter saw only the overcoat of addiction. The dealers saw only the helpless addict who'd do anything for the next fix. If anyone had job security, it was they. His article touched on the addiction aspect of homelessness, but his book, which he had every intention to write, would fully expose the issue in its rawest details.

Then, as if lightning struck twice, Lydia Myers came along. A homeless person. Now there was a fresh twist. She was different, too, in the way she looked at him, believing him to be a drug addict and all the while caring about and not judging him. She even went so far as to give him money. That bothered him. He hated that he had to deceive her. He'd come clean and level with her, eventually. And give her back the money. Maybe they'd still be friends.

But his article for *New York Now* was foremost in his mind. It was the break he needed. Until now he'd felt like just one of the other reporters, a lackey. Insignificant. This would turn it around for him. Fortunately, Maz believed in him, much as he rode his ass and was a relentless copy editor and task master.

He had to wrap the two stories up soon. First, would be the story on homelessness. That would come out in the next couple weeks. Then would come the story of Lydia Myers, once he'd gathered more on the divorce proceedings and anything else he could pick up on Jack Myers. It was going to be good. He just had to pitch it the right way.

Man, when it rained, it poured, and he was loving getting drenched.

Chapter 10

Jack Myers was in the middle of a deposition when his secretary called. Mary Quaile was usually cautious about interrupting him unless it was a matter of extreme urgency. She knew how to field most calls and handle clients he didn't need, or want, to see. He thought of letting the call go to voicemail, but decided it might be one he needed to take. It was a boring deposition anyway. Some insignificant kerfuffle about a death at the nursing home. The family was suing on the grounds that poor old grandma had allegedly been euthanized through an overdose of pain medication. Malpractice, negligent homicide, wrongful death. It all ran together. It happened every day in nursing homes. Par for the course.

"Mr. Myers, I'm so sorry to interrupt, but your daughter is on the phone. She says it's urgent."

Jack excused himself and asked his clients, the daughter and son of the victim, to take a seat in the waiting room outside the office.

"Hey Tori, what's up? You don't usually call me at work. Everything okay?" He tried not to sound annoyed.

Tori wanted to shout into the phone, *No, it isn't asshole,* but bit her tongue. "Hi Dad. I'm sorry to bother you at work, but something came up and I had to get ahold of you quickly or I'd miss the deadline. I've been offered a chance to study for a year abroad in Florence, Italy. It's a real honor to be selected and I'd really love to do it."

"That sounds great, Tori. Congratulations. Do you need me to sign permission?"

Oh, for Christ's sake, Tori thought. *Did he forget I'm not still in elementary school?*

"No, Dad. I have to put down a deposit today to save my place, otherwise they'll offer it to someone else. It's two thousand dollars."

"That's a lot for a deposit. Is it refundable?"

"Uh, yeah. As long as I give thirty days' notice." Tori crossed her fingers. "But I won't. I really want to go. This is a chance of a lifetime and, besides, it'll look great on my resume."

She knew that would impress her father. He was a firm believer in looking ahead to the future and putting your ducks in a row.

"I'll transfer the money to your account within the hour. I have to go now." He hung up. It was just like him to not even say good-bye.

No sooner had they hung up then she called her mother. "Mom, I'm sending you two thousand dollars. Just give me your bank routing number and your account number. Dad's putting it into my account as we speak."

Her mother hesitated, careful to choose words that would not set her daughter off. "Honey, did you ask him for the money to send to me?"

Tori rolled her eyes. "Mom, come on. What do you take me for? I made up a story and he bought it. I'll give you the details another time. Just know that two thousand will go into your account today. Oh, and I talked to Aunt Becky and she called Uncle Tom in Beijing and they said they would send you however much you needed. I told them five thousand would tide you over for the time being, so you should be getting that soon. Aunt Becky said she'd mail you a check. I'd send you a check, too, but you know, snail mail—not the best way to handle emergency funds."

Lydia felt a swell of pride for her daughter's ingenuity. "Thank you so much, sweetheart. You're a life saver. Let me know when you can come up and visit again, okay?"

"I will. Not sure when I'll be done with the summer class I'm taking in Environmental Ecology. I may just drop it, but it's a good class. I don't know."

"No, Tori. Keep the class. You can come up later, after it's done."

Her mother was all about finishing things, which was strange, since she never finished her master's program. She hesitated, not sure if she wanted to know the answer to her next question.

"Mom. Is it really horrible at the shelter? You can tell me. I'll be okay. I mean, are you around a lot of crazy, down and out people, probably all heroin addicts and meth heads? I kind of think it would make a good reality show. Sorry, that probably wasn't the right thing to say. At least you can leave now, with the money coming."

Lydia told her she was no longer at the shelter and was back at the cabin.

Now it was Tori's turn to act surprised. "Huh? How'd you manage that?"

"Someday I'll tell you all about it. It's a complicated story."

Lydia knew it would prompt a lot of questions which she preferred to address face-to-face. In fact, she was hoping to bring Tori to the shelter at some point in the future to broaden her education about people less privileged than she. "Before you go, did you get a chance to talk to Leo?"

"Oh yeah. I filled him in. He's furious with dad, of course. He picked up a picture of him he had on his desk and smashed it. He doesn't even want to speak to him. Oh, and he said he wants to follow him and confront him and his mistress in public. I tried to talk him out of it, but you know Leo, all hot air. I wouldn't worry. I'd place bets he won't do it."

"Please tell him not to. Better yet, give him my number and tell him to call me. It's better I deal with this."

"Are you okay, mom? I mean, seriously. I know you're good at hiding your feelings, but I want to know. Was it very traumatic being at the shelter?"

"During your summer break, you come up for a visit and I'll tell you all about it. And no, it wasn't traumatic at all. It was pretty interesting. I'll sort of miss it, in a way."

After they hung up, Tori sat down on her bed and tried to study, but her mind was preoccupied. Her mom was weird, there was no doubt about that. Who else would get kicked out of her home, end up in a homeless shelter with a bunch of derelicts, find it interesting and even go so far as to say she'd miss it? Unbelievable. Any normal person would have had a mental breakdown. She certainly would have wanted to cut herself, or step in front of a moving vehicle. Well, maybe not that radical. She sure as hell wouldn't say she'd miss it, even if she did manage to survive. Maybe that was why her mom wouldn't say much. Besides being in a scary situation, there was also the shame. If it happened to her, not that it ever would, she'd never have been able to talk to her friends about it. Not ever.

It was always a madhouse in *New York Now's* newsroom. Today was no exception. Too often before this, Simon Vanderlaan wondered how he'd ever gotten mixed up in a rat race like this. By nature, he was in his element in a much simpler, quieter environment, not the frenetic and ofttimes schizophrenic nature of his workplace. Simpler. No wonder he'd taken the name, Simple, at the homeless shelter. Simon Simple, or its reverse, Simple Simon, not that anyone there ever heard the rhyme, *Simple Simon met a pie man going to the fair...* Now, back at work, he thought about his time upstate. If anything would have pushed him to use drugs, it'd be this place. Half the staff were alcoholics or pot heads.

As soon as he got back he was caught up in the frenzy and it was making him edgy. Today was the day he was going to pitch his idea for the new story, on top of the story he'd already been assigned that was in the last stages of copy editing. The plight of the homeless in New York State. It was going to be good.

Living at the shelter had been an eye-opening experience. Once he got over the initial shock of almost getting stabbed in the hand over a piece of Wonder bread at supper, and the fear of having his few personal belongings ripped off during the night, he settled in better than he'd anticipated.

Sleeping in the bunk room had been a trip. A room full of men ranging in age from eighteen to eighty-six, differing in body odor from mildly noxious to clothespin-on-the-nose raunchy, varying from mentally depressed to actively psychotic, and all contending for top-bunk status because it was harder to be robbed there. He didn't mind sleeping on the lower bunk, except for the one time his bunkmate failed to get down the ladder in time to make it to the one bathroom that served twenty-six men. That hadn't been a pleasant experience.

"Hey, Vanderlaan, get your ass in here, we're ready for you." Donnie Maslowski was not just a boss, but a mentor. He'd taught Simon most of what he knew from the time Simon got hired with nothing more than a degree in Journalism and a lot of real-life learning to do. They were friends now, with a certain respectful distance between them. Simon and the others called him Maz. Only one reporter still referred to him as Mr. Maslowski, but then, it was clear to everyone that guy's distinguishing characteristic was the brown ring around his nose.

One of the many words of wisdom Maz imparted was that a reporter had to stand out, make a splash, do the impossible, or at least do something nobody else had thought of doing, and do it better than anyone else could. That's what had prompted Simon to take on the homeless in New York project and to fully immerse himself in it.

He decided early on he wasn't going to hang out around shelters interviewing the homeless, asking them what it was like, how they got there, and so forth. Anyone could have done that. He was going to become one of the homeless. Live the experience. He added the heroin addiction as a side feature that would give him excuses to disappear for periods of time when he had to run back to the city and report in. It was a fortuitous move because it opened up a whole new perspective on the problem of addiction among the homeless.

Simon entered the room and sat where Maz pointed. It was a relief to see only four others around the table. More of a relief when Maz took the floor and began by filling the others in on the progress of the article.

"Okay, so I'm going to brag for just a minute on my protégée, Simon Vanderlaan, so bear with me, or not. Up to you. He nailed the piece on homelessness and took it out of the city and upstate. He gave it a different twist by getting down and dirty. What I mean by that is, Simon took it on himself to join the ranks of the homeless, even so far as to pose as a heroin addict. I don't know about you, but that takes some *cojones* and this dude's got 'em and they're big."

That elicited some chuckles from the room. "No, he's not going to show them to you," Maz continued. "The end result is a tight as your tightest pair of jeans, graphic as your dirtiest porn magazine, and amazingly accurate, not to mention poignant, portrayal of this societal problem we've labeled with the euphemism, *homelessness*."

Maz stopped and looked around the room, as was his style. He wanted to be sure everyone was with him and nobody needed to be jerked awake. Satisfied, he went on.

"I don't mind pointing out that the *Daily Journal* tried to do a similar piece about a year ago and it was a sad-ass flop. Pitifully pandering, as far as I was concerned. Colorless and uninspiring. Fucking white bread, to be perfectly honest. Like it was written by some spoiled rich kid in Jersey. It probably was. So, I have to thank Simon here for getting it right, for calling attention to, no, for literally pushing our faces into the shit hole that is homelessness in this great State of New York. Let's take just a moment here to recognize Simon for *Homelessness—The Face of Courage* which is going to the press this week. If you haven't read it yet, I promise you, it's mind blowing."

The room broke out in applause. Simon stood up, red-faced, took a bow and cleared his throat. "Seriously, I mean it when I say thanks to all of you, but especially to Maz, here. He's been my source of inspiration, not to mention he saved my tuckis on more than one occasion when I had my thumb up it not knowing where to go or what to do with a piece."

Another round of applause.

"I have to say, and I mean it with all sincerity, I owe where I am today to him. I also owe living in a shelter, walking the streets, eating crap out of garbage cans, and schmoozing with drug dealers to him, as well. Maz, I hope I did you proud. If you're ever in need of any needles or heroin, I know just who to see."

Again, laughter filled the room. Simon knew the next thing he was about to say might not go over as well, but he had to take a chance. It was going to be a stretch. He knew from experience and observation that, once someone climbed to the top of the heap, those below were ready and eager to grab him by the ankles and yank him back down. It was rare to get two successful articles published in a row. Maz could do it, but only occasionally.

"The reason I'm here today is to pitch an idea that came to me in the course of my undercover homeless assignment. At the shelter, I made the acquaintance of a woman who was also a resident there. Although she stood out like a sore, albeit attractive, thumb and didn't look at all like a homeless person, she actually was. She was not only homeless, but penniless. The oddity was, there was a huge discrepancy in her overall presentation, not to mention her vocabulary, and just the way she was handling the situation. It got my curiosity up, wondering what the hell a nice girl like her was doing in a place like that. So, long story short, I made her acquaintance. We hung out together and I found out who she was and what her story was."

Simon noticed a couple of his listeners leaning forward. Good sign. There was some interest. If he pitched it right, he might engage the others, as well.

"Maybe some of you remember our coverage a few years back of the People vs. Boyd Enterprises case? A highly publicized case, which I wish I had the experience back then to have contributed to, but such was not in the stars. The attorney for the defense was a certain Jack Myers. He lost the case, as much as he put up a good fight. He's with the firm of Parker, Cross, Epstein and Myers. You've all heard of them. The Saxony Schools incident, the Fellicent trial, the drive-by shooting of Mayor Mauney, the Montclair, Inc. debacle, and others. Jack Myers has won a lot of high-profile cases and earned a reputation, whether noble or not, as a hotshot attorney. His firm, as you may know, represents mostly high rollers, mobsters, and the all-too-frequent corporate violators of civil and human rights."

Simon noticed one of his colleagues yawning, another closing his eyes.

"I'm going to get to the point, but a little back story is necessary. The woman I met at the shelter is the wife of Jack Myers. She was living at the shelter, not long, mind you, only a few days, because her husband effectively put her there. He cut her off, closed all their bank accounts, canceled credit cards, disconnected her cell phone, and basically left her stranded at their cabin on Lake George, a place she'd fled to after announcing she was leaving him. She didn't even have a car to drive because she couldn't buy gas."

He paused to see how the pitch was going. There were frowns, side comments being exchanged, eyebrows arching. A hand went up. It was Sydney Wiseman, one of his least favorites among the group. Sydney always had to take an antagonistic approach to everyone else's ideas. It was just for the principle of it. He couldn't accept anything at first glance without throwing mud at it. Simon pointed to him.

"I see where you might find this an intriguing story, but really, is there even a story here? I mean, bad husband treats wife unfairly, wife ends up in a homeless shelter, wife gets out and tells her tale of woe. End of story. Wah-wah. Everybody gets pissed off for about two seconds, then they move on to the sports page. Now if she murdered the bastard, or blew up his yacht, or he hired a hit man to kill her, we might have something to sink our teeth into."

As much as he hated to, Simon could see Syd's point. It wasn't much of a story, interesting as he thought it would be. Who'd really give a rat's ass if some rich society lady had to rub shoulders with the hoi-polloi. Big deal. Some people would call that poetic justice. He had to find a better angle.

Maz stepped in. "Let's not be hasty and brush off what has the potential of being a good, if not great, story. Suppose we approach it from a slightly different angle? Suppose we uncover a history of abuse that endured throughout the marriage, one that speaks of a disease of corporate corruption that infiltrated the home of a key player in a prestigious law firm? Suppose we not only expose Jack Myers but the entire firm he represents? Instead of making Lydia Myers the victim of his niggardly... sorry, I told you all not to use that one anymore...his inhumane, self-serving behavior, we make her a heroine? An icon for women to look up to and emulate. The Park Avenue pretty woman forced into homelessness by a shrewd and relentlessly vindictive husband. We all know women's lib stories are what's selling and who better to be our poster child than Lydia Myers, wife and soon to be divorced spouse of one of New York's leading attorneys?"

Murmurs of agreement filled the room. Simon took a deep breath, trying to keep his feet from doing a River Dance routine. They were liking it. Well, they were liking the spin Maz was putting in it, which was perfectly fine with him. Maz, of all people, was someone everyone looked up to, with the exception of Syd Wiseman who looked down his nose at everyone, even though he had no good reason to. His articles were mediocre at best, always critical of society and the government. They still got attention, though, which guaranteed him job security. Simon knew Maz would have canned him years ago, except that corporate liked what Wiseman produced. Thus, the resident Eeyore was allowed to stay.

"It'll take some research to find out the firm's history and any possible evidence of corruption," Syd offered. He reached his arms over his head and stretched. "There's also the risk of a defamation lawsuit, so we have to be careful, take our time, and expose only what is public record."

Maz nodded. "You're right about that, Syd. That's why this piece is going to require more than just Simon putting his pecker on the chopping block. We all have to pitch in and do our part. For the research team, I want Syd, Gary, and Christina to work their mojo. Simon, you'll be in charge of Lydia Myers and get a tight-as-your-granny's-girdle angle on her story, plus anything more you can learn about her life previous to becoming homeless. You know what I mean. We want to know what her home life and marriage were like, who she talked to, how she got to the shelter, whether she ever was in danger, and anything else leading up to her runaway to Lake George. The more embellishments, the better. If you play it right, you might have yourself a screen play. I'm in charge of the final copy, but Simon, this is your gig and to your credit. But, I want a lot of input from you all. If we do what we do best and bust our asses, we can get this out for the Fourth of July issue—a showpiece for independence and recognition of oppressed women, an exposé of a corrupt corporate colossus—how's that for alliteration? It'll also be a great follow-up to Simon's article on homelessness and its many facets." He paused as if to gather his thoughts. There was one more thing pressing on his mind.

"I don't think I need to remind you about the prime directive—confidentiality. If so much as a whiff of this story gets out to anyone, and I mean anyone, not only is this story cooked, but so is your ass and your job. Do I make myself clear?"

Maz swept the group with his eyes, clapped his hands once and shouted, "We're done. Now get your butts moving and back to work. We have a paper to write."

Chapter 11

It wasn't every day you found out you were going to be a father. It was even more of a surprise when you had no idea there was a pregnancy to begin with. What really topped it off with whipped cream and a cherry was the fact that you found it out in a letter from the mother-to-be of your child who was living overseas and hated your guts. In fact, hated them so much she probably would have been happy to rip them out with her bare hands and scatter them around just for the fun of it. To be perfectly honest, he couldn't blame her. He'd done her wrong, not intentionally, of course, but then, wasn't it true what his grandmother always said? The road to hell is paved with good intentions?

Vito DeFranco stood holding the letter with all the foreign postage on it. She had nice handwriting, seeing it now for the first time. Nicole Dubois, the bakery counter girl, the one person who made his time in Paris surveilling Lydia Myers more bearable, even exciting, was carrying his child. Or so she said. It would be stupid to ask "How?" or "Are you sure?" They went at it like crazed weasels from their first date on. It was spring in Paris, too, a time for lovers, which maybe had something to do with it. Or so they said. Maybe it was just being in a strange country, not speaking the language, and working undercover that made Nicole's friendship ever so very enticing. And so regrettably reckless.

It had to be true. He knew deep down she wouldn't make up something like this. Not only because it seemed out of character for her, but because the last time he saw her, the way she looked at him standing there on the Pont Royal, flipping him the bird after getting him arrested kind of summed up how she felt about him. The woman wanted him crucified. There was no way she was going to turn around and try to get him back with a false paternity charge. Nicole Dubois wouldn't do that. Rough around the edges, heavily tattooed and wearing her hair in dreadlocks, she was the first woman he'd ever met who knew more curse words in English than most Americans did and she could string them together with finesse. The way they rolled off her tongue in that cute accent of hers drove him over the top. Nicole was a lot of things, but she wasn't a liar. She wouldn't make up a story like this. Birth control wasn't foolproof. He knew that. He really did knock her up. So what now?

It wasn't like she was asking him for anything. She didn't even want him to come back to Paris and she said she wouldn't come to New York, so he needn't worry. She just wanted to let him know she was going to have his child, or, as she put it, "Your little French bastard will grow up in France, be a French citizen, and speak the French language along with English. Fuck you Americans."

If she thought that would sting, she was right. It did.

On the other hand, it was good of her to tell him. He had a right to know. She did add one caveat to her nicely written letter. She said if he even thought for one second she'd name the baby after him, or give it the surname, DeFranco, he could go fuck himself with the torch of the Statue of Liberty. That was Nicole at her best. Besides her amazing looks and a body that didn't quit, she had a talent for coming up with some of the raunchiest things he ever heard. Too bad she didn't want to come here because she'd fit in well in New York.

A thousand scenarios vied for center stage in his mind. Should he reach out to her, tell her he was happy about the news, thank her for letting him know, invite her to New York, offer to marry her, ask her if she needed money? She obviously did, she was almost living in poverty when he met her. She was barely able to pay the rent for the tiny apartment she shared with her roommate. He wondered if she'd drop out of the Sorbonne, give up on her education, stay at the bakery with her prison matron boss who didn't approve of her in any way, or what? Add a pregnancy to the list of her offenses and he was sure it would tip the scales and she'd be out of a job.

What would she do if she lost her job? How would she ever make it in a city as expensive as Paris, where even he found himself scrounging for francs just to afford a cup of coffee? Would she go home to Lyon where she said she was from? He never was sure about the story she told about her family being affluent and her father owning a textile factory. He was pretty good about telling when someone was lying, but, clever as she was, there were a few times she had him guessing. Especially when she talked about being educated in a private, all-girl, Catholic boarding school. It just didn't seem to fit.

The news brought back memories of his ex-wife, Gloria. She'd also told him she was pregnant and, because of it, he married her. It was the right thing to do at the time. The only thing he could have done, given that a family feud would have broken out that would have required the entire NYPD to handle, if he hadn't. But Gloria hadn't been pregnant. She'd made a mistake. They found out on their wedding night. Big surprise.

Back then, he just accepted it as fate. They got along reasonably well. The courtship had been short, but steamy. She was on the pill. They hadn't even talked about having a family. He wondered at the time how a woman couldn't know. Surely there had to be some signs, more than just a late period. Surely she'd have been aware. But Gloria said it was just an "oops" as she tossed the wilted bridal bouquet in the trash, acting like she'd forgotten to pick up the dry cleaning or left a cabinet door open. "Things like this happen all the time," she said.

It was somewhat of a relief, not facing fatherhood so close to getting out of Law Enforcement Training and starting his first job as a beat cop. The real surprise came when Gloria, almost overnight, turned their apartment into a convent. She put up altars, statues of Mary and all the saints she could get her hands on. She put holy water fountains in every room. Then the real kicker came when she chose to sleep in her own bed. There was no need for a husband when you were a bride of Christ, or just as good as one without becoming a nun and taking the vows. His mother loved that about Gloria. She was such a devout girl.

There were some things a guy just couldn't argue over or go to the priest about. And so the marriage went, and so it ended after a year of pretending they were happily married. Luckily the church allowed an annulment. In their case, the reason for an annulment really did apply. They hadn't had sex after the wedding ceremony took place. Now, he could look back and laugh about it, bitterly. It was like all the dessert had come first, before the meal, and when it came time to eat, the kitchen was closed.

There were times in Vito's life, not many, but a few, where it seemed things couldn't get any crazier, but they did. Today was one of them. He was two hours into a surveillance job, organizing his notes, satisfied with the documents he'd gotten and some of the clearer photographs, when his cell phone rang. The number was unfamiliar, probably a solicitor, or someone begging for a charitable donation to one of a million social groups in the city—help feed the pigeons, help clean the statues of pigeon poop, help rescue the ducks in the Hudson, help buy a bike for a kid with prosthetic limbs, help support a heroin addict in recovery…the list was endless. He let it go to voicemail.

During his first break, sucking a diet soda from a can, he decided to see just who was desperate enough to leave him a message, even with his greeting that stated, "You reached Vito. If you're selling something, and I don't care what, hang up." He listened to the message and spit out a mouthful of soda.

Holy Mary Mother of God. It wasn't a solicitor or a beggar. It was Lydia Myers, the woman he'd been hired to surveil in Paris. The wife of Jack Myers, someone he vowed never to work for again. One of the biggest assholes in all of New York City. The man had him dogging his poor wife throughout the city of Paris trying to catch her in the act with another man, all because of Myers' paranoia. Vito dragged his butt all over the city in the foulest of weather, only to have Myers question him about the number of coffees he'd put on his expense sheet. Not only was Myers a dipshit, he was one of the cheapest sons-of-bitches he ever worked for.

All the message said was to please call her. She left a number. Why on earth would she be calling him? Did it have to do with Nicole? Maybe Nicole tried to reach him through her? After all, they'd met in Paris and Nicole had really taken a liking to Lydia. In fact, she said if they'd become friends years earlier, she probably would have tattooed her name somewhere on her body. He didn't ask where. Some things were too kinky even for him. Luckily Nicole hadn't had time to get his name tattooed anywhere, otherwise he hated to think how she would have mutilated herself trying to erase it.

There was no sense wondering or speculating on the matter. He dialed the number. After one ring, Lydia answered.

"Vito, hi. Thanks for calling back so quickly. Look, I'm calling from a phone card and my minutes are limited, so I'll talk fast. I know you're a detective and I know you were working for my husband, Jack Myers, when you were following me in Paris. No hard feelings, you were doing your job. I'm back in New York and right now up living at Lake George. I left Jack and I'm filing for a divorce. I need your help with something. I want to hire you to find out everything you can about his expenses, where his money's been going, phone records, credit card statements, things like that. I need all I can get on him and his mistress. And yes, he does have one. Her name is Serena Castelloes. I'm sure you know the score and I trust you. After all, you followed me for three weeks."

The woman could talk fast. Faster even than his sister Cecilia whose mouth, the family said, moved like pistons on a race car while her brain stalled out at the starting line. She didn't give him much wiggle room or even time to think it over. Was this even ethical to follow her husband's surveillance of her with her surveillance of him? It was a first in his career, to be sure. At least it wasn't happening simultaneously. He'd never done double agent work. He knew guys who did and it usually never turned out good.

"I'd ask you to take photos of him and his mistress, but I have a lot already, including a DVD of them in the hotel room in Paris where he stayed. My room, in fact. I wasn't there. I made him think I was out of town. I also have pictures of him and his mistress in New York. It's a long story. That was after you left. My brother, Tom, you remember him, saw you getting into the cab. We were sorry we didn't get a chance to say good-by to you."

The news was swirling in Vito's head like a mini-whirlwind. She'd been tracking her husband in New York while he was tracking her in Paris? Did it get any weirder than this? And how did she know he'd been following her? He always tried to stay at a distance and never in sight of those outdoor cafés she loved so much, where she'd sit at for hours while his nuts shrank to the size of raisins.

"My attorney is Shawn O'Malley. He can tell you more about what he'll need. Here's his number. I mean, if you're willing to take the job, that is. I guess I'm rushing you a little. Please consider it. He'll pay whatever your retainer is. And he won't be stingy like my husband."

He wanted to help Lydia Myers. He liked her. She was a good woman, even if she did have an obsession with art galleries and led him on a wild goose chase the entire time he was in Paris. It killed him that she found out he was surveilling her. When did she? His mind switched gears. He thought about Nicole. Lydia must have talked to her, maybe saw her again before she left. But, did she know the latest news? He felt it best not to open that can of worms.

He found himself saying, "Yes, of course, I'll take the job. Of course I'll help you out. My retainer is five hundred. No rush, I can send Mr. O'Malley a bill. I'll call him and see what approach he wants me to take and when to get started. Just give me your address and phone so I'll have a way of contacting you. For some reason your number isn't showing up. Oh, yeah, you said you were using a phone card."

He took down the information. It was all happening too fast. He hated to make hasty decisions. He usually liked to meet face-to-face with his clients, feel them out, and take his time deciding if it was worth his while. But he knew Lydia Myers, so it was okay to make an exception. Besides, she really sounded desperate. So, she was going to divorce that bastard of a husband. Good for her. If any man deserved it, it was Jack Myers. He'd enjoy getting as much dirt on the guy as he could, even though it sounded like Lydia had gotten a head start and done a pretty good job of it. A DVD? What the hell?

"Just one question. If you had someone following your husband in New York, might I ask why you're not continuing with that detective?"

Lydia explained how her friend, Ellsworth Witherspoon had done the hiring while she was in Paris. She never met the other detective and decided Vito would be her choice to continue the investigation when she got home.

It was all he needed to know. Worst case scenario, it might have been a friend and he never liked to infringe on another detective's territory, even if the guy was doing a shitass job. Again, he wondered if he should ask if she saw Nicole before she left Paris. She must have because she hit the bakery every day. It was probably best to let sleeping dogs lie or, in this case, pregnant ladies.

"Thank you, Vito," Lydia said. "This means a lot to me. I wish we could meet, but for now, unless you're coming up here, I don't plan to be in the city any time soon. Good luck."

He was about to hang up when Lydia stopped him. "Vito, before I go, I just wanted to ask, have you heard anything from Nicole?"

His stomach took a nose dive. For a few moments he was speechless. The first thought that came to mind, lie though it was, was all he could force himself to say.

"No. Nothing. I hope she's okay. We kind of parted on a bad note."

The sound of Lydia's voice as she assured him Nicole was okay and would probably love to hear from him told him she knew something. What was it with women? They really did have that thing, whatever it was called. A sixth sense. They always seemed to know a hell of a lot more than they let on, and long before a guy ever found out. Maybe Nicole had come right out and told her. If so, it was good of Lydia Myers not to let the cat out of the bag. It'd be out soon enough, though. He'd have to do something.

First, he had to get this job started. Then he'd make sure he and Lydia had a chat. A good long one.

Chapter 12

The trail that wound along the lakeshore meandered at times into the woods, crossing over fallen trees and rocks that jutted up out of the ground making it imperative to have decent hiking boots and sure footing. Lydia stopped to pick up some smooth stones to place in a potted geranium on the deck and studied the gleaming slime trail left by a wandering snail. Red-winged blackbirds perched on cattails growing along the water's edge and called back and forth to each other. She wondered what they were saying. A blue heron moved slowly on stilt legs looking for lunch, while a turtle hovered lazily, watching her until she edged too close, then disappeared beneath the glassy surface like a fading apparition. A grouping of pussy willow trees gave her an idea for supplementing the armful of flowers she'd already picked. She broke off several branches.

Once back at the cabin, she arranged the flowers in a vase and set it on the kitchen table. It gave the room a cheerful country-home feeling. Tonight she was having her first dinner guest at the cabin. Simon Vanderlaan would be arriving any minute. He'd assured her he didn't need to be picked up in the village because a friend—a decent guy and fairly affluent—had loaned him his car. It was nice that people looked out for other people, even going so far as to lend a friend a car, knowing there was the possibility it could be hocked for quick money that would be handed right over to a drug dealer. Not that Simon would do such a thing, but… It wasn't for her to speculate.

She'd thought a great deal about what she was going to do for Simon. He obviously needed help, rehab, counseling and guidance. For all intents and purposes, he was a well-educated, bright young man who could have a good future if it wasn't for those little balls of tar wrapped in colorful balloons. Her maternal instincts wanted her to adopt him and take care of him, though she knew that would not be the solution. He needed professional help and she was going to see that he got it.

It surprised her that she was so excited about having her first dinner guest. She supposed it was because it was the first time she was entertaining someone not associated with Jack's work, not to mention the fact that he was a heroin addict and she had no idea what state he'd be in when he arrived.

She washed the rocks she'd gathered and put them around the geranium, then arranged small vases of the extra flowers around the living room. It was always good to have living things in a house and fresh wildflowers were the best of all. Back home, which she didn't feel she could call home anymore, it was rare when she hadn't had fresh cut flowers on the dining room table.

Dinner was already prepared and though she knew Simon would appreciate anything that wasn't from the shelter's cafeteria or the garbage cans of the fast food restaurants in the village, still she hoped he'd be pleased with the extra care she took to make tabbouleh, hummus, tossed greens salad, and a veggie loaf. She decided not to offer wine, but made a lemonade from fresh squeezed lemons and added some mint growing wild near the cabin.

Keep it simple. She told herself. It's just Simple Simon, after all. She went ahead and did just the opposite, spending most of the day preparing the food and cleaning the cabin. It was too beautiful a day to spend it all inside, so she had her morning run of six miles, followed by her flower gathering walk before her guest arrived.

When a shiny royal blue Honda pulled up minutes before six o'clock and Simon Vanderlaan stepped out, she tried hard to suppress her surprise. She didn't want him to think she doubted his capacity to drive or his worthiness to have friends who were willing to lend him a new car.

"Nice wheels," she said, walking down the steps to greet him.

"Nice digs." Simon looked around and shook his head. "Lydia Chapel. You've done well since your days at the Lake View Rescue Ministry. What's your secret? Another rags to riches story, no doubt?"

She noticed his eyes had a brighter look to them and there was no indication, at least not at this point, that he was under the influence. As much as she wished it would stay that way permanently, she knew that was unrealistic. Nevertheless, she'd come up with a plan and hoped Simon would at least consider it. She couldn't imagine why he wouldn't. It would give him the lease on life he needed, and didn't everyone who was down and out need a helping hand?

She couldn't help but notice that Simon was clean-shaven and wearing what looked like a new t-shirt, at least one with no stains. His jeans were still torn in several places, but looked cleaner than last time. His boots looked new, too. Had he borrowed them?

"So, how's the old gang? Did Janice get that cell phone she wanted? And Lunetta, did she get to see her new grandbaby yet?"

"No, and no," Simon answered. "Janice had a little run-in with the law when she decided to do tricks outside the Hilton one night. What she didn't count on was they were hosting a big Baptist convention and somebody blew the whistle on her. I guess being hustled by hookers isn't something Baptists appreciate when they're attending conventions."

Lydia gasped. Was it because of the advice she'd given Janice about looking for higher class venues? She hoped not.

"Lunetta Loves the Lord hasn't been able to break away to get to Florida, hence no bambino time. But, she talks about the kid ad nauseam and shows pictures of him on her phone every day, whether you're interested not. You'd think it was her only grandchild, but she has five already. She's raising two of them."

Lydia wondered when would be a good time to begin telling Simon about her plan. Perhaps a short walk would provide the opportunity. She had reviewed her course on substance abuse and written some notes. This move on her part couldn't exactly be called an intervention. It was more like a friendly persuasion, one that Simon would have no reason to refuse. He had every reason in the world to accept her offer. The young man was clever, intelligent, and well-educated, even if he did drop out. Surely he'd see the merit in what she was going to propose.

She noticed he was carrying the little notebook he took with him everywhere he went.

"How about a little walk before dinner?"

Simon agreed. She led him to a new trail she hadn't been on earlier. Prepared to lead the conversation, she was surprised when he began talking.

"I want to know more about your story," he said. "I mean, seriously, it's not often you run into a society figure in a homeless shelter. At least not in my experience. I could be wrong, but I think I'd be just about as surprised if Mario Cuomo appeared at the shelter at supper time carrying a tray."

"Well, I wouldn't exactly call myself a society person. Maybe more on the side of a well-to-do housewife whose husband wanted to teach her a good lesson about how reliant she was on him, you know, to impress on her that she couldn't make it on her own."

"Is that what this is all about? Your husband reining you in to teach you a lesson?" Simon picked up a fallen branch to use as a walking stick. "That's one hell of a way to go about it."

"Watch out for poison ivy," Lydia warned. "To answer your question, I'll try to be fair and say it was and it wasn't that. Yes, Jack wanted to impress on me that I couldn't live without his support. But, more importantly, he couldn't live with the fact that I found him out and exposed what he was up to when he couldn't get a thing on me. It infuriated him. Jack never could accept failure and he hates being shown up. He'll do practically anything to win. Even the kids complained they never could play games with him because he was so relentlessly competitive."

"Sounds like a peach of a guy. You told me he works for some big law firm in the city. I wondered about that. One of my cousins is an attorney. I found that you can pretty much tell the character of an attorney by the firm he, or she, works for."

"It's Parker, Cross, Epstein and Myers. Have you heard of them?"

Simon swallowed hard. Had he heard of them? Over the past couple years, he'd produced a prodigious amount of copy on one of New York's leading firms that litigated a surprising number of high profile cases.

"Yeah, I think it rings a bell. They're pretty big, if memory serves me. Didn't they handle the Thisse vs. Future Pro-Gear case where that woman got permanently injured using one of their diving get-ups? And they ruled in favor of the company due to some loophole?"

"Yes. That would be one of the many ignoble cases Jack called a success. Where the big guys trounced the smaller, more vulnerable member of society."

"It sounds like you don't think much of the firm? Or is it just the one particular shithead who works there?"

Lydia gave a rueful smile. "There are so many, and much bigger ones, than that case. So many that have had far-reaching effects on the world. The latest one being Montclair, Inc. They made the news last year and they're back again with more egregious offenses. Jack takes great pride in making them look good and helping them come away scot-free of any culpability."

"Isn't Montclair a known violator of human rights, not to mention a huge polluter of the environment? I followed the case, mainly because my cousin was so up at arms over it. It was all he could talk about. He said they were satanic in their practices and got away with horrific things."

"Yes, that's the one."

"Doesn't it make you wonder how they manage to always get away with it? But then, that's pretty naïve when we all know it comes down to money, and the big money has all the power, and the big money hires the big attorneys who make their big money defending their corporate clients, no matter how nefarious they may be."

"It's sad, but true," Lydia said, stopping to look out at the water. "I really don't want to talk about my husband's work. It's so despicable. Let's change the subject."

They stood for a while listening to the sounds of bullfrogs and watching a hawk circle high above the lake, appearing nonplussed by the harassment of several small birds who were darting in its path but failing to upset its graceful drift. The evening air rippled the surface of the lake and brought a coolness to the land that was refreshing after what had been one of the warmest spring days so far.

"Let me know when you're getting hungry and we can head back."

"Are you kidding? I've been starving for the past day." Simon laughed as he patted his belly. "As good as it is to get a free meal, my God, that shelter cooking does a number on your gut. I think it would kill you dead if you ate it for too long."

Lydia thought about something else that might kill him faster.

"This morning we had the fake eggs and some kind of stale hash browns I think were thrown out by that greasy spoon, Little Abner's, down the road. But hey, I can't complain. A full barrel, even if it's full of crap, is a lot quieter than an empty one."

It was good to hear Simon laughing and in such good spirits. Now it was time to fill him with some decent food. They headed back to the cabin where Lydia gave him the task of bringing in some firewood while she set the table and brought out the food.

"I hope you don't mind vegetarian cuisine. I made fresh lemonade, too."

Simon set down the load of wood in the stand next to the fireplace. He hoped they'd have wine with dinner. It might get Lydia to open up a bit more about just how despicable her husband and his firm were.

"I think I might be able to stomach it, although I may have to hit the chef up tonight for some left over shank of rat or a dogfood burger." Simon watched as Lydia brought dish after dish to the table. "Jesus Christ, did you cook like this for your husband?"

Again, before she could suppress it, Lydia burst into a laugh. "Jack hated my cooking, at least when I served all vegetarian meals. He didn't like much of anything I made, unless it included chicken, pork, fish, or beef and, of course, cheese. He loved cheese. He said it was a sophisticated food and those who didn't appreciate it were plebian."

"Plebian, eh? I just thought they were cheese intolerant, or crazy." Simon reached for a pita wedge and scooped up some hummus. "Sorry, but I have to see if this is edible." He dipped and ate several more wedges. "Don't worry, I'm not telling anyone you forced me to eat food that should be illegal. A person could o-d on this."

Perhaps this was the time to segue to her plan? Something told her to wait until after the meal.

Throughout dinner, they laughed as Simon told jokes and stories, pausing intermittently to rave about how good the food tasted. "You should write a grant so you can open up a concession at the shelter and get everybody into healthy eating," he suggested. "Of course, most of them would probably prefer fast food to this. It's way too foreign. Disgustingly healthy. I'd seriously consider becoming a traitor to the carnivorous cause and cross over to the vegan side of the force if I could eat like this all the time."

When the meal was over, Lydia suggested having dessert in the living room. Simon got a fire going while she laid a spread of fresh fruit, nuts, and chocolate chip cookies on the coffee table. Simon spied the cookies and put a whole one in his mouth. He eyes became huge as he chewed, swallowed, and put a hand to his heart.

"Roll over Mrs. Fields, here comes Mrs. Myers. These cookies are to die for. I mean they are so seriously good it's hard to believe they're healthy. I really think you should forget counseling and consider a career as a vegan chef. I'm serious. You'd help more people getting them to eat this food than talking to them about their problems. I should write down the recipe." He took out his notebook. "Speaking of things that are awesome and rich, I want to jot down some notes about your story and what went on before you became a homeless woman. Also, what happened after you left the shelter. I mean, obviously, you have a great story to tell and I, unfortunately, have only bits and pieces. It's worthy of more detail, I think. Don't you?"

Lydia sat back and lifted her eyes to the ceiling. "Do you really want to know?"

"Does the pope wear a jewel-encrusted miter?"

Taking a deep breath, Lydia lowered her eyes to stare at the fire. "Where do I start? Are you sure you want all the details?"

Simon opened his notebook. "Well, not all. I'm not interested in your sex life with your husband, or what size jockey shorts he wears. I would like to know what led up to your going to the shelter and what happened that got you out, other than that little windfall you so generously shared with me and the others. By the way, everybody's still talking about their night at the Lobster Trap and the great time they all had. Antoinette, God love her, got drunk and fell over the rail and into the water. They had to call the rescue squad. Janice got into a fist fight with one of the waiters. Diego got smashed and put the moves on DeShaun who, in his homophobic way, punched him out. Poor Cody almost coded blue when he walked out in front of a tour bus because he was so smashed."

"You mean they all got drunk?" Lydia was stricken with his account of the dinner she intended to be a treat—a nice dining experience that would be a departure from shelter food.

"Come on, Lydia. Don't look so surprised. You gave them all a gift certificate to a restaurant that sells alcoholic beverages and you expected them to buy food and not booze? Is it me or are you an alien from another planet? Or is that completely innocent, trusting and naïve façade you put on for real? Maybe it is. Maybe you're just too nice for this world."

Lydia shoulders slumped. "Jack always said I was hopelessly naïve. Maybe he's right. Maybe I do trust too much and expect more from people than I should. I don't know how to be any different."

Simon reached over and patted her hand. "Hey, Lydia Chapel, reigning queen of the cookie kingdom and, well, of the whole goddamn vegetable kingdom, for that matter. Let's not indulge in any self-flagellation. How about we get back to your story? So you left for Paris and your husband hired a detective, then you somehow got someone to track him in New York, then he came to visit you in Paris and you tracked him. How the hell did you pull all that off?"

Lydia explained the details of her time in Paris, her friend, Ellsworth Witherspoon's hiring of the detective who followed Jack, who provided ample evidence of his flagrant escapades in infidelity, and her own undercover surveillance of her husband during his brief stay in Paris. Surprised at his interest, she went on to describe her homecoming and how she confronted her husband's mistress in their home on the morning of her arrival.

Simon was scribbling furiously in his book.

"You have got to be shitting me. She was really wearing your bathrobe?"

"Oh, yes, and my turban. I have to say it looked damned good on her, too, the bitch."

"And right after that, you went to the office and confronted Jack? Is that when you demanded a divorce?"

"It was more like I told him I wanted a divorce and that I was leaving to come up here." Lydia stood up and headed for the kitchen. "Want any more lemonade? Need anything while I'm up?"

"No, thank you. But please, continue your story. I haven't been this entertained in years. You came up to the lake, found out you were cut off, literally, from all manner of monetary support and then somehow you managed to get to the shelter?"

"I was brought there by the police, actually. I purposely hitchhiked so I'd get arrested. A very nice officer named Paul Mancini gave me a ride to Lake View Rescue Ministry, only because he didn't want to lock me up. Besides, he thought I was crazy. And that's the whole truth and nothing but the truth." Lydia set down the plate she'd refilled with cookies. Simon had devoured a half dozen so far. He eagerly seized two more from the plate.

"So where is all the money now? I mean, obviously you're sustaining yourself on something, even if you did squander a bundle on me and the others. Has Jack come to his senses and reinstated you back into the domain of domestic support?"

Lydia shook her head, hesitating to tell more than she needed to. After all, Simon had his own problems and she didn't want to burden him. On the other hand, he seemed so animated and interested in what she had to say. It helped to talk to him about it. Here was someone who could appreciate being out in the cold with nothing but the clothes on his back, except that she had other outfits she'd left behind in the closet.

"Essentially, I sold much of what I brought, or wore, to the others at the shelter, then I begged from my kids and relatives. My attorney advanced me the largest amount with the assurance, on his part, not mine, that he'd get it all back after the divorce settlement. Money started coming my way and now I can take care of myself, buy food, and put gas in the car."

"Does Big Jack know you have a pipeline? Or is he just assuming all those men he suspected you of screwing are taking care of you?"

"Honestly, I don't know what Jack thinks, and I don't care. He can think what he likes."

"If he finds out, what do you think his next move will be? Would he do anything drastic?"

"Like what?"

"Oh, I don't know. Come here and let the air out of your tires? Burn down the cabin? Hire a hit man?"

"No. Those would be too risky and Jack doesn't take needless risks. He would try to get me committed. He's been pushing the crazy card on me for quite some time."

"You're not serious. Really? He wants you in the loony bin?"

"He's so much as intimated that I'm not in my right mind. That I've made all this up. It assuages his guilt over all his affairs."

"So there've been more than this latest one?"

"I suspect he's been continually involved with someone else throughout our entire marriage."

"Shit. What a guy. What do women see in him, I mean, besides the obvious?"

"You'd have to know him to understand. He has a way of manipulating people. My brother once said he could sell pork to a Jew, ice to an Eskimo, and porn to a priest. He's a charmer, a conniver, and a brilliant liar."

"Sounds like your average sociopath."

"That diagnosis has crossed my mind."

"And women like him?"

"Oh, I'm sure he has a way of presenting himself as a victim. A poor unfortunate man saddled with a crazy wife who he can't leave because of the children. You know the score. Women fall for that kind of thing. Especially needy ones."

"Yeah, and I'll bet they go for the fuck therapy, as well."

Simon ate another cookie and took a sip of lemonade. "Is this stuff alcoholic? I'm getting a buzz from it? Never mind, back to the story."

Lydia finished telling him the latest developments, her contact with Shawn O'Malley, and her plan to support herself as a counselor after her master's program was completed. She asked him for his stories and he said he had a million of them. He joked about the shelter, all the people he'd met, all the stories he'd heard, and went on to describe some of the more flamboyant characters.

"There was this one guy, Nick Rapozo, who loved to make up poetry, or rhymes, actually. He told everybody he had a published book of poetry and it turns out he did. One of those rackets that has you send in a piece of your work and talks you into paying them to publish it because it's so 'refreshing, new, spirited, creative, alive' and other such bullshit. Well, he made up a poem about shelter life and somebody put it to music. Would you believe somebody sent it to Nashville and before you know it, it was on the radio? I think it might have won an Emmy. You might have heard it sung by Gracie Newbury? *The Way It Is.* It's just another testimonial to the richness of homeless living and what a lot of talent is out there going to waste. Except in Nick's case."

"I don't think I met Nick," Lydia said. "Was he the tall guy with the cowboy hat and chaps?"

"Oh no, that would be Caleb. Caleb Car Thief, from Georgia. Lunetta told him he couldn't call himself that, so he told her she was Lunetta

Lunatic, which got him thrown out for a night. No, Nick wasn't around when you were there. He had, well, let's just say his drinking and drug use got the better of him. The brief sojourn into fame and liquidity, no pun intended, was more than he could handle. I believe he's right now regaling the angels with his poetry."

"I'm so sorry. It's hard to maintain that life style and, well… stay alive."

The time had arrived. It was now or never. "Speaking of talent going to waste, and Nick's misfortune, or should I say, misappropriation of fortune, I've been thinking a lot about something and I wanted to hear your ideas."

Simon sat up straighter. The tone in Lydia's voice has suddenly changed from fun and light-hearted to funereal.

"Simon, you know I care about you and I'm concerned for your well-being. What I'm trying to say is, I don't want anything bad to happen to you. I want you to be able to live your life and accomplish your goals. And be happy. You are a fine person and you deserve better."

Simon lifted a hand in protest. "Whoa, Lydia…let's not get carried away here."

"Please, hear me out. I'd like to help you get into a rehab program. I'll pay for it. I'd also like to be your coach, so to speak, while you're in it. I mean, someone to talk to and encourage you. I don't have the credentials yet to be your counselor, but I will. There's a very good program not too far from here called Liberty Farm. It's a three-month program that includes detox and counseling. It even has a work component where you can do chores on the farm, work with horses, even help with their therapeutic riding center. I went for a visit and it looks great. I talked to the director and she told me all you needed to do was call for an intake appointment to get started."

Simon put down the cookie he had in his hand and sat silent for a few moments. He looked as if his eyes were stinging.

"Lydia, I have to say that you are one of the kindest, most thoughtful human beings I've ever had the pleasure of knowing. I find myself speechless right at this moment, which is foreign to me since I'm seldom at a loss for words." Simon picked up his glass of lemonade from the coffee table and flicked some cookie crumbs from his lap. "Let me just think about it, okay? I won't say yes or no right at this moment, but I promise you, I will give it some thought."

Lydia got up and went to the kitchen counter, returning with a manila envelope. "Here's some literature about the program. Keep it. Whenever you feel ready, just let me know and I'll take you there myself."

Simon peered into the envelope, again, at a loss for words. Clearing his throat, he said, "Lydia, I want you to know I'm here for you, too. Whatever happens from here on… whatever is coming down the pike…what I mean to say is, whatever might befall you or me, or what the future may bring, I'd like to think you'd always be my friend and think well of me."

He stopped talking and looked down at his lap.

Lydia felt her throat tightening. Every impulse was compelling her to wrap her arms around him and assure him everything was going to be alright. She knew she couldn't do that. But she could talk to him and assure him she'd be there and help him get through it. It would be a long and difficult haul, but she was willing to stay the course. She could see it was all too overwhelming for him, so there was no need to add to the emotional impact. Instead, she reached out and put her hand on his.

"You got it, buster. We're pals, right to the end. We're going to get through this."

Chapter 13

Women were infinitely more frustrating than what he had to put up with in most court cases. In fact, if Jack Myers had his way, he'd find a woman who had no voice and no needs of her own. That way he'd get his needs met without all the added bullshit. Serena was ragging on him all the time now, and he just got a nice little package served to him, compliments of none other than Shawn O'Malley, that flunky Lydia hired to handle her side of the divorce. Ha. As if that jackass could stand up to his attorney, Maxinne Gunderman, even on a good day.

Jack Myers had his fill of demanding and irrational women. At least the Montclair, Inc. case was going well and he was pleased with his progress. So far, everything was moving along swiftly and according to plan. No matter what those attorneys in that pathetic Thai village could produce, they'd never be able to present anything to topple the defense he was building. In no time at all he'd have them licking his boots.

The death toll from the chemical leak was now up to 1,115 and rising. It was still minor and would only strengthen his case, given what he had planned. He'd done his research of similar cases where judges had thrown out cases due to extortion and fraud on the part of the plaintiff's lawyers. Some recruited fraudulent plaintiffs to make claims against a company, while others lined their pockets with bribes. Thailand was noted for such corruption. Little did they know it would play right into his hand and provide just the platform he needed to launch his defense.

If only his personal life was going as smoothly. First, Serena had just about gotten on his last nerve with her whining and clinginess. Then it was his daughter, Tori, coaxing two grand out of him for a college-sponsored trip. Then Leo had the nerve to call him and say he was dropping out of college unless he did something to help his mother. Tori's trip was a good idea, he agreed. It would look good on her resume and would help her get into graduate schools. Leo was just too immature to understand. That wasn't the point, though. It was the way they approached him. Tori was just like her mother. Always knowing just what to say that sounded reasonable at the time and he couldn't argue with. And Leo was whimpering and sounding like a damn baby crying for his mother. He didn't need a weakling for a son when he had a dingbat for a wife. Which reminded him, he needed to have Mary Quaile make an appointment for him to see Dr. Aronson, Lydia's psychiatrist. He'd make it appear that he was seeking help, coping with Lydia's demand for a divorce when, in fact, he'd find out just exactly what took place on Lydia's last, and only, visit with him. It might prove to be useful during the divorce trial.

Back to Serena, constantly needling him about the divorce, already making plans for the home they'd live in and what her favorite wall colors and furniture were. She was smart enough not to mention wanting children, although he knew she did. He nipped that one in the bud years ago. No sperm were swimming down his tubes. The only way Serena could get pregnant would be by another man, and if she tried to nail him with a paternity suit she'd be in for a big surprise. Even if he did lead her to believe he wanted children and supported her idea of having a big family, she wasn't going to get away with pinning a paternity suit on him. She was so common and predictable. He didn't let on that three dependents were enough for him to support. And soon to be two. Getting rid of Lydia in the way he planned would save him thousands, probably even millions, in the long run. He couldn't help smiling at how strategically he had it all worked out.

Reflecting back on the past few weeks, the trip to Paris had been worth it in every sense, even if it hadn't turned out exactly as planned. It wouldn't have mattered if Lydia had been there. She already had her mind made up. In fact, it turned out better that she wasn't there because it furnished him an ally in Emmanuelle Jobert, one of the senior Montclair executives he'd had the good fortune to meet. In just a short day and a half, he got to know her quite well, both professionally and in the Biblical sense. Their intimate relationship was proving to be rewarding in ways he hadn't expected.

They'd slept together the night before he returned to New York and, much to his surprise, the pillow talk had been most informative. The woman was a gold mine of information, having worked for Montclair in the village of Sumar Pakan where the factory was located. She could even speak Thai. She knew the village, the workers, and what's more, the managers. She shared some very useful information on some of the higher ups—local boys who thought they could play the corporate game, but failed miserably at it. They'd be some of his targets, along with the lawyers. He'd prove it was negligence on the part of the managers and fraud and extortion on the part of the lawyers. In no way would Montclair, Inc. be liable for the disastrous leak. It was all a matter of small town corruption and greedy lawyers.

Montclair, Inc. would then step in and offer its humanitarian support, help with the clean-up of the spill, offer compensation to the families, gain tighter control over management. He'd even suggest a company-run health clinic to deal with the on-going medical issues. From what Emmanuelle said, every day new people were showing up maimed, sick, and permanently disabled by the disaster. She said it would go on for years. More litigation was likely to follow. Bread and butter for the firm. Montclair would come out as an icon of corporate virtue, showing compassion for the little guy.

Mademoiselle Emmanuelle Jobert gave him a lot of good ideas. She was indeed a generous woman. It was amazing, too, how she could excite him, but not in the same way as Serena Castelloes. Serena was a loyal and devoted lapdog who didn't assert herself very often and always strove to mollify and placate. Emmanuelle was a woman who knew what she wanted and went after it with ruthless abandon. She was a lot like him. Generous in her information sharing, among other things. He liked that. A professional woman who knew her mind and wasn't afraid to give and take. Their lovemaking had been enjoyable. At least she seemed to have been pleased. He would have performed better had he not indulged in so much wine over dinner. It was that way with Lydia, too. She always let him drink too much.

Yes, Emmanuelle was proving to be a real asset to the case. They had to be careful, though. At least where email was concerned. Phone calls were the rule whenever they discussed company business and, of course, whenever they had sex talk.

The Montclair, Inc. file was getting thicker as more and more lawsuits were pouring in. It was conceivable that Parker, Cross, Epstein and Myers could work exclusively with Montclair and have all the work they'd ever need for at least a decade. He was already spending seventy-five percent of his time on this one case alone.

The long and short of it was, people wanted to believe Montclair, Inc. was a monster that stomped on and annihilated everything in its path to achieve profit. In reality, it was the big sugar-tit in the sky, a colossal benefactor whose main interests were in promoting the economic development of third world countries. A company that generously compensated those who may have suffered minor losses due to unfortunate accidents caused by the negligence of its management. They were the ones at fault. The locally hired yo-yo's who misappropriated company funds, ignored safety policies, and brought about the disaster. And he was going to prove all of that in court. Montclair, Inc. would come out clean and it would take him to a whole new level in the firm.

It was good he had his first experience representing Montclair only a year ago. This time, he'd do things a little differently. He'd see to it that the corporation came out shining like a newly minted silver dollar. He regretted not doing that to the degree he needed to last time, but he was just cutting his teeth on that case. Representing a corporate giant wasn't something you did every day. In fact, he didn't know a single colleague who had a similar experience. This time was going to be an even bigger win with Emmanuelle Jobert helping.

Mason Parker stopped by his office just about every day to hear what was happening. Today, the old fool poked his head in and said, "How's our best pit bull today?" Usually it was something equally corny. "How's the big bulldog doing?" "Bit any legs today?" It was getting old, but some things you just had to put up with, especially with senior partners.

Pitbull? Bulldog? Not hardly. If there was a dog he should be likened to, it would be a Belgian Malinois. Emmanuelle Jobert had pointed that out. They were stealthy and cunning. Highly intelligent. If he was going to stretch it just a bit, Emmanuelle was like that. It was unusual to find such qualities in a woman. He found it alluring and wondered if they spent more time together, if she came to work in the United States, that is, would their relationship get old. Probably so. Women could so easily become boring and tedious.

Thinking about the firm and his record so far, Jack realized he was the sharpest one of all, the one who'd rise to the top while the old codgers got older and more senile. Sure, they could still work, he'd allow that, but the order of the names would change. One day, his name would be heading the list and he'd have to answer to no one.

At least Lydia was being quiet for the time being. She was no doubt being driven crazier by her neurotic mother who she must have fled to when she found out she was cut off. But, that was her problem. So what if they were trashing him over what he'd done. He was within his rights. His name was on the accounts, not hers. None of the money was hers and he planned to keep it that way. Thank goodness Serena was somewhat financially secure, though she did manage to bring her budget into the conversation a little too often. It was a ploy to get him to pay for meals, taxis and theater tickets. He had to wonder if the pleasure was worth the cost.

She was driving him to distraction now that Lydia was gone. It put him in a place he didn't like to be. He wasn't about to drop her, though he had every reason to. That wouldn't work for him. There had to be someone to take her place first. It was too bad the distance between him and Emmanuelle was over three thousand miles. Serena was only a fifteen minute drive away, when she wasn't staying with him at the house which was, again, a new turn of events he was beginning to find taxing and downright annoying.

She'd already moved half her wardrobe in, was using his toothpaste and was forever leaving her stuff on the vanity in the bathroom. It was like having a bad dorm mate in college. He wasn't going to put up with it much longer. Still, he needed the sexual release she provided so willingly and expertly. It made him wonder sometimes if she hadn't been a working girl some time in her past. She seemed to have perfected the art of lovemaking, like someone who'd gotten plenty of practice. If it weren't for that one aspect of the relationship, she'd have been history long before now.

Which reminded him of two things. He should be meeting with his divorce attorney, Maxinne, and he had to figure out a way to get those photos and that DVD Lydia had out of her hands and into his. She had the unmitigated gall to suggest an uncontested divorce. Ha! As if she had it all over him with her so-called "evidence." Wouldn't that work in her favor, getting half of everything, probably going for spousal support and even child support till Tori turned twenty-one, besides getting all the kids' college expenses paid for. She'd be entitled, too, given that she didn't have an income. She thought she had a winning hand and could have it all her way, but she was in for a surprise. He had other ideas and knew just what he had to do. It would be easy to build a case of mental impairment and have her institutionalized. That way he'd be able to keep all the assets while he generously agreed to cover all her medical expenses and long-term care.

What puzzled him was how Lydia had gotten all those photos she'd thrown in his face the day she returned. And what about that DVD? Surely she hadn't gone so far as to videotape him in the hotel room. If so, wasn't that a nice wifely thing to do? Did she really think she could intimidate him? Scare him enough to give in to her demands? It was all hubris. Unless she walked into that hotel room and videotaped him and Emmanuelle in the act, there was no way. She was calling his bluff. Lydia could be a real ball buster when she wanted to be.

But how did she get the photos? Surely she must have hired someone, and if so, she must have done it before she planned her trip to Paris. Was it was all premeditated, or had she possibly hired someone later, after she found out he was having her surveilled? Whatever the case, it was devious. Far more than he would have expected of someone who professed to be a peacemaker, an advocate for human and animal rights. Shit. A self-righteous vegan. Well, this carrot muncher was going to find out quickly just how little she knew about the law, and about him. He'd fight her with everything he had.

Still, it bothered him that she'd even suggest she had something on him. The photos could easily be written off as a photo-shopped attempt to frame him. She thought she had him, naïve little fool that she was. The joke would be on her when he produced enough evidence to have her declared incompetent. It wouldn't be hard. He'd helped a client do the same in the past. His wife had been a little more unstable than Lydia, going off for weeks at a time and gambling away fortunes. She, too, had tried to get half her husband's assets. He first put her in a mental institution in Poughkeepsie, then ended up giving her a ticket back to her family in Puerto Rico. He saved millions and she got to go home where she belonged and be a burden on her own relatives.

He thought about the kids. Sure, they'd want to take their mother's side, at first. It was only natural. But when they understood what was really going on, how she used them for her own gains and manipulated them, they'd come over to his side. He'd convince them she'd been draining all his assets and he was just trying to stop the bleed. Stop her from sucking him dry. They'd come to see that she was out of control and he had to stop her for her own good. They'd get it, in time.

Even if they didn't, he knew what he needed to do. He had to make Lydia face reality and take responsibility for her actions. It was too bad the cabin was so available and ready for habitation when she left. If he'd had the foresight, he'd have arranged for the plumbing or electricity to be non-functional. Or he could have arranged to have it flooded or damaged by fire. Those possibilities still existed. He'd use more drastic measures if needed to convince her she couldn't keep going on as before, having it all her way.

It was what she deserved, traipsing around the globe, living the high life with her gay friends. No lover, though, not that he hadn't suspected it. The fact that it hadn't been proven irked him, especially after all the money he shelled out on that inept excuse for a detective he hired. The idiot. Which reminded him he had to hire someone else to get back the DVD and photos.

He called Mason Parker. He'd had his wife followed a year before she left him.

"Hey, Mason. Question for you. Remember that detective you hired to surveil Elena? I was wondering if you still had his number. I have a client who needs someone followed."

Mason put him on hold and came back on the line. "His name's Gormann. Erik Gormann. Only I think he's serving time. If I recall correctly, he was sent up the river on a B & E charge. Seems he broke into a suspect's house to gather evidence and got caught. Rotten luck if you ask me. He was good at his job."

Jack felt a surge of excitement. It was just the boost he needed. "I'll take his number and give it a try. Chances are he might be out by now."

"Well, good luck. But if he's unavailable, there's also somebody else I'd recommend. Let's see if I can find his card. Yes. Here it is. Vito DeFranco. I've been told he's a real humdinger."

"That's great, Mason. I'll take his number, too." Jack paused and waited while Mason read off the number. "Okay, got it. I'll pass this along. Thanks."

Jack wondered if Mason had ever used DeFranco's services. He never let on, so maybe he had and was just as disappointed in him as Jack was.

He dialed the number. The call was answered by someone who sounded like he'd just awoken from a nap.

"Yo, Erik here. What's the buzz?"

"Mr. Gormann, this is attorney Jack Myers. I was referred to you by a co-worker, Mason Parker. You did some work for him in the past."

There was silence. Then Jack heard some clicking noises and what sounded like a glass breaking, then, "Oh, Jesus...aw shit!"

The drowsy voice returned. "Sorry about that. Where were we? Oh yeah, Parker, Parker...let me see. Oh yeah, Mr. Mason Parker, downtown, office of Parker, somebody, somebody, and somebody. The dude whose wife was gambling and running around on him. Yeah, yeah. It's coming back now, man. Whew. Now I remember. She was pretty old...what I mean is, old to be fucking some younger dude, pardon my French. What can I do for him...I mean, for you, sir?"

Jack wasn't at all sure this was the person he needed to be talking to. The man was obviously under the influence. On second thought, that could be as asset. If anything went awry with what he was having him do, it would work in his favor if his detective was already on record for at least one B & E and was a drug user on top of that.

"I have a situation where my estranged wife is now living in a cabin at Lake George and she stole some vital information I had on a client I'm working with. It consists of an envelope of photos and a DVD I need to get back soon. What I'd like you to do is get them and return them to me."

Again, there was another pause. "So, what I think you're asking me to do is break into the cabin, steal the photos and DVD and return them to you. Is that about right?"

"That's it." Jack rolled his eyes. The man was definitely two brain cells ahead of being a cretin.

"Well, man, I really really wish I could help you out here, but it's like, well, I'm still on probation and, like, I really couldn't risk it, you know?"

Oh brother. Why hadn't natural selection removed this guy from the gene pool long ago? "There'd be no risk involved, whatsoever," Jack said, trying to keep from sounding annoyed. "I'll tell you where the spare key is and where the photos and DVD are likely to be found, in a desk drawer or in one of the bedroom dresser drawers. All you'd have to do is let yourself in, take them, and return them to me. I think anyone of your talents would find this, well, a no-brainer. A piece of cake, so to speak."

"Hmm…I'm not so sure. My probation officer would have my ass and cut off my jewels if he found out…"

"And I'll pay all your expenses to and from Lake George and give you five hundred dollars, once the material is in my hands."

He heard a moan coming across the line.

"Oh, shit, man. When do you want me to do this for you, bro? I'm free just about any time."

"Tomorrow."

Chapter 14

Memory lane. That was where Lydia and Shawn O'Malley departed from current events and took a lengthy stroll during lunch. It was a refreshing departure from their conversation the other night. They'd talked at length about Lydia's experience in Paris and all the events that led up to coming home and asking Jack for a divorce, and then what followed.

Initially, Shawn had been angry when he heard about how she'd been cut off and found herself with nothing, no money, not even a phone. It was a relief that his sense of humor was back. Today, over lunch at the cabin, they enjoyed many good laughs recalling past times at Columbia University. She felt she needed to divert his attention away from her present situation and lighten the mood somewhat. It wouldn't bode well for her divorce attorney to have homicidal thoughts about her husband.

She'd forgotten how witty and charming Shawn was, and what a great memory he had for details she'd long forgotten. Now, after deciding to show him the village and the homeless shelter, they continued laughing as they shared more memories and stories in the Plucky Goose Bistro on Main Street.

At one point, she felt a sharp pang of regret. So many years had passed when they weren't in contact with each other and weren't even a presence in each other's life. So many missed opportunities, changes of plan, and other intervening relationships and conditions, marriage being one of them. They'd worked their way into the script and altered the course of their lives and it all happened before she even realized it. Now Shawn was bringing it to the forefront and, while she was enjoying his sometimes shocking, mostly hilarious reminiscences, the memories were overshadowed with twinges of remorse.

Shawn's eyes were twinkling as he recalled story after story of their antics. "Remember the time you decided to come to that frat party you really didn't want to and I ended up tying up your friend, what was her name, Suzanne, with curtain cords or whatever those things are called? What was I thinking? What on earth were you thinking? I don't remember how you talked me into it, but I do know if that happened today, I'd be behind bars enjoying a career as a prison mail room worker. You'd be baking me cakes with files in them." Shawn took a bite of his roast beef sandwich and a sip of his IPA.

"That wasn't quite the way it happened," Lydia said, dipping a stalk of celery into a ramekin of tofu dip. "I suggested we play the game, "I dare you," and one of the cards said to tie up a player of your choice. Suzanne had a crush on you, so I whispered in your ear that she'd be a good choice. So you did."

"Nice advice from a friend, eh? So when the cops showed up, there I was frantically trying to untie that poor girl who was screaming bloody murder at the top of her lungs because something about being tied up freaked her out, and there you were, telling me to hurry and pounding me on the back. And I was almost wetting my shorts because I saw my whole future pass in front of me. I could see me behind bars in a striped uniform trying to avoid getting butt-raped by my fellow prisoners."

Lydia had to take several minutes to stop laughing and dry her eyes. "You were so scared. So was I, for that matter. Then, if I recall correctly, we all went back to the Rat and drank more beer and I think you and Suzanne ended up having a fight. Or am I mixing that with another memory?"

Shawn shook his head. "You know, I honestly can't recall. Suzanne and I never hit it off, and then she found solace in the arms of that Anthropology professor, Dr. Furst. Remember him? A great guy. All the girls loved him. Some of the guys, too. Everybody wanted to congregate in his office. Ha. Only Suzanne got to jump his bones."

"I wasn't enamored of him. He gave me a B on a paper I felt deserved an A."

"Overachiever. He nailed me with a C once. I argued it up to a B, though. He didn't like my take on prosimian mating rituals. All I was trying to point out was the fact that they were very similar in many ways to homo sapiens' mating practices. He thought I was being crass."

"I can vouch for your theory. I wish I had read the paper. I could have given you some first-hand anecdotes."

"All I know is, I have never, not once, ever tied up another person since Suzanne. I think I have a phobia of curtain cords." Shawn leaned back in the seat and ran a hand through his thick, wavy black hair. "I swear to God, what a nightmare college could be, at times. All the binge drinking, the drugs, the crazed partying, pledging for fraternities, spending most of your time recovering from hangovers. Using what few brain cells were left over for studying. How did we ever get through it all?"

"As I recall, Shawn, it never seemed to affect your scholastic performance. You were a consummate brain. You always managed to pull the highest grades. You know, Jack was jealous of you."

"Seriously? As I recall, he was no slouch in the law department, at least. His moot court made me look like a piker, while he practically got a standing ovation. I thought he was a pretty slick operator back then."

"He was, back then. Still is."

"It gets old, doesn't it? Somebody who's too damned confident for his own good."

"It does. But, I have to say, you've gained a lot of confidence and I'm happy for you. You're a shining star in your profession, even if your moot court didn't measure up to Jack's. I'm proud of what you've become."

"Aw shucks, now, Miss Lydia," Shawn said, slumping his shoulders forward and feigning a drawl. "You shouldn't aughta go sayin' such kindly things."

"Shut up. You know you came highly recommended."

"What? For my good looks and savoir faire? Or was it my Jeep? It had to be my Jeep."

Lydia smirked. "Mostly your Jeep, but it also had something to do with your being a hell of a good attorney. Face it. You had to be good to get Jack to hate you."

Shawn cocked his head. "So, Jack hates me, is it? Is that maybe the reason you retained my services?"

"I'd be lying if I said no, but it wasn't the only reason. I know you and I heard good things about you over the years. Even when Jack was castigating you, he was effectively lauding your skills. I also heard you were fair and a fighter for justice. That means a lot to me. I've lived too long with someone who was also a fighter, but only for what was best for him."

Shawn sat back and frowned. "Shit, Lyd, what happened to us? How did we ever fall apart? I mean, what happened to our friendship? It seemed so solid back then…then I blinked an eye and it was gone."

Lydia closed her eyes because they were getting close to overflowing. "Life. Just life. And choices."

"But you chose Jack Myers. I have to tell you, as much as I have always tried to see the good in people, and I did even with Jack, what the fuck did you see in him? He was the biggest asshole at Columbia. Okay, that's not fair. I rescind that. He wasn't the biggest. There was also Kent Sherman, the Olympic torch bearer and gold medalist for the asshole team. He's a tax attorney today, by the way. But Jack was a close runner up. Bronze, maybe silver, but not gold. Seriously, Lydia. Why?"

It was a perfectly reasonable question, at least in the context of their reminiscing about old times, but the words had a lowering effect. Lydia didn't have a good answer. She didn't know exactly what it was that attracted her to Jack. And she couldn't exactly say what made her gravitate away from Shawn. It was largely due to the fact that he'd always treated her like his little buddy, never once having made any advances of a romantic nature. She wished he had. Her life would have taken a different turn had he shown her any interest beyond having her play Gilligan to his Skipper.

"I really can't say," she lied, taking another sip of her smoothie. "Jack was ardent in the beginning. I was flattered. He seemed so confident, always knowing the right thing to say and do. He was never unsure of himself. I was in awe of that. I think that was what drew me to him. His overpowering sense of security sucked in my insecurity like a pull of gravity into a black hole. I found myself floundering, then I lost myself in it. I'm now just finding my way out."

"I can see that. It happens with couples. Couples with shitty marriages, that is."

"I was swept off my feet quickly. I didn't really have a chance to set them back down on solid ground when Carl, my first, now called Leo, was born. I wasn't even ready to become a mother and there I was, trying to do my best, hoping every day I wouldn't fall on my face and mess my child up. Then Victoria came and I was little better prepared, but still trying to figure it all out. Jack was rising in his career. I was expected to be the dutiful wife and mother. I tried to keep up with everything, but you know how it goes. I dropped out of college. There was no way I could handle it all by myself. Jack was never there."

Shawn shook his head. "I know. I was so sorry when you quit Columbia. Bereft, to be honest." He reached awkwardly for his napkin and pretended to wipe something from his lips. "You know, sometimes I argue with God about that free will deal. I mean, talk about a double-edged sword. It's like giving a kid in the ghetto a loaded gun. I'm not trying to be prejudiced here, but I represented so many of them who just, for sheer lack of maturity and guidance, made horrendous choices. Choices that ruined their lives. And they were good kids. Kids who could have had a future, who could have gone to college. Kids who could have had a shot at realizing their dreams. Instead, they took a shot and it ended them in a cell, for life." Shawn paused and leaned his head against his hand. "Stop me here before I start singing Mother Machree. I hate to cry in my beer. I know it's permissible for the Irish, but other people aren't so understanding."

"By the grace of God, we didn't let our free will take away our freedom. At least not permanently. What I mean is, I hadn't felt really free till I left for Paris this last time. Then I started to see that my life had possibilities. I could do the things I'd put off for so long. I know it sounds selfish and maybe I am self-centered, but I like being me and doing what I want to do."

"It doesn't. And you're not. You're tasting real freedom, maybe for the first time in your life. Think about it, Lyd. First, you were with your parents. Then you were in college, which is like a big institutional babysitter that makes sure you do what you have to do and don't completely destroy yourself. Or at least it tries to. Then you jumped right into marriage, then kids. When did you ever have a chance to taste freedom?"

Lydia looked down at her hands. "What about you? Do you feel free since your divorce?"

"Hell, yes. Someday I'll tell you the whole story, but not right now, I think we have to take care of a little business first. Namely, your divorce. I want to know what your plan is, if you have one. What you want, what you need, how you want this to go. Are you ready to talk about that?"

"Yes. That would be good."

Noticing the drop in mood, Shawn said, "Hey, buddy, I didn't mean to dig up a grave here. Let's talk about how we're going to make Jack Myers writhe in agony as we leach everything we can from him. How does that sound?"

Lydia looked into his eyes. She was struck by the cerulean blue orbs that locked onto her gaze. "I don't want to do it that way, Shawn. I want an uncontested divorce and I told Jack that. The only problem is, he doesn't."

"Most couples think an uncontested divorce goes something like this. Both parties agree to divorce, both agree on how the assets will be distributed, and both behave as sane, intelligent people without an ax to grind. Both come out unbattered, hardly bruised, and financially stable. From my experience, that's practically non-existent. In fact, I've never seen it happen."

"But that's how it should be. How it could be if both parties were mature enough to communicate and agree on everything."

"I rest my case, Mary Poppins. You know, they'd serve ice cream in hell if the souls of the damned asked for it. Lydia, be reasonable. Consider who you're dealing with."

"I know. You're right. It's just…" A feeling of hopelessness descended on her like an opaque cloud.

Shawn wasn't about to lose her to a wave of depression. "Okay, listen, bud. I think what you would like in terms of an uncontested divorce means you will accept everything that's gone on between the two of you, let Captain Hook off the hook, so to speak, and ask for what the law says you're entitled to. Am I right?"

"Yes."

"That sounds good and reasonable and it would certainly be a win for Jack and decidedly a nice consolation prize for you, given his assets. So, I have to say, sure, let's propose that first. I'll write it up and send it to him. I'll first initiate a legal separation and propose the uncontested divorce. Should he refuse, we'll go for the adultery allegation and Jack will have the option to plead nolo contendere. Should he not, then we initiate a suit against him not only for adultery but cruel and unusual punishment."

"Seriously? It would have to go that far?"

"If little Jackie doesn't want to play ball our way, yes. I mean, why would he not go for an uncontested divorce? He has everything to win, nothing to lose. Except his wife, of course."

"It sounds reasonable, but..."

"It is reasonable, and for that reason, I think it's the best action to take. Jack will refuse, and when he does, we'll have to haul out the big guns. It will likely go to trial unless he changes his stance. And it may take some time, Lyd. I'm sorry, but that's the way the system works."

While Lydia saw how much Shawn enjoyed strategizing, still, it was daunting to think that the divorce procedure would go on for...what? Weeks? Months? Years?

"What would you have to do if it went to the next contingency?"

"Good question. You said you have evidence of his affairs and that's good. I need to see it. All of it. If push comes to shove and we have to charge him with adultery and mental cruelty, we need all the evidence we can get. You'll need something from the shelter, even the police officer who drove you there. Maybe even something from the residents you got to know. What's more, if they could come to the trial, it would be icing on the cake."

"So you're saying, in effect, we'd have to drag Jack through the mud."

Shawn winced. "Hmmm...not exactly the words I'd use. We wouldn't so much drag him, as lead him to it in his bare feet, so it squishes up around his ankles, if he chooses to do what I think he'll do. We'd have no choice. It might be the only way he's going to give you a divorce, buddy. What I mean is, the court will decide for him."

"And if he doesn't go along with this? I mean, if he somehow turns it around that he has evidence against me, that he's really the innocent party..."

"Lydia, what could he possibly have as evidence against you?"

"He's been trying to convince me I'm crazy for the past year."

"Yeah, well, just about every guy who's porking another woman likes to make that plea." Shawn reached his hand across the table and laid it gently on top of hers. "Seriously, for Jack to let this go to trial is tantamount to putting his pecker on the conveyor belt to the meat grinder. Not that I'd mind or try to stop him. Hell, I'd be pushing the button."

"So what do you need me to do?"

"Help me get into his head. I need to know what nasty little drama is playing out there. You said you think he may want to prove you incompetent. Maybe so. What else would he be capable of doing?"

"I believe Jack would want complete and total revenge. I think going to Paris and then not being there when he came, then telling him I had evidence proving his affairs pushed him over the edge. I was gone for almost four weeks. The entire time, or the greater part of it, he had me followed by a detective. Then I had him followed. I got results. He didn't. That infuriated him. Then I asked for the divorce."

"You horrible crazy women. You should be locked up in an institution and lobotomized. Seriously, Lyd, so far, nothing has been your fault. Is there anything you're not telling me?"

Lydia hesitated. She hadn't wanted to mention this. "When I told him I wanted a divorce, I saw something in his eyes I'd never seen before. I know it sounds strange, bizarre, in fact, but the look was demonic. Even the energy in the room changed. It felt cold and dangerous. He looked like he could have killed me right there on the spot. I believe he would have if he thought he could get away with it."

Shawn sat quietly for a moment, turning his beer glass in one hand and studying the design on the placemat. This was something he should have taken into consideration. He cursed himself for overlooking a vital part of the equation. He knew exactly what Lydia was talking about.

Chapter 15

When Shawn spoke again, his tone was different. "Lydia, I have concerns for you. It's just a feeling, but for some reason everything in my head is telling me you have to proceed very carefully. Jack isn't a stable person. Yes, he's a brilliant attorney. Yes, he knows who to manipulate and how to get his way. But it goes beyond that. I know exactly what you're talking about. I saw the same look in his eyes when he lost the People vs. Boyd Enterprises case to me. It was, as you said, demonic, and you know me. Regardless of the fact that I practiced for two hellish years in Alabama," he said, switching to a slow drawl, "I don't cotton to that demon shit, no how." He reached out for her hand and cupped it in his. "Look what he's already done to you. I'm still trying to wrap my head around the shenanigans he's pulled. Oh, and in case you didn't know, 'cotton to' is Southern for 'believe in.'"

"I'll be okay, Shawn. Don't worry. I have friends, family, even a shelter to go to if I have to. I'm not afraid of Jack. His threats and his bark, even his bite, aren't enough to deter me or get me to back down. I offered an uncontested divorce. He laughed in my face. We'll offer it again and he can turn it down. He'll bristle when he sees you're representing me, but that's okay. You'll just have to count on him being ugly and trying every way to undermine you. We'll go along and play the game his way and do what we have to do. I know you know all the legal aspects, but I do know at least one thing. In our great State of New York, which is still an at-fault state, one can obtain a divorce on the grounds of adultery."

"You are partly right there, but it's not foolproof. Believe it or not, adultery is difficult to prove. I know you have the evidence, which I can't wait to see, but to push adultery as the reason, it has to be clear that you, the cheatee, were not aware of Jack's, the cheater's, extra-marital affairs and still opted to remain in the marital relationship."

"I didn't know. I only thought he might be."

"We'd have to make that our case, but Jack could counter attack by saying you knew and you agreed to stay for...what? Monetary support? Religious reasons? He'd have to take that tack."

Lydia paused for a moment to think. "I did mention to him that I thought he'd been cheating all throughout our marriage."

Shawn rubbed his hand over his chin. "He could and probably will make the case that you were aware. But don't let's get bogged down with that. We can still make adultery the issue, but I will also bring out the cruel and inhumane treatment charge. After all, he put you in a homeless shelter, endangered your life, cut you off from all monetary support and left you with nothing, not even spare change. No phone, no money for food, electricity, gas, not even a damn phone card...I'd call that cruel and unusual. I suppose he could say you got to stay in a luxury homeless shelter and were well taken care of...but, then, what asshole would buy that?"

Lydia laughed, even as her eyes were stinging. "I hate doing this. As much as I want this to be fair and settled amicably, I know better. Jack won't have it. He'll do everything he can to prove I'm the monster, the abandoner, the crazy one. I don't want the father of my children to be exposed for who he is. Jack is bad, but the whole world doesn't have to know, and the kids certainly don't. I shudder to think how this will affect Tori and Leo. This is their father. They'll have to live with this the rest of their lives."

Shawn leaned back and stared at the cream-colored faux tin ceiling overhead. "All we can do is present the evidence. Jack always has the option of agreeing on the divorce and the proposed settlement. If he chooses not to, it lies with the judge to decide. But Lydia, you have to understand. A divorce, at least in this state, is not a walk in Central Park. You step in dog do-do. Well, you still do when some lazy slob doesn't scoop the poop. Feelings are hurt. People suffer. If it wasn't so painful, I truly believe the divorce rate would sky rocket. I know men I work with who are so damned afraid of divorcing for fear of what it would do to them. They're living lives of marital misery, shackled, literally imprisoned by their marriages. And I'm not saying there's not an equal number of women, maybe more, who feel the same way. Staying married, to some, is preferable to having your balls ripped off and all your assets taken away. What the female counterpart of that is, I'm not sure."

Lydia wondered what Shawn's divorce had been like. He had strong feelings about the topic, but they could have come from the course of his work and not his own personal experience. That conversation would have to wait till another time.

Now, for the first time, she was beginning to see that others would be hurt in the process. Her children, first and foremost. It was inevitable. She'd help them as much as possible, but, in the end, they'd have to deal with it in their own way. If it taught them one thing, and she knew the chances of that were slim, they'd learn that marriage was not something you entered into on the basis of romantic love and intoxicating feelings, or being wowed by another person. She hoped they wouldn't assign the word, "love," to that peak time of hormonal overload, but wait till it subsided and let real emotion and reason come to play. She'd made the mistake. She'd taken the bait and fallen headfirst into the trap. It was hard to acknowledge the truth and accept the many years it took to finally wrench herself out of it.

After lunch, she walked Shawn to his Jeep and they said their good-byes. Lydia waved to him as he backed out of the parking space, then watched as the black Jeep leapt forward, screeching the tires and leaving a black streak on the pavement. That was the old Shawn from college days. Her heart gave a leap.

She felt sure of one thing. Shawn O'Malley was going to fight for her. It was a new and different feeling and it settled well on her mind. She'd made a good choice of attorney. More importantly, she liked him. Not so much that she'd let it interfere in her judgment, or his, but enough to make working with him a pleasure. Hopefully for both of them. For now, she'd be happy to have him as the Skipper, and she, his little buddy.

Smiling, she walked to her car, daydreaming about what it would be like to be lost on a remote island in the Pacific with nobody else around but Shawn O'Malley.

Chapter 16

"Get your asses in gear and gather round, my little lambs," Maz shouted out to the crowd gathering in the newsroom. The bullpen, as he liked to call it, was filling quickly.

"I'm going to say this fast, and I'm going to say it once. We have got to get our act together pronto or we lose our chance to get this to press in time for the Montclair, Inc. trial. My goal is to have this out the exact same time as Day I coverage hits the press. Anything before that leaves open the possibility of a continuance. Anything too far after leaves the gate open for every goddamn tabloid and rag dog to come into the yard, walk all over it with his grubby paws, and lift his leg on it. Timing is everything with this release. We had a lucky and unexpected break here. I'll let Simon fill you in with more details later."

The others looked around at one another and nodded, some in full agreement, some with fear in their eyes. Only Simon smiled and gave a thumbs up. "We're going to do it, boss. I know we can."

Maz clapped his hands. "Our legal team is ready to punt the first round of libel accusations and whatever lawsuits may, and most likely will, arise. We're going up against a giant here, you all know that. So remember, if you feel like backing out and working somewhere else, there's the door. The door is also there, may I remind you, for anyone who so much as lets a whiff of this fart out. There will be no silent but deadlies here. Not a word is to be spoken to your lover, your spouse, your mother, your granny, your rabbi, your priest confessor, your spirit guide—no one. You are mute until this newborn crowns and comes out of the birth canal screaming."

Recently, most of Maz's analogies centered on childbirth and babies. His wife had just given birth to their first child, a nine-pound boy they named Trent. Christina shielded her eyes, her shoulders shaking. Some of the younger men rolled theirs.

"Simon, you finish the Lydia Myers component and don't over-dramatize, got it? We just want to illustrate the fact that the son-of-a-bitch she calls a husband, or soon-to-be ex-husband, is just that. In case the rest of you aren't up to speed on this, Jack Myers is Montclair's attorney. You can write a whole damn book on Mrs. Myers later, for all I care. Just tell her story in a way that shows Jack Myers for who he is and Montclair for what they are. Got it?"

Again, Simon signaled with his thumb.

"Thanks to our Paris liaison, Bob, aka Ro-bear, Rutledge, aka Sledge, we've been deluged with the facts about the Sumar Pakan tragedy. This all came about quite unexpectedly when he was approached by one of Montclair's own, or so they thought. She's an undercover agent for the French equivalent of our Environmental Protection Agency, and don't expect me to pronounce her real name because I can't. Her name, or pseudonym, is Emmanuelle Jobert.

Sledge tells me she's an eleven on a scale of ten and it's making it hard for him to think about taking any assignments outside of Paris. Poor Sledge, the schmuck. He's smitten."

A hand went up. It belonged to Syd Wiseman. Several faces turned away to look around the room.

"I'm just wondering if we considered the possibility of Montclair having the power to shut us down. You remember the Berkeley Injunction several years back that temporarily slammed the door closed on the Berkeley Voice. I think we should…"

"Thank you for sharing that, Syd," Maz interrupted and looked around the room. "Are there any other relevant questions?"

No one raised a hand.

"Okay. Let me just close by saying, we have to diaper this baby up and get it locked and loaded in its car seat very soon. Needless to say there'll be late hours and don't even ask about overtime pay. Your facts have to be airtight as a dirty diaper pail and stronger than a newborn's cry. I expect there'll be a shit storm of retaliation, but we're used to that. Just suit up in your best ebola protective gear and have your prescription anxiety meds on hand if your toes start to curl. Wear your adult diapers because there're going to be times you won't make it to the potty and others when you just may want to drop a crab cake in your shorts. Or panties, to be non-sexist."

Eyes were now either staring at the floor or darting around the room.

"I'm not trying to scare you, boys and girls, but we're walking into the dark cave of corporate malfeasance and we have to be ready for the Lernaean Hydra. Every head you chop off, a new one grows back. Don't tell your kids that story before they go to sleep, by the way. Okay, let's get this mother to the delivery room and get her pushing. Push! Push! Get the hell out of here and get some work done."

Chapter 17

The rusted matte-green Chrysler Newport eased into the driveway of the unoccupied cabin, its bald tires crushing pine cones in its path. If he'd read the directions right, Erik Gormann was in the driveway next door to the Myers' cabin. He saw what looked like light piercing the darkness of forest through an opening in the trees. Closing the car door quietly, he advanced toward it. Sure enough, there was a path. He flicked on his flashlight, even though the natural light was still bright enough to see the trail. You never knew what you might run into or step on in the woods. He hated the country. It was so freaking foreign and, well, dangerous.

So far the operation was moving like clockwork. He'd seen the woman in the Subaru leaving the driveway and watched her as she passed him. She glanced his way and saw him parked on the side of the road, probably figuring he was just another person looking for an entry point to the lake. He'd pulled his baseball cap low over his eyes so she didn't get a good look at his face, even though he got an eyeful of her. She was a pretty nice looking broad, with that color of red hair that made a woman look daring and hot. He wondered if she was.

He also wondered why a nice looking woman like her would be up in these woods all by herself. Was she nuts? Did her husband mind her being here? He knew about it, so maybe he didn't care, or maybe he was glad to be rid of her. She'd stolen the photos and DVD from him, after all, so there must have been something going on between them. It wasn't his job to find out, but still, it made him wonder.

If it was his wife camping out in the wilderness, he wouldn't be so agreeable. Not that he had one, or even wanted one. Maybe he would, someday. But, seriously, a woman alone in a cabin in the boondocks was a target for any pervert who might wander by. Of course, there was also the possibility she wasn't alone and doing the big nasty with somebody her husband didn't know about. Something was going on between them, for sure, otherwise why would he want the photos and DVD and why did she take them? There had to be more to the story, which was none of his business. All he was hired to do was get the stuff back to her husband and collect his money. In and out. Nothing risky. His probation officer would never know.

Erik felt good. Great, in fact. The hit of crystal meth he took right around Saratoga hit the spot and lifted him out of a funk he'd been in for a while, ever since he got out of Attica and hadn't been able to get any new jobs. This one came out of the blue and was literally a shot in the arm. Not like a hit of heroin, which he stopped doing a while back, but still a pretty great feeling. Heroin was too risky. Too many friends lost to overdoses. Besides, he liked the effects of meth better. Longer high, energy that wouldn't quit, until he came down, of course, which was always a bummer. Shit, he might even take a jog around the lake after he got what he came for. He sure as hell wasn't looking forward to the long drive back to the city, so he made a plan to stop by Albany and stay the night with his aunt. She'd love to see him and he wouldn't mind seeing her, as long as her asshole of a boyfriend wasn't hanging around. How she put up with twenty years with that windbag was beyond his understanding. One word from her and he would have off'd the guy in a New York minute and gotten away with it. He knew how. He'd worked enough cases to know what to do and what not to do. People got away with murder every damn day.

He walked up the steps to the door, knocked loudly several times, and waited. No one answered. Good deal. Now for the key. It was exactly where the boss told him, under the lantern mounted on the wall next to the door. The dumbest place they could have picked, but then, morons from the city often were under the mistaken impression that the country was safe and no baddies every pulled their shit there. How stupid could you get? He walked inside and called, "Anybody home?" just to be safe. Nothing. The coast was clear.

The cabin was about one of the nicest dwellings he'd seen in a long time. Far better than any of the places he'd ever lived. Shiny polished floors, scatter rugs that looked like the pricey kind Macy's carried. A long wooden kitchen table and a fancy granite-topped island and counters. All top-of-the-line appliances. Flowers even. Shit. It was a fucking House Beautiful place, not that he read the magazine, but he saw it in one of his foster homes.

The fireplace in the living room was what really caught his eye. And those nice overstuffed recliners and a couch covered in pillows. Christ, there were real flowers in vases everywhere he looked. This was a quality joint. He should have hit Myers up for more money. Maybe he might find some spare cash the wife left around. Hell, he earned it for all the time it took to get here. Not that his travel expenses weren't more than adequately covered.

He checked out all the rooms and found the bedroom with the desk, almost hoping it would take a while to find the photos. But, as luck would have it, there was a manila envelope with a small square case on top, obviously housing the DVD. Hey, no time like the present to take a break and check out the movie. He had time. Even if the lady ran down the road to get a six-pack, it was a good ten miles away, so he'd have ample time for a little entertainment. And what better way to enjoy a good movie than to have a snack?

He went back to the kitchen and opened the refrigerator. Holy crap, God was smiling on him again, for lo and behold there was a plate of cookies with plastic wrap over them and a carton of... What the fuck was this, soy milk? Who drank that shit, anyway? Oh well, the rich had their quirks and he needed something to wash the cookies down with, so he poured himself a big glass. Outside of it tasting a little chalky, it wasn't all that bad. One of his foster moms used to drink it. This job really was turning out to be cake, but not just ordinary cake. It was more a hot fudge brownie with whipped cream topping. One of his foster moms used to make that. He couldn't remember which, there were so many.

He brought the envelope, DVD, cookies and milk into the living room and set them on the coffee table, turned on the DVD player, and popped in the movie.

Jesus Christ on a bicycle, it started right out with a bang. Literally. Two stark naked people going at it with gusto. He was getting horny just watching the first few minutes and it went on for another ten. Huffing, puffing, bumping, grinding. It was no porn flick, but you got the idea. The bitch was something to look at, too. What tits, not to mention a world class booty. If he wasn't imagining it, she had some kind of foreign accent, too. French, maybe.

The man was obviously super-excited and who wouldn't be nailing a woman like that. He felt a twinge of sympathy when the guy shot his wad pretty early in the game, not that he could blame him. A chick like that was deadly for a guy's endurance. Too bad it was such a poor filming job, all shot from one angle, but at least it gave a good idea of what was going on. The woman alone made it an award winning performance.

He wondered who filmed the fuck fest because it didn't look like the couple was even aware of being videotaped. Maybe they set up the camera themselves, but he didn't think so. There was something so raw and natural about the whole scene, it got him questioning. If they did it themselves and were cheating on their spouses, they were pretty damn stupid. It was like those dumbass kids who filmed themselves robbing a convenience store or beating up another kid on the playground. The evidence was irrefutable and not something you could bullshit your way out of. "Gosh, your honor, I'm sorry if that makes it look like me screwing that fine looking woman, but I don't have a clue where this came from. Or, yes, that is the same mole I have on my ass, but this clearly is a case of mistaken identity." Shit. Kids could be that stupid, but grown-ups? They should know better.

He finished a fifth cookie, went to the kitchen to replenish his drink, and came back to eject the DVD. Now it was time to look inside the envelope. What the…? Oh, whoa baby, here was a different story altogether. It was the same dude with a gorgeous hunk of a woman sporting a rack on her that could sink a ship, and hips that could, well, launch a thousand ships, or however the saying went.

There were a lot of kissy face shots and one boob fondling but, for the most part, they weren't remarkable, as least as far as the couple getting it on and doing the horizontal mambo. Who were these people? Obviously it was somebody's husband, or wife, getting it on with somebody they weren't supposed to. The photos were good, too. Obviously taken by a pro because of their quality and crispness. Whoever took them had to have one of those honking bazookas of a camera with a lens the size of a pony's schlong. He always wanted one of them. It would have helped him in his work. Unfortunately, the over four grand price tag kept them out of his reach and, unless he wanted to lift one, he had to content himself with his Canon Point n' Shoot. Outside of not having the best photographic equipment, he had a decent firearm and a good knife. He was a good detective, too, when he wasn't serving time. He made enough to cover his living expenses with enough left over for drugs. What else did a person need?

The times he wasn't working, when he was "on vacation" courtesy of the New York State Department of Corrections, it was a relief not having to keep up with bills and all the other hassles of daily living. Life was good, inside or out. It wasn't like the drugs weren't available in the big house and he learned to adapt well and follow the rules of survival. The first rule being, be a bigger motherfucker than the next guy so nobody messes with you. If somebody so much as went for the cold toast on his plate he didn't plan to eat, the second rule was to lay him out swiftly and painfully. It instilled fear and respect and that's what kept you alive.

He learned this after the first time he'd been incarcerated. He was only eighteen and small for his age. He got shoved around a lot, collarbone broken, and some other things he didn't care to think about. After that, he handled himself differently. He worked out and buffed up, even earned a black belt in karate so that, whenever the doors clanged shut and locked behind him, he turned into the mighty Hulk. Everybody steered clear of him. He already had under his belt several broken noses and ribs, a dislocated shoulder, and one guy who spent over a week in the infirmary for multiple injuries. He earned the title of badass and it suited him.

Erik also prided himself on knowing when to quit and not take it too far. It didn't make sense to kill anyone in the lock-up, though there were a hundred guys he would have and could have. It was the consequences that mattered. He could lose his freedom entirely, even if it was in self-defense, and he didn't particularly want to grow old behind bars. Not everybody felt that way, but he liked being only an occasional visitor.

He jumped when he heard a car door shut. Toasted shit on a shingle, the lady of the house was back. He had to think fast. She was already coming up the steps. The door opened. He was on his feet.

Before Lydia could scream, he shouted, "Ma'am, Mrs. Myers, it's okay. I'm a detective. My name is Erik Gormann and I was sent here by your husband to check on you. He was worried about you. Are you okay?"

"How did you get in?" she asked, standing halfway in the door with a grocery bag in her arms and keys in her hand like she was ready to bolt any second.

"Mr. Myers gave me a key. I would have waited for you to return, but you see, I have to get back to the city tonight. I waited a while, but then decided it would be okay to come in. I'm sorry to say, I had to take a wicked...I had to use the restroom."

Lydia slowly closed the door behind her and glanced down at the coffee table. "Did my husband also tell you to look at those photos and the DVD? Did you get a chance to watch it?"

In situations like this, which weren't the usual way his investigations went, Erik always found truth to be the best way out. Getting caught up in a string of lies was just amateurish and plain retarded. "Yes, ma'am. I did."

"And did my husband want you to take those photos and that DVD to him?"

"Uh, yes ma'am. You are right on the money, again."

Lydia walked over to the coffee table, gathered up the photos, put them in the envelope and slipped the DVD back in its holder and tucked it in the envelope. She turned to the detective. "Here. They're yours. Take them back to my husband and don't say a word about meeting me. He wouldn't be pleased if you did. Trust me."

Erik took the envelope and turned to leave.

"And the key?"

He fumbled in his pocket and handed it to her saying, "I'll let him know you're okay."

Lydia glared back. "That wouldn't be advisable. Remember, you didn't see me. It's for your own good. Trust me."

Erik nodded. "Right. Okay, then. Thanks for everything, ma'am."

Before he closed the door behind him, he got an idea. "Ma'am, here's my card, in case you ever need anything. I work in the city mostly, but I wouldn't mind coming out here. The lake's pretty and, well, I don't mind the drive. Seriously. You take care, now. Living out here alone, I mean, if you are alone, isn't the greatest idea. There's a lot of weirdos and perverts out there."

Before shutting the door, he poked his head back inside. "Sorry about making myself at home, but I have to tell you, those were the best cookies I ever ate."

He walked out the door and down the steps, slipped on an acorn and almost lost his balance. That's all he needed, a graceful departure after getting caught red-handed with his pants down. Damn nature!

Back in his car, he wondered about what just happened. Who were those folks in the photos and the DVD? And if she stole them, why was she so willing to give them up? It didn't jive. Shit. If he'd known she'd be that agreeable, he would've parked in the driveway and spared himself the walk through the woods. It was even darker now when he came out. God only knew what was lurking there.

All in all, though, he had to admit it turned out to be a primo job, an easy five hundred dollars. It all went according to plan, except for the last couple minutes. Thank God the woman was level-headed and didn't start screaming her head off or call the police.

She didn't buy his story, though, and that was okay. It bugged him that he couldn't figure out what was going on, unless that guy in the photos and DVD was her husband, which would mean Myers was trying to cover up his own romping with sexy women and wasn't trying to protect a client, as he said.

So his wife had gotten her little mitts on the evidence and man, wasn't that the worst kind of hand-in-the-cookie-jar kind of experience? So what was he doing screwing other women when he had a real looker like her for a wife? Shit. If that was Myers, and he figured it had to be, the guy had to be a total loser. And a piss poor lover, at that. A real monkey's patooty. But then, even monkeys had more class. Probably better stamina, too.

No sooner had the detective left than Lydia called Shawn. He didn't answer so she left a message. "Just as you predicted, Jack sent someone to get the DVD and photos. I happened in on him in the process and scared the daylights out of him. Don't worry, he wasn't violent. In fact, he told me why he was there and was rather polite about the whole thing. I gave them to him. I also took down his license plate and he gave me his card before he left. Can you believe that? The only thing I'm mad about it is that he drank half the soy milk and ate almost all the cookies I left in the fridge. Okay, then. Thank you for having me make the copies. You were right. Hope you're having a productive day. Good night, Shawn."

Lydia changed into her pajamas, made a cup of chamomile tea and flicked on the TV. There was a movie she'd seen several times but wanted to watch again. It was one of her favorites. *Notorious*, starring Ingrid Bergman and Cary Grant. Ingrid's character, Alicia, was being poisoned slowly by her husband to prevent her from revealing his nefarious dealings with the Nazis. Cary Grant came to her rescue and whisked her away to safety. She shuddered to think this could be her story. Was Shawn going to play the part of Cary Grant's character, Devlin, and come to her rescue?

She sipped her tea and glided easily into sleep just before Ingrid Bergman was being carried away to safety.

Chapter 18

Lydia opened the envelope with the return address of *New York Now* and a scribbled name above it. It was from Simon Vanderlaan. She removed the contents, to which a note was attached.

> *Lydia,*
>
> *I know this will come as a shock. I never intended to deceive you and I hope we can continue to be friends. I had to maintain secrecy and not disclose my identity to you or anyone. I hope you'll understand. None of this was meant to hurt you. Please read the enclosed and try to understand.*
>
> *Your friend,*
> *Simon*

She read the manuscript.

Defending the Lawless Giant
By Simon Vanderlaan

Citizens are required to pay their taxes. Citizens are held accountable for their actions when they infringe on or violate the rights of other citizens.

They are tried for their crimes and when the system works as it is designed to, they are punished.

We, the people, live in a society governed by rules, regulations, and laws. Large corporations live outside this sphere. They are not subject to the same laws. They are not held accountable. They are exempt from paying taxes. They are allowed to operate with impunity in their disrespect and disregard for the well-being of others and for the planet as a whole. When citizens rise up in protest and they are brought to a kind of "justice," it is served to them differently. They are not punished or held accountable, but allowed to make amends instead of being found guilty and prosecuted. One such corporation is Montclair, Inc., a giant that operates with freedom from censure as it stomps on fragile and vulnerable third world countries as though they were anthills.

Montclair, Inc. is leaving its print wherever its leviathan foot sets down. It operates in zones of lawlessness amassing gargantuan monetary gains in its silent assault on the planet and its people. Its weapons are chemicals. Chemicals tested in its own laboratories and extolled as catalysts for economic development, touted to be environmentally safe, and even safe for human consumption. These chemicals are used exclusively outside the United States. One such Montclair engineered chemical is Kali-chlor4, a pesticide designed to promote agricultural development throughout the world. To date, Kali-chlor4 has taken the lives of over 2,400 people and the numbers are steadily rising.

A recent chemical leak in the Montclair plant located in Sumar Pakan, Thailand eclipses that of the last leak one year ago in Indonesia, with a death toll surpassing 1,854. The figure rises daily as continuing repercussions are recorded. The myth of legal intervention perpetuates the crimes perpetrated by Montclair against these countries where the law merely serves to camouflage and protect these acts of aggression and hold the aggressor harmless. Lust for power and profit combine with internal corruption to allow Montclair to practice in an environment exempt from regulation and oversight.

One might be led to believe that the efforts of Montclair, Inc. are vastly humanitarian and focused on enriching the lives of the less fortunate. Nothing could be further from the truth. Their advertising budget exceeds three billion dollars annually, creating a screen of propaganda that extols the virtues of their presence as a force of good as it carries out its work in a secret society of noncompliance with regulatory agencies. It safeguards its hold on power by pointing the finger at local sources of noncompliance and human ineptitude to explain away its own negligence and disregard for compliance. Montclair, Inc. purports to comply with fair labor practices and markets itself as a benefactor when, in fact, it is a persecutor and a liar of astronomical proportions.

This is an American company, represented and legally defended by American attorneys. Its corruption and inhumane practice is not restricted solely to third world countries. It promotes lawlessness by surrounding and insulating itself with those who would support and defend its conduct. Its henchman are well-known and well-respected men in society. They, too, operate with impunity. The attorney leading the defense of Montclair's most recent scandal in Sumar Pakan is Jack Myers, partner in the firm of Parker, Cross, Epstein and Myers—one of New York's finest. Myers is credited with Montclair, Inc.'s victory in Indonesia only one year ago.

To understand Montclair's corporate mentality, one must only look to the character of the lawyers who defend it. Jack Myers is a brilliant man and a successful attorney, to all outward appearances. A Columbia graduate, husband, and father of two, this juris doctor might be considered a man of integrity, but he is far from it. Jack Myers recently put his wife's life in danger when he deprived her money, electricity, a home, a phone, and all means of monetary support which required her to seek sanctuary in a shelter for the homeless in Lake George, New York. While Jack drove his Lexus to work and consorted with his mistress in their Manhattan home, his wife, Lydia Myers, found refuge among prostitutes and drug addicts. Because of overcrowding, she slept in the shelter's chapel on a wooden pew. The reason for her husband's action? He wanted to punish her because she asked for a divorce.

Jack Myers is just a cog in the wheel of a corporate machine that operates outside of the law as it levels oppression on the aggrieved classes. He represents the cadre of corporate lawyers who see the rule of law for the myth it is and who uphold the law of power and greed. With the help of such lawyers, Montclair, Inc. shields itself from all accountability as it hides its unrestrained tax evasion and unaudited expenditures behind a smokescreen of corporate largesse. Its biased research goes unchallenged and its criminal exploitation and egregious violations of basic human rights are swept under the rug.

Although due process of the law is one of the hallmarks of Western civilization and something we should be proud of, corporations such as Montclair, Inc. undermine its bulwarks and render it impotent. Montclair, Inc. is a mega-corporation that amasses fortunes as it annihilates those who need humanitarian support and true economic development the most.

What you will hear and read about in the coming months in other publications is how Montclair, Inc. is assuming responsibility, providing compensation, bolstering economic growth, and rendering humanitarian support in Sumar Pakan, as it did in Indonesia. Its advertising campaign with its three billion dollar budget will be busy at work bringing you all the untruth it wants you to believe.

Two centuries ago Senator Daniel Webster referred to the legal system as the "ligament that holds civilized beings and civilized nations together." When no one speaks out against such lawlessness, this ligament begins to tear. When no one hears the feeble cries for justice, we cease to exist as a society. In the end, we fail ourselves and our world.

Lydia put down the manuscript. She'd been holding her breath and now inhaled deeply and let it out with a long sigh. She sat down to steady her wobbly knees. Simon Vanderlaan. Simon Simple. He wasn't a homeless heroin addict, but a reporter. A New York City reporter who worked for *New York Now*, the paper Jack always read because, as he put it, "They walk on the edge and don't mince words."

Simon had fooled her. How could she have been so blind? He was that good, that's how. He could have fooled anyone. Stay calm, she advised, and took another deep breath. Do nothing. Just sit with this for a while.

What in God's name was he thinking not to tell her what he was up to? He was doing his job, of course. That was all. Using her to get a story. But why her? Her connection to Jack Myers, what else? She wasn't sure if she wanted to cry or laugh hysterically. There was no appropriate reaction for something like this. She'd been taken by surprise, blindsided by someone she thought she was going to help. Someone she was going to resurrect from addiction.

There was a hurt somewhere deep within but she couldn't feel it yet. Only numbness and a feeling of betrayal. Her hands were trembling as she picked up the phone to call Shawn. As always, he didn't answer. She left a long message. The machine cut her off before she was done.

Never before had she felt such a mix of emotions. Did she want to slap Simon, hug him, knock him silly, or make more cookies for him? She thought about Jack. Should she laugh in his face or run and hide from him now? When this hit the papers, and she had no idea when that would be, Jack would be beside himself. Livid. Possibly even homicidal. And he'd think she was behind it. He'd blame her.

Such was the whirlwind in her mind and the tumult in her body, she felt like she was going to either throw up or jump out of her skin. The call that came in later from Shawn went to voicemail. While he left a lengthy message, she ran down to the lake, stripped off her clothes and plunged into the icy waters of Lake George. She screamed, cursed, swam some more and stayed in the water until her limbs were stiff and her lips blue.

Chapter 19

The psychiatrist's office was grungier than he expected. For all the money the guy was charging, it should have been a palace. Then again, it was an older downtown Manhattan building and offices were hard to keep up due to decades of disrepair and the unpreventable decrepitude of age. Unless they were gutted and rebuilt from the studs on up, they tended to look like this one. Neglected and shabby. What some people liked to think was "character," but Jack found it to be a pitiful waste of prime real estate. They should all be torn down and replaced with modern buildings.

It also depended on how many patients Dr. Aronson saw whether he wanted to put a fortune into creating a nice environment for his clients, or patients, as he probably called them. His own firm had spent four million on renovations to their offices and it showed. Parker, Cross, Epstein and Myers was a showcase. You walked in the door and smelled money.

The aquarium was an okay touch, but something the office could do without. No matter how well maintained they were, they served no purpose other than to give the air that fishy smell and cost a bundle in maintenance. This one was badly in need of cleaning. Even the fish looked tattered. His firm considered having an aquarium but ruled against it for these very reasons. Their offices were avant-garde and minimalist. This place was a turn-of-the-century dilapidated relic with an overlay of dust. Lydia probably loved it.

Another patient walked in. Jack looked up from the article he was reading in the *New Yorker*. He couldn't help but notice this man was exactly the kind of nutcase he'd expect to see in a psychiatrist's office. He had the air of someone in need of a lot of help, or a backbone. The man was carrying a bowler hat and wore a pair of rubber galoshes, a black trench coat that was stylish two decades ago, and a black umbrella. He walked slightly hunched over and looked like a puff of wind would knock over his ninety-pound frame. He had a look of someone who might faint if someone shouted at him or worse, raised a hand to him. The word "wimp" came to mind. Someone like this fit the bill as a psychiatric patient, whereas Jack was a fish out of water in a place like this.

He never thought much of the psychiatric profession or psychotherapy. It was all a lot of psycho-babble bullshit, and high-priced bullshit, at that. Maybe some people needed it, but not him. He also couldn't help but notice how the man carefully wiped the seat with a handkerchief before sitting down, then folded it neatly and tucked it in his coat pocket. As he hung his coat on a coat tree, he moved it slightly to better align it near the door. Then he sat down and smoothed the creases in his pants before taking out a can of breath freshener and giving his mouth a squirt. A real head case, for sure. Jack smirked to himself, thankful he wasn't here as a patient, though he led Dr. Aronson to believe he was seeking help with his divorce.

When the door opened and Dr. Aronson came out to the waiting room, he looked at both men as if trying to decide, then turned to Jack and said, "It's your time now." Jack understood he was letting the other man know he was way too early and simply had to wait. The man mumbled something, but didn't look up from examining his cuticles as the two men went into the office.

At least he could say he liked the look of the doctor's office. It was how a psychiatrist's office should look, even if it could have used a good polishing and dusting.

"So what brings you here today, Mr. Myers," Dr. Aronson said as he shuffled papers on his desk to clear a place for his notepad. In so doing, he upset a chipped mug with the inscription, "Super Dad," on it, sending a splash of coffee on some files.

Jack cleared his throat. "You saw my wife, Lydia Myers, about two months ago. She'd been depressed. Since then, things have gotten worse and I just wanted to find out, hm, I wanted to learn from you how I should cope with her moods and some of her more alarming behaviors. Any insights you could share would be appreciated. I realize you can't talk about her visit with you, but maybe I could give you an idea of what she's been doing since she last saw you. Frankly, Dr. Aronson, I'm very concerned about her well-being."

Dr. Aronson sat staring at Jack with a puzzled look on his face. "Lydia Myers, you say?"

"That's right. My wife, Lydia Myers."

"And you say she came to see me, what, a couple months back? For depression?"

"Yes."

The doctor ran a hand through his thinning white hair and looked up to the ceiling as if he was searching for something there. "I'm sorry, but I don't recall seeing a Lydia Myers recently. I could check my file cabinet to see if I have any record of a session. Allow me a few moments."

Jack shifted in his seat. "No rush. Take all the time you need."

Dr. Aronson opened a file drawer in his desk and sifted through a number of files, murmuring, "Myers, Lydia…Myers…depression…now where the deuce is that file?"

"Ah ha, here I have it." He opened the file and bent closer to look at the one sheet of paper in it. "Why, there's nothing here. Nothing except a note that says she was going to re-schedule her appointment because…let me see…oh yes, now I recall. We didn't meet that day because I had an emergency and had to leave the office. I did see her, in fact, and she was kind enough to close the office for me and leave a note on the door."

Dr. Aronson sat back in his burgundy leather chair and smiled, pleased that he remembered an event so far out of range for his normal recollection.

"You say she never saw you?"

"Oh no, she did see me, and I saw her, but she didn't meet with me."

"And you didn't suggest to her that she was bored and needed time away, a month by herself, to travel and sort things out, or something like that?"

"Absolutely not. I would never suggest anything of the kind to a depressed person. They need stability, not the upset of traveling or being away from their support systems. I only suggested that she re-schedule. And she did not. At least not yet. I hope she's doing well."

Jack said back, silently processing this new information. It was not what he expected or was led to believe. Lydia told him she'd seen Dr. Aronson and given details of their conversation. She told him Dr. Aronson had not found her depressed, but bored. She said he recommended some time apart, travel. She lied to him. What's more, she conned him into a month in Paris on the basis of Dr. Aronson's recommendation.

His only comment was, "I see. I guess I was mistaken. I thought my wife had had a session with you." He stood up. "I'm afraid I've wasted your time and my own. I came here under the false impression that you had worked with my wife and might be able to shed more light on her condition. There is no reason for this session to continue. Just send me the bill."

He strode out of the office as Dr. Aronson trailed behind him. "Wait, Mr. Myers, wait. Lydia did come to see me, but I wasn't able to see her. She was actually very helpful. Leaving the message on the door, letting the next patient know I wasn't in. I'm sure there's more we could talk about."

Jack stopped at the door to the hallway and said over his shoulder, "Yeah, I hear you. I need to get back to work." Just as he was about to close the door, he saw the little man seated in the waiting room raise his hand.

"May I have a word with you, sir?" The man's eyelids were fluttering like bird wings.

"No, I'm busy, I have to go."

"It's about your wife." He hesitated, then said softly, "May we go into the hall?"

Jack gave a disgusted sigh and held the door for the man as he tiptoed to the door and eased past him. Closing the door behind him, Jack folded his arms across his chest.

"What do you know about my wife?"

The tone of Jack's voice made the man tremble. "Excuse me for bothering you. I just wanted to ask if you would tell Dr. Myers that Terrence Warshawsky said hello. And tell her I still think she's one of the best psychiatrists in the city. She's most definitely the kindest one."

Jack's fist knotted as he raised his eyes to the ceiling. "You're mistaken. My wife is not..." He stopped. "What are you saying? You said you talked to my wife, Dr. Lydia Myers...the psychiatrist?"

"Yes, yes. That's what I'm trying to say. She talked to me when Dr. Aronson wasn't here and...well, please don't think there was anything, well, untoward about it, but we went to a health food store and had smoothies together. She listened to me and I told her..."

"She told you she was a psychiatrist."

"Yes. I mean, no, I don't know that she told me, but I knew she was."

"She led you to believe she was a psychiatrist?"

Terrence Warshawsky's lower lip was trembling. "I hope I haven't said anything out of turn. She was most helpful and I…"

Jack turned abruptly and headed for the elevator. Before he stepped inside, he looked back down the hallway to see the little man standing like a child, dejected, with his head drooped down and his hands folded in front of him.

Back at the office, Jack called his attorney, Maxinne Gunderman. He'd worked with Maxinne over the years and had to give her credit for having earned the reputation as an 'iron maiden.' He'd seen her take down plaintiffs and grind them to dust in her inimical style. "Maxinne, it's Jack. I have some very interesting news. Something's that's going to help us tremendously in the divorce proceedings. Are you ready for this?"

The voice on the other end of the line expressed interest. Jack related his news and waited as the attorney scribbled notes.

"Sounds very promising, Jack. We pretty much have a solid case for incompetence, what with the running away to Paris, then to Lake George, then the false allegations against you that affirm her paranoia, and now this. Lying about seeing the shrink and posing as a psychiatrist herself. It's pretty damning evidence. I'll go ahead and subpoena the psychiatrist's records, or lack thereof. If push comes to shove, we can get this guy, what's his name, to testify."

"Warshawsky. Terrence Warshawsky."

"Got it. Back at you later." Gunderman was about to hang up when she thought of something. "Hey, Jack. Changing the subject, but when's the Montclair case going to trial? I have a couple interns here who want to be in the courtroom. They want to see how a real pro operates."

Jack shook his head in disbelief. His own divorce attorney wasn't keeping up with current events. It was already in the news and the press was prepped and ready. "You asked just in time. Tell them to be there tomorrow morning before 8:00 if they want to get a good seat. It's going to be packed, just like last time. Tell them to expect a media blitz, too."

Gunderman laughed. "I'll tell them. You go get 'em, Jack. Do what you do best."

Chapter 20

Shawn looked at his notes and gave a low whistle. The problem with most divorce cases was that the conflicted parties weren't willing to compromise on even the smallest of matters, like who got custody of the family pets or who got the cheap porcelain vase they purchased together on their honeymoon trip that sold in Macy's for thirty bucks. Such was not the case with Lydia and Jack Myers, at least not from the wife's standpoint. She was willing to concede it all, let her husband have everything, and all she really wanted was the right to change her name and be free of him. He wasn't about to stand for that.

He understood her need for independence and to feel she could survive on her own without her husband's support, but Lydia was overlooking the fact that she'd given the man twenty-two years of her life, raised his children, took care of the family home, and supported him throughout his career. She even surrendered her counseling education to carry out her duties as wife and mother, handled all the home and family responsibilities while her husband worked and played to all hours and did pretty much whatever he wanted, including straying outside the marriage. That didn't surprise him. The self-serving bastard hadn't changed over the years. If anything, he'd just honed his skills.

As her attorney, it was his job to keep Lydia focused and on track. She was trying too damn hard to be kind, fair, and way too tolerant. She was taking generosity to the extreme by offering to let Jack have everything, as long as she could keep the Subaru and the cabin. It was ludicrous, of course, which made the case all the more interesting and challenging. Usually he was trying to temper the emotional reactions of his clients. With this one, he was trying to ignite a spark of retaliation, a fighter instinct, in Lydia.

Over the years, Shawn had dealt with the many absurdities divorce seemed to generate. There was the case of the wife who tried to take her husband to the cleaners and strip him down to bare bones while she turned the children against him. Then there was the husband who wanted to render himself penniless, at least to all outward appearances, to avoid paying alimony and child support. Those were the typical cases.

Lydia's was different. Her biggest concern was how it would affect her kids and how she could best shield them from the truth about their father. Divorce cases were often sticky and messy, but they never ceased to be fascinating. In this case, he felt he needed to up the ante and inspire Lydia to be at least a little greedy and vengeful, not placating and conciliatory.

Something in the daily news caught his eye. The Montclair, Inc. trial. It was starting tomorrow. Attorney for the defense, none other than good ol' Jack Myers. Oh, he was their man, no question. Sleazy and underhanded all the way. Jack would present an airtight case, proving the company to be flawless and most probably magnanimous in its dealings with whatever the latest place was where they desecrated sacred grounds, exploited workers, and polluted the environment. He read on.

Wait a minute. This one was even worse than last year's case. The death toll was up to 2,446 people? Holy Mary Mother of God. This corporate megalosaur was eating up the planet as it tromped its way through third world countries. Jack would have to really build a good case to overcome these statistics. If anybody could, it'd be Jack. He'd pull some angle, like a malfeasance or corruption charge against the local government, something to divert attention away from the facts. He'd have to put the blame somewhere. Just like he was doing in his marriage. Blaming Lydia for its demise. Well, this divorce was one case Jack wasn't going to win. Shawn was going to make sure of that.

He listened to his voicemail and the message from Lydia. What the...? Now he hired someone to steal the photos and DVD? It was no surprise, really. Jack had enough henchmen surrounding him to do his bidding. What worried him was how far Jack would go to stop Lydia from going through with the divorce. Or worse, what harm he might inflict on her if things didn't go his way.

She was alone, in a cabin in the woods, for God's sake. Lake George was a huge lake. It would be easy to drop a body in the middle and not have it found for a long time, if ever. Surely Jack wouldn't go that far, but it was never good to disbelieve the human capacity for capital crime when they saw it as the only way out. Jack should have taken the offer of an uncontested divorce. He had nothing to lose if he did. It only proved what an ass he was to push this divorce to trial.

The more Shawn thought about it, the more he wondered what Jack's real motivations were. Maybe he wasn't being an ass. Maybe he really was insane and his actions were symptomatic of that. Should he be worried about Lydia being alone in the cabin? He decided it would be wise to take some precautionary measures. He picked up the phone and called his secretary. She could handle this for him. It would just add to his expenses and he could only hope to be compensated later on. This was more important. Lydia needed protection. One of the calls he decided to make himself. He found the number online and dialed the Lake George Police Department.

After introducing himself, the person who answered said he would check with his superior officer. A different voice came on the line. It was Officer Paul Mancini. Shawn told him his concerns.

"You're talking about a red-head living in a cabin on the Lake, right. A Lydia Myers? Yeah, I know her. I brought her to the homeless shelter in the village myself. She was violating the law, hitchhiking on Highway 9N. Nice lady. She didn't look homeless, so I figured she'd been out on a binge and lost her way. I didn't charge her. It just didn't seem right at the time. I thought a night at the shelter would sober her up, or at least give her a chance to come to her senses. Honestly, I thought she was pretty normal acting for someone who'd overindulged."

Shawn gave the officer more details about the situation.

"You don't say," Officer Mancini whistled through his teeth. "I think she said something about being cut off from her money. Her husband really did that, did he? What a piece of work. So what can I do to help?"

Shawn explained what he wanted and how he would compensate the Police Department for their help.

Officer Mancini agreed to offer assistance, but added, "You know, we don't normally do this kind of thing, but in this case, I see your point. She could be in danger. Tell you what. I'll have a patrol car cruise by her place, say, two, three times a day. How does that sound?"

Shawn approved and asked that Lydia be informed.

"Will do," Mancini replied. "It wouldn't hurt to let her know we're looking out for her. I'll keep you posted."

Shawn hung up the phone and dialed Lydia. He left her a message telling her what he'd done. She'd been out planting flowers and called him back immediately.

"Shawn, I appreciate what you're doing, but do you really think it's necessary?"

"I would rather err on the side of being overly cautious than to speculate on what Jack might or might not do. You know he's obsessed with winning. And this article, coming out now when he has all his ducks in a row and probably thinks he's invincible...well, I just think it's worth taking precautions. Look, I can arrange for someone to be up there to look after you. It won't be for long, just until this whole trial business blows over. Then we'll face the divorce court and be done with him."

Lydia interrupted. "Shawn, don't find someone for me. I have someone in mind already. I'll contact him today, right after we hang up."

"Who? Not a relative, I hope?"

"Give me more credit. I would like it to be Vito DeFranco. He has time now. He's just about found out all he could about Jack. I think he'd be willing to do it."

Shawn paused, trying to decide if he liked this plan. He didn't want to upset Lydia, but he wasn't sure this was the best course of action. After all, the man was already working on getting all he could on Jack. He didn't want him to overlook anything that might develop.

"Why him?"

"Because I know him and I trust him. There's a lot more to the story, but believe me, he'll do the job right. Don't worry Shawn. He'll be fine. Can you continue paying him?"

Shawn assured her that Vito's expenses would be covered. All DeFranco had to do was contact his office so they could discuss this new arrangement.

After they hung up, Lydia stood rooted to the spot in the kitchen. How did all this come about? Had she been that blind, that ignorant to not see this coming? Was all her freedom ephemeral and she was just living in a fool's paradise, or in a *Punch and Judy* show where Jack held all the strings and could make her life miserable any way he saw fit.

She had enough. It was over. No more being the arbiter, the peace seeker, the one who wanted to make everybody else happy by living the lie she'd lived for twenty-two years. She was done. She wasn't going to live in fear of what Jack's retaliation would be like.

She walked outside and headed down the trail to the lake, her mind already swimming with possibilities before she reached the water. If Jack could manipulate and control and call the shots, so could she. She certainly had the best role model all the years of their marriage. But it wasn't going to be about revenge. No. That was more Jack's style. The stage was set and she had a plan. She stripped down to her underwear and plunged in. Icy needles pierced every inch of her flesh as she dove under and came up screaming from the shock. Once again, the water had a cleansing, revitalizing effect.

This was round one and Lydia was prepped and ready. She was determined to beat Jack in his own game. If only Witherspoon, her mentor in Paris, was here. She would channel him and his incredible talent for creating disguises. He'd taught her well and she knew his style. She needed only one thing. A shiny, shoulder length black wig.

Chapter 21

The knock at the door startled Serena Castelloes. She hadn't been expecting anyone to visit today. Jack had left for work early to get ready for the trial he'd been preparing for over the past several weeks, much to her disappointment. He hardly had any time to talk to her, let alone take her out to dinner or a movie. She was just finishing her second cup of coffee and watching *Good Morning America*, so whoever was banging on the door better have a very good reason for upsetting her morning routine.

As she headed for the door, she scooped the plates, wine glasses and bottle left over from last night and carried them with her to the door. Whoever was there would see how busy she was and wouldn't take up too much of her time. She really did have to clean house today. Jack hadn't been thrilled with her idea of letting the maid go, but she finally managed to convince him she'd do a much better job making a comfortable and tidy nest for him, and it would cost him nothing. He gave in and let her have her way, so she really couldn't fall short, especially not during her first week on the job.

She opened the door, expecting to see a salesperson or someone collecting for yet another charity crying for help. She was prepared to slam the door in their face and tell them if they returned, she'd prosecute them. Instead, an attractive woman in a crisp white suit, high heels, and shoulder length black hair stood glaring at her. Before Serena could say a word, the woman shoved her out of the way, barged in and slammed her purse down on the table in the entrance way.

"Mrs. Myers," Lydia said in a French accent as she reached into her purse. "I would greatly appreciate it if your disgusting, deceitful, lying husband would leave me alone and never, ever, set foot in my bedroom again. You should be ashamed to allow him in your bed, honestly. Mon Dieu, he isn't even that good a lover. Who knows how many other women he has done this to? If he even tries to call me again, or get back with me, or shows this video to anyone, I will make very sure he suffers very, very much." She pulled a DVD out of her purse and tossed it on the table.

Serena stood speechless as Lydia came closer pointing a finger in her face.

"Tell that lying sack of merde to take this video and shove it up his derrière where it belongs. Tell him that if he calls my cell phone again, or sends me any more text messages, or letters, or dares to send me another email, I will send someone to cut off... how do you say, 'les testicules?' Oh yes, his balls."

With that, Lydia turned on her heel and marched out the door, slamming it behind her.

Serena had to catch her breath. What on earth just happened? Who was this woman? Was Jack really seeing someone else? A French woman? But how? And when? He never seemed to have any time. He was always busy, always working late, always too tired, too stressed, too something. He was always making excuses. He never had time anymore for...her. But he had time for this woman. He was seeing her on the side. He was fucking her!

Serena grabbed her head with both hands. He was cheating on her with this obviously well-to-do French woman who probably just wanted to have a fling. Or maybe not. Maybe there was more to it. Maybe this woman was his real paramour and she was, what, just the housemaid? The fucking housemaid picking up his dirty dishes and wine glasses? Cleaning up the messes he left behind while he was out screwing around with someone else.

She stormed into the kitchen and flung the bottle, glasses and dishes into the sink with such force they shattered and sent shards flying over the counter onto the floor. Then she walked back to the living room, turned on the DVD player and slipped the disc into the slot. She'd see what Jack Myers was up to and whether this woman had any real claim to him. What on earth would she be doing with a video involving Jack?

Her answer came quickly, in living color. Jack's backside dominated much of the opening scene, not that there wasn't plenty to see of the black-haired woman he was pleasuring. She stood up, let out a long scream, then pulled her hair until she had a fistful of it in her hand as she stood riveted, watching the movie to the end.

Gathering her forces, she ejected the DVD, threw it across the room, and went into the bedroom. On the unmade bed she threw what clothes she'd been allowed to store in the closet onto the bed, then some articles on the dresser—a brush, comb, her diaphragm, nail polish and all her jewelry. In the kitchen pantry she found garbage bags into which she packed all of her belongings, filling two large bags. There were no suitcases because Jack had complained about them taking up too much room, so she'd brought them back to her apartment.

Next, she set to work making the bed very specially, just for Jack, pouring the remains of the coffee pot and crumbling her unfinished toast on the sheets. She thought of relieving herself on them, too, but decided that would take too long. She spit on them instead. Next, she found a sharpie in the utility drawer and went to the closet where Jack kept his wardrobe of suits all lined up in perfect order by color. Charcoal, light gray, navy blue, black, and off-white. On the sleeves of each she wrote, "Fuck You!" "Bastard" "Liar" "Cheater" "Fucker." When she ran out of English words, she switched to Portuguese. "Bastardo" "Trapaceiro" "Mentiroso" "Porco" "Và se foder." He could sue her for all she cared, the scumbag. Let him try. She had her men who could lay him out in a moment flat and make him sorry he was ever born.

After she dragged her garbage bags to the door, she got dressed, went to the master bathroom and took out one of her least favorite lipsticks. Across the bathroom mirror she wrote, "FUCK YOU AND YOUR FRENCH WHORE! WE'RE DONE!!!"

Serena Castelloes left the home of Jack Myers in a different state from the way he'd left it that morning. As she lugged her bags down the stone steps to the taxi waiting alongside the curb, she held her head high. She gave the driver her address and said nothing more the rest of the way home. Her only wish was that she'd done one more thing. She wished she'd taken all of his shoes and thrown them in the tub for a nice long soak.

As if the day wasn't going to be hectic enough, there was Mason Parker's niece reading the newspaper, blowing bubbles with her chewing gum in between sipping a soft drink out of a quart-sized container. She probably stuck the gum on the underside of the desk when she was done chewing her cud. He had no say in her hiring and couldn't exactly complain about what a complete waste of humanity she was, given she was the boss's relative. How she managed to find herself in the same gene pool as Mason was beyond him. The girl had no clerical skills at all and was nothing to look at. She was still fighting the onslaught of teenage acne and the braces were yet to come off. The least she could do was look up when he walked in and give some kind of intelligible greeting. Instead, she popped another bubble and took a noisy sip.

"Brandi," Jack said, standing in front of her desk, "As busy as you are, do you think you might be able to find time to get me the morning paper and a cup of coffee, black?"

Brandi looked up at him through her thick glasses, stared for a moment, then said, "Why not?" She eased herself out of the chair carrying her drink with her, straw stuck in her mouth, and went to the anteroom where the coffee pot was. Several minutes later, she returned with the mug she'd filled to overflowing and set it down on his desk, letting the coffee slosh over the sides. No napkin. No coaster. She dropped the morning edition of the *New York Times* next to it, in the puddle.

"There's an article you might want to read in *New York Now*. I'll give it to you when I'm done. It's pretty interesting and..."

Jack cut her off. "That's fine. I'll read my own paper."

"Suit yourself." Brandi walked back to her desk, smiling as though Jack had given her a compliment. She picked up the paper and read on. When she was done, she folded in and tucked it in the desk drawer. She smirked as Jack left the office on his way to court and continued filing her nails.

The courthouse was vibrating with activity. Jack loved big trials and this one already had half the press in the city clamoring at the door. He'd been accosted three times on his way in. Later, it would be different. He'd have to fight his way through a gaggle of reporters and pose for camera shots along the way. The usual demonstrators were outside holding their picket signs and yelling something, "Montclair, Inc. really stinks. Montclair doesn't care, Montclair beware, Montclair unfair…" Brilliant. But then, demonstrators weren't noted for their high IQs.

It was all part of the show, and what a show it was going to be. He thought about gladiators in the colosseum with crowds screaming for their blood. This was just a modern day version of it. If he did his job well, no company blood would be shed and a lot would be gained. He had everything he needed for a sure victory.

The trial started with the reading of the allegations against his client. It was a long and tedious list intended to make Montclair, Inc. out to be the big bad wolf that gobbled up the poor village of Sumar Pakan. Nothing surprising there. He could have written it himself. The plaintiff covered the gamut: damage to the environment, severe human rights violations, loss of lives, support for military who harassed and even killed those who protested against the company, promotion of technology that operated solely from a profit motive, disregard for safety, exploitation of workers, misrepresentation of the facts, corporate greenwashing through advertising and lobbying campaigns, disregard for the health, safety, and welfare of an entire village and its ecosystem. Yada, yada.

Jack kept his fingers laced on the table in front of him, trying not to smirk. What did they expect? That the very same industrial development that lifted them out of the lowest ranks of the least developed countries in the world wasn't going to be without its risks? Didn't people realize there was economic logic to the infiltration of dirty industries in countries where there was little or no pollution? The world was a dirty place. The underbelly of development was pollution. Countries around the world were waiting in line begging to be lifted out of poverty into the world of economic development, which meant getting more than just a little soiled. Lives would be lost along the way. There was a price to pay for entry into the first world.

Hell, the air quality in Los Angeles made Sumar Pakan seem like a paradise. Then there was the outcry about the dangers of cancer-causing chemicals and cancer rates rising in these small countries—countries where people were lucky if they lived past the age of thirty-five.

People just didn't get it. To have development, you had to take the good along with the bad. It was the way of commerce. Of development. Montclair,

Inc. was no different from any other large corporation engaged in lifting entire nations out of destitution.

Jack was going to prove the logic behind the practice of corporations moving to lesser developed nations to avoid costly environmentally oriented measures and protections, where regulations were reduced in economic agreements that directly benefited the third world countries and their citizens. He was going to educate the courtroom about how Montclair's lucrative gains were funding schools, clinics, and hospitals, providing food and housing to the masses, all of which promoted small businesses and cottage industries. Furthermore, with their capital, knowledge, and resources to conduct research, Montclair, Inc. was helping the country develop and market environmentally friendly/sustainable products. Being environmentally friendly was, indeed, a concern of Montclair, but not to the extent that it would slow down progress that would ultimately lead to improved living conditions and contribute to the greater good of the nation as a whole.

Much of the allegations were monotonous repetitions. Rehashing the same arguments, pointing out minute details and transgressions. What Jack was waiting to sink his teeth into were the witnesses. That was where he would shine.

Finally, it came time to call witnesses to the stand. The first one was the manager of the Sumar Pakan factory. He was nervous, sweating, and even trembling. No wonder. Being in a foreign country facing a foreign legal system with all the hype going on would make anyone shake in their boots. Jack saw his prey and was ready to leap.

In a matter of minutes Jack had the man contradicting himself, agreeing that Montclair was a positive force in the community and lauding the company for the good work it was doing, in spite of the mistakes it had made.

The second witness wasn't quite as agreeable. It was clear he had some background in debate as he tried to point out the corrupt practices of the company and the false claims it made about improving the environment when, in fact, levels of pollution were increasing and having a severe impact on the environment along with claiming lives. He made several good points and even evoked cheers from the courtroom which had to be silenced by the judge.

The witnesses testifying on behalf of the families who'd lost loved ones were perhaps the most convincing and detrimental to Jack's defense. He showed compassion for their suffering and made the promise that the company would, as it always had done, compensate them for their losses.

It was getting close to breaking for lunch and time for one more witness to be called. The next one was a female attorney who represented the French Environmental Protection Agency. Her name was Emmanuelle Chiasson. Jack looked up from his notes and dropped his pen as a volt of electricity passed through him, almost lifting him off the chair.

The woman approached the bench and was sworn in. Jack felt the blood leaving his head and thought for a split second he might vomit or pass out. No. This wasn't possible. Yet there was no mistaking it. It was Emmanuelle Jobert from Montclair's Paris office. What the hell was she doing here and on the side of the plaintiff? Yet, it was she, with that familiar stride, the shimmering blue-black hair, only this time she was wearing a silver-gray tailored suit with a white blouse every bit as form-fitting as the suit she wore in Paris. The suit he removed from her body and tossed on the floor of the hotel room before they made love.

She sat down, turned her head and looked straight into Jack's eyes. Her expression was cold, unsmiling. It was the most frightening face he'd ever seen. Something inside his gut was burning and wanting release. He had to press both hands against the table to steady himself. It was a relief the attorney for the plaintiff questioned her first.

She spoke with confidence and a command for which he would have congratulated her, under any other circumstances. She talked about a company without a conscience, a company that exploited people, raped the land, took huge profits from lesser developed nations and gave little in return. A corporation that indentured whole populations to carry out its work as it took credit for being a friend and ally in the world of industry and commerce.

As she spoke, she continued to turn to look at Jack, each time causing a different reaction in him. At first, he couldn't stop staring at her as he feigned a look of confidence. He didn't want to give the impression she was getting to him. He had to maintain the upper hand. This was his courtroom, his country, his legal system. He'd crush this foreign upstart with words alone, but he had to be careful. She could play her hand and crush him, too. It was his turn to cross-examine.

When he approached the bench, Emmanuelle smiled.

"So we meet again," she said.

Jack saw the judge's eyebrows raise.

"Yes, we meet again, Miss Chiasson." His pronunciation made her wince.

Then, as sweat began pooling under his shirt, he began his questions.

Chapter 22

A huge uproar was taking place outside the courtroom. Cameras were rolling, some people were shouting and waving placards, others were raising fists and pounding the air. A cadre of police officers was getting nervous. It was more than anyone had expected. The extra law enforcement brought in was clearly not enough for a crowd like this. In fact, they were quickly realizing the augmented numbers couldn't stand a chance as the numbers of protestors was growing by the minute. Too late now. The scene was tense, people were incensed and anger was fomenting. What had started out as a peaceful demonstration was fast evolving into an enraged uncontrollable mob.

"Take him out, take him out. Take Jack Myers out." People were chanting something the officers didn't understand. They expected all the slurs to be against Montclair, Inc. This was something no one had warned them about. Who the hell was Jack Myers anyway? A defendant? The judge? What was happening wasn't exactly clear. Walkie-talkies were transmitting messages back and forth at record speed. No one seemed to know who or what was inciting the crowd.

Officer Paul Mancini stood next to his brother, Gino. They'd been among the officers called in for the increased police presence. Now he was shaking his head, wishing the NYPD had thought of riot gear. He would've felt much better wearing a helmet with a face shield and a full-body riot control suit. A well-placed rock thrown by a strong arm could easily take out an eye or give him a seriously bad headache, if not a concussion.

His brother looked at him and shook his head. "Welcome to New York City. I never thought this was going to be such a deal. I bet you don't see this in Lake George. I know Albany never heats up this bad."

Paul shook his head. "Nope. Not even close. New York always has to do everything in a big way. I wonder what the story is behind this poor sucker they want to crucify. Jack Myers. Funny, the name sounds familiar to me, but I just can't place it.

A young woman with blue hair and a penetrating voice walked past the barricade behind which they were standing. She was shouting something about some low-life bastard wife abuser. "Put the lawyer on trial," she yelled. "Put the wife abuser on the stand. Put Jack Myers in the lock-up."

Paul waved to her and gestured to her to approach. "So what's the deal about this Jack Myers guy? What's everybody so upset about? I thought this was the Montclair trial?"

The blue-haired woman gave him a look that would have seared his flesh had he not seen it so many times before in his work. "Like, duh. Don't you dudes read the paper? Get with it, man. It's like, all over the news. Check out *New York Now*. The lawyer in there defending the corporate bastards is an even bigger bastard himself. He abused his wife. The shithead put his own wife in a homeless shelter, you know. Left her penniless. Get with it, man."

Officer Mancini listened intently, nodding throughout her narrative. A lightbulb went on in his head. There was no way. It was too much of a coincidence. Surely this wasn't the same woman he'd picked up for hitchhiking on Highway 9N? But didn't she tell him she was from the city and her husband was an attorney? Didn't she tell him her husband took away all her money and she was basically homeless? He didn't believe her, of course, because he knew what homeless people looked like. She didn't fit the picture. Now it was beginning to make sense. It had to be her. Lydia Myers. Now the details were coming back. This was the one that attorney O'Malley called him to check on. She was the lady living at the lake. So, this was her husband they were ranting about. Did it get any better than this?

Turning to his brother, he said, "Hey, Gino. You're not going to believe this. I swear if this isn't the freakiest coincidence ever. Remember that classy lady I told you I picked up for hitchhiking up at the lake? This is her husband they're talking about. Jack Myers. He's the attorney for the Montclair side. The story of what he did to her came out in the papers this morning."

Gino Mancini rolled his eyes. "No shit. Are you serious? This is unbelievable, man. I mean, what are the odds?" He called his sergeant and filled him in. The word spread to the other officers with a warning. In Gino's words, the message was transmitted loud and clear. "Be prepared. Things are about to get ugly here."

Lydia positioned herself on the outskirts of the esplanade where the protestors had gathered. The crowd seemed angry, unlike the more peaceful demonstrations she'd participated in during college. The street was barricaded to stem the tide of arriving protesters who were carrying signs and chanting. More were arriving outside the barricade, while buses were offloading passengers who were joining the protest. An atmosphere of general chaos was somehow being expertly controlled by a handful of police officers attempting to establish some semblance of order.

Before taking the taxi downtown, she had changed her outfit and was no longer wearing the wig. Instead, she had on sweat pants, a t-shirt and a baseball cap. As she expected, Serena had left the house door open, so she waited till the cab pulled away to re-enter her home. She knew her old key wouldn't work as Jack surely had the lock changed, so she searched and found a new spare key in the vestibule sideboard. She pocketed it for future use when she'd need it to come get the rest of her belongings. The hassle of negotiating a visit with Jack was a debacle she was not willing to face.

She'd first gone into the guest bedroom, formerly Tori's room, to change her clothes, then into the kitchen. There she found a mess of broken bottles, dishes and wine glasses in the sink and shards of glass on the floor. Curious, she walked around to the other rooms to see what else Serena had done as a parting gesture. In the master bedroom, she took two framed photos of her and the kids to put in the cabin. She saw no more evidence of destruction, only the bedclothes rumpled as if hastily made, until she went into the master bathroom. The mirror screamed out its message in blood red. It was obvious her visit, or more precisely, the visit by Emmanuelle Jobert, had an impact on Serena.

Now, as she stood leaning against a store front, she saw police officers scuffling with one group of demonstrators, while mounted police were trying to maintain control over their nervous horses. She hadn't expected such a turnout, let alone such an outcry over the trial. It was both startling and exhilarating to know that people were taking a stand against corporate crime. Perhaps the zeitgeist of the sixties was returning—a time when people displayed more compassion for their fellow man and concern for the environment. The Vietnam War had been the catalyst back then. Unfortunately, no one around her was handing out flowers or holding up peace symbols. She said a silent prayer there'd be no violence.

The demonstrators were chanting different messages. "Down with corporate greed." "Free the exploited." "Save the planet. Stop corporate rape." "Get him out. Get Jack Myers out."

The last chant took her by surprise. Was she having an auditory hallucination? Surely they were chanting something else, only her brain was interpreting it differently. *Get Jack Myers out?* No, it was very clear what she was hearing. Some were screaming, "Wife beater," others, "Misogynist." One group was shouting, "Only criminals defend criminals."

Was this just another protest against the whole Montclair ordeal or were they taking out their wrath against Montclair by singling out its attorney? She decided to ask someone standing nearby what they were protesting about regarding Jack Myers.

The woman she spoke to looked her up and down before answering. "It's all in the news, girlfriend. You gotta read this morning's *New York Now*. The article is called *"Defending the Lawless Giant"* and let me tell you, it's explosive. I kid you not. The lawyer inside that monkey house who's defending the Montclair, Inc. marauders just got exposed for domestic violence. Ha! Can you dig that? Seems he abused his wife and forced her to live in a homeless shelter. Go figure! I guess it happens to the rich as well as the poor. What a world we live in, huh?" As an afterthought, she said, "Hey, girlfriend, you got any weed on you?"

For a moment, Lydia felt disoriented. Then she looked all around her and saw a kiosk nearby. Running to it, she grabbed the last issue of *New York Now* and began searching.

"Ya gotta pay for that, ma'am," the vendor said. "Buck fifty."

Lydia handed him two dollars. "Keep the change."

There it was. The article written by Simon Vanderlaan on the first page. She read down to the part about her. It read exactly as the copy he'd sent her. They'd timed it perfectly. *New York Now* chose today to release the story. She should have known, but how could she? She'd been trying so hard to process the whole situation with Simon and how she'd missed the cues that he was a journalist. It now occurred to her that the timing of her visit with Serena had been poorly planned. Or maybe not. Maybe it was perfect timing. If Jack was going to get his comeuppance, he might as well get it in one fell swoop.

She wondered if Shawn knew anything about what was happening right now. His office was just blocks away. She pulled out her cell phone and called.

"Shawn, it's me. Lydia. I'm downtown outside the courthouse and there's something really strange going on. Have you heard anything?"

"You're where?"

She repeated what she said.

"As a matter of fact, we're all sitting here watching it on Channel 6. According to the reporter, it started out as a protest against Montclair, then suddenly it turned to the lawyer defending them. It seems that *New York Now* ran the article about Montclair that talks about Jack. I haven't seen the paper yet, but it sounds pretty much like the story you told me. Very damning, in fact. The crowd got wind of it and now the brush fire is spreading. It's surreal, Lyd. I've never seen anything like it."

"Tell me about it. I'm standing right here in the middle."

"The irony is, Jack's inside doing his best to snow the jury and rack up points for the defendant, while right outside the door the crowd is calling for his blood. Sorry, but I can't help but be ecstatic. This is unprecedented. Are you okay? I didn't know you were planning to be here for the trial."

"I wasn't, at least not until late last night. I woke up early, realizing Jack would be in court all day, so I thought it would be a good time to stop by the house. I did, and of course, *she* was there. I'll give you the details later. After I left, I decided to come down here just to see if anything was happening before I headed back. Frankly, I wouldn't have come if I'd known what was going on. It's scary, actually. It looks like it's becoming a mob."

"I'll meet you there. Just tell me where you are and stay put, if you can. If you can't, text me."

It took him twenty minutes to run down five blocks to where Lydia was standing. It was far too busy to even try to get a cab and several streets had been blocked off. He needed the exercise, but cursed himself for not taking his bike. It would have gotten him there much faster.

"Sorry it took so long," he said, reaching out to Lydia and putting an arm around her shoulders. "Let's get away from these glass panes." They moved to an area where there were no windows behind or above them. "Better to be safe than sorry, my grandma Gertrude used to say."

Lydia continued to hold Shawn's hand even when they both felt they were in a safer zone. She noticed the sweat on his brow and how wet his pale blue button down collar shirt was under the arms. "Good run, I see. Bad running clothes."

"Uh huh. Sweating like a pig in mud on a July day in Alabama."

"You say that with some conviction."

"You're right, I do. I represented a pig farmer when I lived there. Smelliest home I ever went to, but the nicest client. He and his wife had me over for chicken and dumplings. Have you ever eaten that? With homemade biscuits? It almost had me thinking I'd make Alabama home."

"Sorry, I missed out on that experience. Vegan, remember?"

"Oh yeah, you really did miss out. I bet you never had shrimp n' grits either. Too bad. Maybe you can find a good recipe for tofu and dumplings, with butterless biscuits. Or tofu and grits. Sounds gruesome, but hey, worth a try, right?"

Shawn had a way of making Lydia laugh, even in the most serious of situations. She thought it would be best to tell him more about her morning.

"I have something to confess. I hope you won't think the worst of me."

Shawn looked into her eyes and said in a serious tone, "Don't go telling me you joined the convent. Or worse, you want to get back with Jack. Oh, please don't tell me you decided to give up being vegan and want me to buy you a hot dog."

Lydia pulled her hand away. "Stop. Nothing that bad. Especially not the Jack part."

"What, then?"

Lydia told him the whole story of what she'd done and how Serena had reacted. When she was done, she looked up to see Shawn's eyes wide and shining. He burst out laughing.

"If that is not the best revenge against a mistress story I've ever heard, I don't know what is. That was brilliant, buddy. God, I wish you could have videotaped it." Shawn pulled her toward him and hugged her for several seconds. "You're unbelievable, Lyd. God, I'm having fantasies of you in a black wig. You know you really haven't changed a bit since college."

"Is that supposed to be a compliment?"

"What do you think?" He suddenly grabbed her by the shoulders and pulled her away from the building just as a beer bottle smashed against it only three feet from where they were standing.

"I think this is our cue to leave. Let's blow this taco stand."

Hand in hand, they ran down the street, crossed to the next block and ducked inside Flannigan's Tavern.

"Might as well have lunch while they build the gallows for Jack's lynching." Shawn helped Lydia onto a barstool. "I think this calls for an adult beverage, don't you?" Signaling the bartender, Shawn ordered two Guinness stouts and a bowl of peanuts.

Lydia had never tasted Guinness before and was dubious until she took her first sip. "Hm. Very robust. Spicy and sweet like molasses, only colder. I like it."

"I'm sure Guinness would love to hear that critique." They raised their steins and clinked them together. "To Lydia, lady of disguises and soon to be the former Mrs. Jack Myers."

"Amen to that."

They stayed the afternoon until Lydia called recess and said she had to be sober enough to drive back to the lake.

Shawn took her by the shoulders. "No, don't do that. Stay the night. You can sleep at my place and I promise I won't let you have my bed and you must take the lumpy couch. It's only right since I'm your attorney and you're still married."

Lydia debated, but the effect of three Guinness's on an empty stomach won out and convinced her she didn't need to face a five-hour drive. Shawn called a cab and they went back to his apartment. As Shawn prepared a supper of pasta and marinara sauce, she told him the story about sleeping on the pew in the chapel of the homeless shelter.

He listened, fascinated. "I always knew you'd end up sleeping around once you got free of Jack, but a chapel? Come on, Lydia. Couldn't you come up with anything a bit more risqué?"

Lydia enjoyed the meal and felt surprisingly relaxed and comfortable in Shawn's one bedroom apartment. It was tastefully decorated, if somewhat Spartan. She could tell he had a cleaning service because it was spotless. His sports equipment occupied most of the free spaces, a tennis racket here, a racquetball racket there, a treadmill dominated the living room décor and it all felt homey and cozy. It was like a trip to the past, to a college dorm room, only cleaner.

The feeling as she sat next to Shawn on the couch and they watched an episode of Bonanza was exactly as she'd felt being with him in the past. Comfortable, and utterly platonic. Nothing had changed over twenty-two years. She wished he'd drag her to the floor and have his way with her. Or, better yet, pick her up in his arms and carry her off to the bedroom like Rhett and Scarlet. He did neither.

Shawn kissed her on the forehead before she fell asleep, while he stayed up to watch the news. What he saw was astonishing. Twice he wanted to wake Lydia up to see what had transpired that day, but he stopped himself when he saw how peacefully she was sleeping. He'd let her be. She needed the rest. The news could wait till morning.

She awoke early, roused by the aroma of freshly brewed coffee. Shawn was setting down a steaming mug on the coffee table in front of the couch when she opened her eyes.

"Good morning, sleeping beauty," he said, pushing aside the sheet and blanket to make a spot for himself next to her. "The word of the morning is, 'brace yourself,' which is actually two words, but you get the gist. A lot went down yesterday." He handed her the mug. "Mrs. Myers, it is with the utmost dismay that I must report to you that your husband is no longer representing Montclair, Inc. I would also venture to guess, he may not be practicing law again, at least for a while."

Lydia grabbed the remote and turned on the TV.

Chapter 23

The atmosphere transformed from moderately charged to high-voltage electric with the opening of the courthouse doors. A swell of bodies moving like a school of fish pressed toward the man now being escorted down the steps of the courthouse by a cadre of police officers. The men in blue pushed and shoved their way through the sea of shouting reporters intent on thrusting their microphones toward the face of their person of interest. Cameramen cursed in the wake of the surge that jostled and threatened to topple them.

Jack looked around, fascinated by the unexpected attention the trial was getting. It was only a recess for lunch on the first day of the trial. Surely they didn't expect anything to be settled by this early hour. He was used to being interviewed by reporters, but never assailed like this. What's more, even though all the others, plaintiffs and defendants alike, were making their way down the steps, the crowd seemed to be converging on him. He couldn't help but be astonished and flattered. Then he heard their questions.

"Mr. Myers, is it true you put your wife in a homeless shelter?"

"Jack, what do you have to say about the allegations being made against you?"

"Jack Myers, you've been accused of domestic violence. What do you have to say?"

"Jack, rumor has it you're to be removed from this case. Any comment?"

Jack's eyes narrowed and his smile turned to a grimace. "Whoever is making such slanderous allegations will be prosecuted to the full extent of the law. Let me pass. I have nothing more to say."

He continued fielding the barrage of questions being hurled at him with a repeated, "No comment." Around the reporters, he heard the crowd jeering, chanting and calling for his arrest.

"Get Jack out!"

"Lock the louse up!"

"No justice for Jack!"

"Myers must go!"

The rest of the way to his car strained the resources at hand as the police officers did their best to protect him. At one point, someone let off a firecracker causing the officers who were flanking him to yank him off his feet and push him to the ground."

"Stay low, sir," one officer cautioned. "We've got a mob here."

"What the hell is going on?" Jack's face was crimson, his lips trembling. "I demand some answers."

One of Jack's partners, Abraham Epstein, pushed his way toward him and grabbed him by the arm as an officer seized him and tried to pull him back.

Epstein fired back, "Let go of me, you ape. I'm here to help. Get him to that limousine parked over there." He pointed toward the street where the crowd was thinner.

The officers steered them both through crowd to the waiting limo and helped them inside. Doors slammed, tires squealed, and the limousine took off, trailed by a small crowd of protestors running behind.

Mason barked an order to the driver to take them back to the office, while Jack leaned back against the plush leather seat and brushed dirt from his pants and sleeves.

"Christ almighty, what the hell was that all about?"

When he looked up, he saw that the limousine was fully occupied. Seated beside him was Mason Parker. Across from him was Abraham Epstein and James Cross. None of them were smiling.

Jack laughed nervously. "What a relief to be out of that fray. Thanks for the rescue."

No one responded. Jack's eyebrows arched. "Hey. This is some trial, eh? Frankly, I hadn't expected such an outcry. It's not going quite as expected, but nothing we can't pull ourselves out of. That last witness, the woman from the French EPA, tried to bring the house down with some unfounded allegations, but I shut her up. Then the judge called for a recess."

Jack was hoping he could say something that would lift the mood. The atmosphere inside the limo was thick with tension. Their concern for his safety made him realize how valuable an asset he was. He didn't expect his partners would be taking the protests outside so seriously, as if they had any control over that. Crowds were unpredictable. One person could ignite a spark and the rest of the crowd were like kindling, taking fire and getting out of control fast. He figured they had cause for concern. Losing him would be like, well, losing their star performer.

"I only have an hour for lunch. I hope Mrs. Quaile thought to have some food brought in. I'm starved."

No one even acknowledged that he had spoken.

Jack loosened his tie. "I'm getting the feeling that something's up. Is there anything I should know about?"

Mason Parker spoke first. "We're taking you off the case, Jack."

Jack laughed as he worked on removing a spot on his trousers. "You're what? You're not serious. So, what's the joke? It's way past April Fool's Day."

James Cross spoke next. "You're not going back. We're taking over from here. We'll discuss the rest later."

Jack didn't laugh this time. "Okay, good one. You had me going there for a second. I gotta hand it to you, you really know how to keep a poker face, though, as far as jokes go, your timing is pretty off. It's been a harrowing morning. I really don't need this."

Abraham Epstein spoke next. "I'm handling the Montclair case from here on, Jack. You're to go home and not come back till we tell you. You're effectively on suspension. Don't make it worse on yourself. We have no choice."

Jack looked from one face to the other, realizing that no one was playing a practical joke on him. In fact, they were more serious than he'd ever seen them, except perhaps at a funeral for one of their colleagues.

"What the hell's going on? It's me, Jack. Remember? What do you know that I don't? Come on. I'm working my ass off and now this? I don't get it."

Before anyone could answer, the limo pulled up to the curb in front of the office building. Fortunately there were no demonstrators outside. The three men got out, but as Jack reached for the armrest to make his exit, Mason Parker put up his hand. "You don't have to come up, Jack. The driver will take you home."

Now he was outraged. "What the fuck? What do you mean I don't have to come up to the office? This is going way too far." They couldn't tell him what to do. Not after the time he had this morning doing his level best to discredit that bitch from France, all the while trying to keep his cool while she was making libelous accusations about things he allegedly told her in Paris. This was far beyond what any man needed to put up with. And now his own team was giving him grief.

"I'll fucking get out and go up to my fucking office, if you don't mind, so get out of my way, goddammit."

Mason and Epstein grabbed him by the arm. "Don't make it any worse on yourself, Jack. We understand you need time to cool off. Here. Take this and read it on the way home. We think you'll get a clearer picture of what's going on. We'll call you when things settle down. Just don't go back. The judge called a mistrial. You're off the case. It's best if you don't make a scene. It won't help your situation."

Jack sat back down and caught the newspaper James Cross tossed to him before he shut the limo door. His head was spinning. He couldn't catch his breath. Was he having a heart attack or did the air suddenly become extremely hot? He ripped off his tie and unbuttoned his shirt, forcing air in and out of his lungs. His heart was racing and every pore of his body seemed to be opening up to dump its payload of sweat. When he managed to get his breathing under control, he picked up the newspaper in his lap. Something he needed to read, one of them said. But what?

He scanned the first page, then saw the headline. *Defending the Lawless Giant*. Was this what they were talking about? He glanced down the column and saw his name.

By the time the limo reached his house, he was shaking uncontrollably. He left the limo door open as he headed for the steps and gripped the handrail, pulling himself slowly up the steps. He put his key in the lock, but the door was already open. His ears were buzzing. He needed to get inside fast and have a drink. Serena would make him a triple martini. Yes, that's what he needed. Hell, he'd have her massage his feet, too, while he thought about what to do next. If she so much as asked him one question, he'd slap her across the face and tell her to shut the fuck up.

In the kitchen, he found the broken wine bottle and shards of glass in the sink, on the counter and on the floor. "Serena," he bellowed. "What the hell is this?"

No response. She must be out shopping, damn her. And she left the front door open, the stupid bitch.

He walked into the bathroom and saw the writing on the mirror. For a moment he thought, again, someone was playing a joke on him. French whore? How the fuck had Emmanuelle come into Serena's sphere? And when?

He went to the closet and flung open the door to hang up his jacket. It was there that something snapped inside his head.

Nothing mattered to him anymore. He returned to the kitchen and poured himself a tumbler of gin and splashed a healthy dose of Vermouth in it. Screw the olives. He guzzled half the tumbler without stopping.

In the living room he turned on the television. The news station was airing the coverage of the trial and the demonstration outside. The words of the reporter were shrill, the din of the crowd almost drowning her out. He watched as if it were someone else's life and he was merely a spectator.

He heard his name mentioned several times, right along with the words criminal, abuser, domestic violence, spousal neglect, homeless shelter, wife, Lydia Myers, victim.

He finished the first tumbler, mixed another and drank it down. When he reached the third, the bottle of Bombay was spent. He threw it against the wall in the kitchen sending shards across the floor that mingled with the others.

In the space of four hours, three women had colluded to destroy his life. Three banshees had descended on him and tried to rob him of every vestige of dignity and self-worth, even his livelihood. Three fucking bitches attempted to ruin him. But they wouldn't succeed. Oh no. They'd regret every move they made. He'd see to that.

Jack Myers didn't get to hear the eleven o'clock news that night. He was in a cell in the 112th precinct, passed out. Two police officers had responded to a call placed by a hysterical woman, a Serena Castelloes, who reported a breaking and entering at her home in Queens. The man was intoxicated and, for all intents and purposes, completely out of his mind and too drunk to be dangerous only to himself. Further charges included disorderly conduct, destruction of property, and driving while intoxicated. A Lexus, no less. Nice toy to smash up in a DWI. The woman knew him and it was evident she didn't think much of him. In fact, she spat at him as the arresting officers led him away in handcuffs.

"Go fuck yourself, you lying son-of-a-bitch," she shouted as they lowered him into the patrol car. "Go back to your fucking French whore, you bastard. I hope you rot in hell."

Early the next morning, as a golden-pink sunrise illuminated the Statue of Liberty and set fire to the waters of New York Harbor, Emmanuelle Chiasson boarded a plane for Paris. She was headed back to her work as an agent for the *Ministère de la Transition écologique et solidaire*. The trial was over. At least the part she had to play in it. She had accomplished her mission.

Lydia Myers began her trek upstate after a leisurely breakfast with Shawn as they watched the morning news. She looked forward to the quiet of the country and some time alone, although it would have been nice to have had a couple more days in the city for one reason only.

Serena Castelloes called and talked to an old boyfriend at the same time Jack Myers was leaving jail. He'd been bailed out by a friend who worked for another firm. The firm of Parker, Cross, Epstein and—no longer Myers—wasted no time in enlisting a sign painter to scrape his name off the door. By email, they informed him he was no longer a partner, but would be allowed to remain at the firm if he chose. The small windowless office reserved for interns was now his. Someone moved the contents of his office to the new space, but there was hardly enough room to accommodate all of it, so they left the boxes stacked against a wall.

Jack spent the day at home nursing a raging hangover, which he treated with the remainder of the alcohol left in the house.

Chapter 24

Vito DeFranco couldn't remember a time he enjoyed a motorcycle trip more. The weather was perfect and the traffic, with the exception of a few asshole drivers, was manageable. Some people just didn't get it that a motorcycle had as much right to be on the road and required the same amount of space as a car. The last idiot who cut him off got the high sign—something he rarely did, given the high incidence of road rage on the Northway.

It'd been years since he'd taken his Harley upstate. He used to visit friends at the State University at Albany, and his relatives in Troy, particularly Uncle Tony and Aunt Rose. In summer, he'd come up to Saratoga for the horse races whenever he could. It felt great to have the cold air rushing past him, his helmet sitting firm on his head, and the awesome feeling of seven hundred pounds of metallic power between his legs. It was the rush he loved whenever he took his hog out for a spin.

It was good to get out of the city. Upstate seemed so much calmer, even as the scenery sped by and he had to do some fancy maneuvering around slowpokes and Sunday drivers. People seemed happier upstate. Less stressed and worried, for the most part. Even though he grew up in the city and most of his family still lived there, he often thought of moving upstate to get out of the rat race. It probably wouldn't be any different, though, crime-wise. Just on a smaller scale.

He appreciated getting paid up front by Lydia Myer's attorney, Shawn O'Malley. He seemed like a good guy. The thousand dollar retainer he forked over reassured him he wasn't going to have a repeat performance of what Lydia's husband, Jack, had put him through. It was ironic, too, to be working for his wife now. Well, guarding her safety instead of following her like last time. Also, what a joke that he got the lowdown on Jack, the skinflint, and found out the guy had no reason to be stingy. The man was worth a fortune.

Vito congratulated himself on his work so far. He'd already amassed credit card information, DUI reports, phone records, and even got some nice shots of him and his mistress. She was quite the woman and attractive in every respect but one. She seemed to be puppy-dogging Jack and clinging to him like her life depended on it. She looked Mexican or Central American, definitely some Hispanic lineage, because he heard her accent when he followed them into a crowded lunch room on Thirty-Forth. A real brick house was his first impression. She made Lydia Myers look like a school girl in uniform.

His assignment changed as of a few days ago. Apparently a lot had happened between Lydia and her husband over the past several days, or so her attorney told him. Mr. O'Malley thought it best if Lydia had someone looking out for her up at Lake George. Providing personal security wasn't necessarily his line of work, but since it was Lydia, and it was outside the city, he figured it'd be a nice relaxing assignment. A getaway from the hustle and bustle. Besides, he'd never been to Lake George and always heard from friends and relatives it was a beautiful spot with great hiking trails, swimming, boating, and a funky little town with decent bars and restaurants when you needed a break from all the natural beauty. Maybe Lydia would accompany him to some of them and they could talk about the future. His future. With Nicole.

He wasn't much of an outdoor person, but he did like the water and took swimming lessons as a kid at a pool in the Bronx. He even made senior lifeguard. Swimming came naturally to him, which is why he spent six years in the U.S. Navy's amphibious force before deciding to get out to pursue a career as a cop, which all led to where he was today. Now he was a detective and a bodyguard. The road of life sure had some very interesting twists and turns, no doubt about it.

The most interesting twist of late was the news from Nicole. He couldn't wait to talk to Lydia about it, maybe get her help in figuring out what to do.

He trusted she'd be objective and maybe be able to give him some good advice. She was a mother, after all, and probably the most creative woman he'd ever met. He found out all about that when he followed her for over two weeks in Paris.

Lydia was waiting for him, sitting on the front porch of the cabin doing what she always did in Paris—working on her sketches. She put down the sketchpad when he pulled into the driveway and turned off the engine. As she came down the steps and walked toward him, she held her hand outstretched and took his, giving it a warm, friendly shake.

"It's wonderful to see you again, Vito. I hope the trip wasn't too grueling. I find it challenging enough in a car. I can't imagine how it must be on a motorcycle."

Vito grinned as he looked around, admiring the scenery. "You should try it sometime. It's worth the sore seat you get." He paused to take in more of the surroundings, then saw the lake behind the cabin. It seemed to go on forever. "Man, this place is beautiful. You're looking good, too, Lydia. I can't believe I'm here. What are the odds I'd be working for you? I have to say, I'm glad it isn't your husband again. I wouldn't have taken the job if he asked me."

Lydia nodded in agreement. "Jack doesn't know about this, of course. In fact, I don't know how much Shawn told you, but I asked him to have you come here."

"He told me. As you know, I've been keeping busy checking up on Jack and I have to say, it's been pretty revealing. So, you think he'll be a problem?"

"I honestly can't say, but Shawn felt that, in light of everything that's happened, it would be best to err on the side of caution." She looked at Vito's black jacket, peppered with the remains of a population of flying insects. "Looks like you could probably stand a shower, maybe some fresh clothes. You have your own bathroom and shower, so feel free. Come on in and I'll show you to your room."

Vito followed her inside and whistled. "Nice place. You won't find this in the city. This is about one of the choicest cabins I've ever seen."

"It is nice," Lydia agreed. "The perfect getaway, even if it is isolated. Like I said, Shawn, being a worrier, didn't want me to be up here alone.

He insisted on having someone look out for me, so I thought of you. I hope you don't feel put upon."

"No way, not for a minute." Vito chuckled to himself. Yeah, it was a really tough assignment having to spend time in one of the most beautiful parts of the state with someone he was fast considering a friend. "Lydia—and I hope you don't mind me calling you by your first name—this is a real treat, trust me. And I think I'll take you up on that shower and put on something a little cleaner and less buggy. That's about the only downside to motorcycle trips. You gotta eat and wear a lot of bugs."

"I'll take your jacket. Maybe I can scrape it clean. I do have some leather cleaner under the kitchen sink. I'll give it a whirl while you're showering." She carried the jacket to the sink, smiling to herself that this was the article of clothing by which she spotted and even named Vito when he was surveilling her in Paris. "Bomber jacket" was the name she'd given him. Her friend Witherspoon would have loved the irony of all this.

When Vito rejoined her on the porch, he looked like a freshly scrubbed schoolboy in his white t-shirt and jeans. Lydia glanced up at him from her drawing and wondered where he kept his weapon, if, in fact, he had one. A pocket on the leg of his jeans told her he was equipped with a knife. When he walked to the porch rail and leaned over to look up at the sky, she saw the gun tucked behind in the waistband of his jeans. Somehow she expected a bigger gun, like the long barreled ones she'd seen in Westerns. This one looked pretty compact. Surely Vito would know what kind of gun he needed. She thought about asking him if he could teach her how to shoot it, then chided herself. She definitely had watched too many crime shows on TV.

She excused herself and went to the kitchen, returning with two tall yellow glasses with daisies etched on them. "It's unsweetened tea, but I have sugar if you want it," she said, handing him a glass.

Vito sipped, licked his lips and said, "This is fine just as it is. I'm not big into sweets. My nephews love it and always want to get cotton candy when we go to the fair. I can't see how they can eat all that sugar, but they do. Of course, they're loose cannons right after."

"Oh yes, how well I know. I lost the battle of trying to keep sugar out of the hands of my two. I have a boy and a girl, but then, you probably already know all that."

"I did have to check out your background, in the line of duty, so yeah, I knew about Victoria and Carl."

"Now they go be Tori and Leo."

"Some things you just don't find out in the snooping business."

Vito sipped more of his iced tea, wondering when would be a good time to really talk with Lydia. He figured there was no time like the present, so he started right in. "I hope you don't mind me asking for your help with something. I mean, advice, really. I'm in a bit of a predicament and not sure what I should do...or what I can do. It's a touchy situation."

Lydia put her sketchpad down. "It's about Nicole, isn't it?"

He almost spilled his iced tea. "You know? I mean, what do you know? And how? Did you talk to her?"

Lydia nodded and reached over to put her hand on Vito's. "First, may I say, congratulations, even though that may sound a bit strange. A baby is a joyous thing, no matter what the circumstances. Nicole told me the day before I left Paris that she was pregnant. She'd just found out."

Setting his drink down. "Was she happy about it? I mean, did she seem okay with it?"

"I think she was mostly scared. It came as quite a shock."

Vito stood up and began pacing back and forth. "I can't believe it happened. I mean, I can believe it, but I, well, I just wasn't expecting it. I had something like this happen to me before. Six years ago, in fact. I got married then. It lasted about a year. My girlfriend at the time, Gloria, told me she was pregnant, so I did the only thing I could think of. I married her. Then on our wedding night, she found out she wasn't."

"Why didn't you have the marriage annulled? I mean, if you didn't want to be married?"

"At first, it never entered my mind. I felt like I took a vow and it couldn't be broken. At least not that easily. Gloria pretty much ended it, though, when she decided she preferred being a nun rather than a wife. Then we did get an annulment."

"I'm so sorry, Vito. No children, then?"

"No. Thank God." Then he realized how that must have sounded. "It's not like I don't want kids. I really do. I love them. My nephews are little rascals, but they're the coolest kids. I always wanted a big family. I can't believe I'm saying this, but I'm even hoping it's a girl. The problem is, I don't think Nicole wants a family. She so much as told me she's not giving it my name and she's not coming to the states."

Lydia sighed. "Yes, that was the impression I got the last time we talked. Maybe she'll change her mind as the pregnancy progresses. She's still in the early stages of morning sickness and feeling overwhelmed by the whole thing. The good news is, my friend Ellsworth Witherspoon has befriended her. You remember the Englishman I spent a lot of my time with? He's a good man with a heart of gold. He took a liking to Nicole after she..." Lydia stopped, realizing Vito knew nothing about the escapade involving Nicole and Jack which happened after he'd left Paris. She decided to tell him the whole story of how Nicole had gone out in disguise and met with Jack. Even recorded some of their conversations.

"Seriously? She did that? Man, I gotta hand it to her. She's a very attractive girl and I could just see her pulling that off. I wish you had a picture of her dressed up and in a blond wig."

"I do." Lydia brought up the picture on her camera and handed it to him.

"Holy Toledo. It doesn't even look like her. I think my mother and my grandmother might even be able to accept her if she looked like this, if her cleavage was covered up, that is."

He continued to study the photo as they talked.

"She hates my guts and I don't blame her. I really hurt her bad. I didn't mean to, but I did."

"No, Vito. She doesn't hate you. She was hurt when you left. She blames you for not telling her sooner. Then this happened, the baby, I mean, and, well, I think she blames you for it, too. Not that she doesn't take responsibility for her part. She does. You two just have to spend time together. You have to get to know one another, here, on your home turf. She had the advantage in Paris, but here, you could show her around and be there for her. You need to let her know you care about her. I don't know how deep your feelings are, but I can tell she loves you. Otherwise she wouldn't be so angry."

He had to think for a moment about this. "I do love her. She's the craziest and most different woman I've ever met. Something about her makes me feel like...well, stupid as it sounds, she makes me feel like the missing piece of the puzzle is in place. When I see her, she lights up everything. I feel like I'm whole with her. I know that sounds dipshit crazy."

"Not at all. It sounds beautiful."

"But how could it work? She says she won't come here. And she doesn't want me in her life. And I honestly don't want to live in France. And I don't know if she could be happy here, I mean, in the city."

"If she loves you the way I think she does, she could be happy wherever you are. Vito, Nicole feels trapped right now. I know because I felt the same way when I first got pregnant. But she'll get past that, just as I did. When the baby comes, everything will change."

"But you're so different from her. You were married when you got pregnant. You chose to have children."

"Yes, married, but I wasn't ready to become a mother. It happened quite unexpectedly and I was frightened. Jack was angry about it and I felt desperate. But, in time, it all worked out. I have loved my babies more than anything else in the world. Nicole will love hers, too. Trust me, Vito. She'll come around."

Looking woeful, Vito shook his head. "You make it all sound like a fairy tale with a happy ending. But, the truth is, I can't live over there and she doesn't want to live here. She has a family there and from the sound of it they must be pretty well off. At least she's going to a high-class university. The *Sore-bone*, it's called."

Lydia smiled at his pronunciation, even though it was better than most. "If she wants to, she could continue her education here. Having a baby doesn't mean the end of all your goals and plans." She was stretching this, of course, having dropped out of college for the very same reason. "Nicole can do anything here, whatever she chooses. And just think, she has an advantage. She speaks English perfectly."

"Yeah, and she curses perfectly, too."

Lydia couldn't argue with that. Nicole's vocabulary was rich and colorful, if nothing else.

Vito was now wringing his hands. "I sent her some money, but she sent it back. She said she didn't need my help and she told me where I could stick my stinking schmuck money. I wish I never told her the word, schmuck. She uses it all the time."

Lydia reflected on her last conversation with Nicole in Paris. He was right. She had a particular fondness for the word. "Look, Vito. All I ask is that you don't give up hope. Okay? Give this some time. You'll have plenty of time to think things over up here. And you can call her from here. I have international calling on my phone. I call Witherspoon all the time. Oh, and speaking of which, she moved into his apartment, at his insistence. He said she wasn't safe and neither was the baby where she was living. They needed a good environment so they'd both flourish. She took him up on it and so far, they seem to be getting along just fine."

Vito's eyes brightened. For the first time that evening, he looked genuinely happy. "Could I call her right now?"

"Not unless you want to wake her up at two in the morning. I think it'd be better to wait and call tomorrow, don't you?" She stood up. "Let's talk some more over dinner. I hope you like spinach lasagna. It's made with tofu, not cheese. Even my kids like it, even though they usually stage a protest over my vegan cooking."

"I'll try anything once. Got any beer?"

"Absolutely. I got a German pilsner because you liked it so much in Paris."

Vito walked over to Lydia and reached out his arms. "Don't take this the wrong way, Mrs. Myers, but can I give you a hug?" He wrapped his strong arms around her and held onto her for a few moments. For the first time, Lydia understood completely how charmed Nicole must have felt being with this man. He gave a first-class hug and he smelled good.

Chapter 25

That evening, in front of a crackling fire, they sat in the living room and talked over a glass of wine and a second beer for Vito. The plate of a dozen cannoli she'd made sat in front of them on the coffee table, now reduced to seven.

"First, spinach tofu lasagna, then tofu cannoli that tastes like the real thing," Vito said, reaching for his fifth one. "This is unbelievable. My grandmother on the DeFranco side is probably rolling over in her grave. You know, I just might consider going vegetarian, except that my mother would kill me if I stopped eating her meatballs. I kid you not. Meatballs are like a sacrament to her. If you don't eat at least three, she feels insulted and won't let you forget it. I'd have to be a meatball eating vegetarian."

"Trust me, many vegetarians cheat once in a while." It pleased her that Vito was willing to try her concoctions. Many people wouldn't even give her dishes a taste, as if the very word, vegan, connoted poison. "I think I'd like your mother. I mean, meatballs aside, she sounds like a woman with strong opinions."

Vito laughed. "You don't know the half of it. I keep having visions of her fainting if and when she meets Nicole. Just the sight of the dreadlocks and tattoos will send her into orbit. My mother isn't exactly the most open-minded person in the world. Neither is my grandmother on the Patricelli side, for that matter."

"You know you can't make them like Nicole if they choose not to. I think it'd be best to just see how things go, and don't worry. There've been stranger matches in the world and you know people get married under all types of circumstances. Please don't think I'm pushing marriage on you, though. You two may just decide to live apart and have the child together. It doesn't mean you have to be enemies."

Vito drained his second bottle and smacked his lips. "Hey, all we've done is talk about me and my tragic life story. I want to hear more about you. Mr. O'Malley, Shawn, I mean, filled me in on some of the details, but I didn't get the whole gist. So Jack got fired from the trial and demoted at his job, and then there was a brief stay in the jail after he got drunk and busted up his girlfriend's, sorry, mistress's place. Then what...? And where do you fit into all this? You're up here and he's down there. Why does Shawn seem to think you're in danger? Does he think Jack'll get drunk and go berserk again?"

Lydia took a deep breath. "You've heard the expression, 'I don't get mad, I just get even,' right? Well, that describes Jack, except he does both. Apparently his mistress, Serena, found out about another affair he had while he was in Paris. I'll tell you that whole story later. At any rate, she went a little crazy and trashed the house, so when Jack came home, right after he'd been dismissed from the trial and his partners informed him he wasn't a partner anymore, he apparently got really drunk and broke into Serena's house. He ended up in jail, according to Shawn, for one night."

"How did Shawn find out all that? I mean, about Serena and the affair in Paris, and the house getting trashed and the arrest? Did he have somebody surveilling Jack besides me?"

Lydia hesitated. Was it that important that he know all the details? She figured it was. "Actually, I was the French woman from Paris he had the affair with who came to the house and told Serena about it. I gave her the photos and a DVD of the two of them going at it in my hotel room."

Vito shook his head vigorously. "Wait a minute...you were...what? You dressed up and pretended you were the woman? And of course, you speak French, so you must have sounded like her. And you somehow had photos and a video of her and Jack together...but how?"

Lydia told him the story of how she'd followed Jack in Paris disguised as a man when he was having his fling with Emmanuelle Jobert who turned out to be a key witness in the trial. The DVD was something outside of her scheming, but it came in very handy. She also told him how Jack had sent a man to steal the photos and DVD from her, but because she'd made a few copies, knowing he would, she let the man have one and she gave one to Serena. Shawn had the originals in his office file.

Vito sat speechless for a few moment, shaking his head, eyes beaming. "Can I just say one thing? You really should be the detective here. I mean, you have more balls, excuse my language, and more disguises, and more crazy ways to find things out than anybody I've ever known, including me. I gotta hand it to you, Lydia. You really should consider a new career."

Lydia lowered her gaze and played with her wine glass for a moment. "You know, when I was younger I always wanted to be an FBI agent. I used to watch that TV show, *The Man from U.N.C.L.E.* and I thought being a spy was the most glamourous job a person could have. My mother almost had a heart attack when I told her I was going to major in criminal justice. So, being the dutiful daughter I used to be, I switched to Art, then Sociology, then Psychology. My daughter is following in my footsteps. She can't make up her mind, either."

"How much of this does Jack know? I mean, does he know you impersonated his French mistress and came to the house?"

"No, I don't think so. I think he thinks she really did. She was in town for the trial."

"So what's he so mad about? Because you're up here? Because you asked for a divorce?"

"I wish it was just that. No. I'm sure Jack sees me as the reason why he was dismissed from the trial, basically fired as the attorney, and why he got demoted. What happened was, I met someone at the shelter who was an undercover reporter for *New York Now* and he wrote an article about the company Jack was defending, Montclair, Inc. Only he decided to take a swing at Jack, as well, pointing out how he abused me and put me in a homeless shelter. He did, in fact, but all Jack would see is that I caused this whole problem and I'm the one to blame. And knowing Jack as I do, I'm also the one who deserves to be punished."

Vito ran a hand through his shiny black hair. "Geez, this is sounding more serious than I thought. I guess Shawn was right. He's not just worried about you being here alone. He's worried about what Jack's going to do next."

All of a sudden there was a loud cracking sound outside the cabin. A vase flew off the fireplace mantle and broke on the hearth, sending pieces of porcelain flying across the floor. She thought she heard someone curse.

Vito grabbed Lydia and dragged her off the couch onto the floor, covering her with his body.

Someone was shooting at the cabin.

Chapter 26

Vito stayed low, squat walking as he inched his way across the floor to the hallway leading to the front door. He remembered they came in from the porch without locking the door behind them. Along the way, he turned off the only lamp that was on in the living room and the light in the entranceway. When he reached the door, he stood up and kept to the side, so as not to be seen through the frosted glass pane. He turned the lock on the door handle and set the dead bolt. Another shot rang out. This time he heard a crashing sound as if something large fell to the porch floor. It must have been the wood stand. He thought he heard a moan, or it might have been wind bending the trees next to the cabin.

He crawled back to Lydia.

"Where are the other doors?" She pointed out a door to the kitchen, and whispered. "There's also a sliding glass patio door off the master bedroom."

"I'll take the kitchen. You stay low and get to the master bedroom, then come right back here."

They locked the doors, returned, and huddled in front of the couch, waiting. Only the sound of the fire crackling disturbed the silence. The flames illuminated the room and cast moving shadows on the floor and walls.

Vito warned, "I know it sounds crazy, but the best thing is to let whoever it is out there in here. I want them to think they hit their target.

Lydia, move over to the middle of the floor in front of the fireplace and play dead. Watch out for the shards."

Lydia crawled across the floor, brushing away pieces of the vase and sprawled herself out on her stomach with her arms and legs splayed. She wasn't sure this was the best idea, but Vito seemed to know what he was doing.

It seemed an eternity before they heard footsteps coming up the porch steps, then stop. He heard a man's voice. "Oh no. Oh damn." Vito was poised with his weapon drawn, keeping out of sight from the entryway. Lydia was in full sight of anyone who came in. She had her face turned away and was doing a good job of lying still. He hoped she wouldn't scream when the person walked in.

They heard a key enter the lock and turn. Then came another curse. The deadbolt was an obstacle. Whoever it was didn't have the other key. Already Vito knew the guy was an amateur. Firing his weapon, then walking straight up to the door, then trying to open it with a key. What a goofball. Now he'd have to kick the door down or find another way in.

Lydia was doing well in her dead pose. He couldn't hear her breathing overly hard or making any noise. Another woman would be shaking and sobbing in terror. He should have known she could play dead as convincingly as any actress. His only hope was that the next gunfire wasn't aimed directly at her, to make sure the job was done right.

He heard the steps moving around to the side of the cabin. He'd be in view of the kitchen door if that was the next stop, so he eased his way to the kitchen and crouched under the table. Most people, even the experienced ones, wouldn't stop to look under anything when they were first getting their bearings. Besides, it was dark in the kitchen. He counted on not being seen until he had the advantage and could stop the person, or take aim, whichever seemed the best course of action at the time.

The key turned in the lock and the kitchen door opened.

A voice called out, "Lydia? Are you here?"

Vito reached out, grabbed the man's legs and yanked him off his feet. The man fell hard and no wonder. He was a big guy, probably tipping the scales at three hundred. Not your average hitman, but then, they weren't exactly chosen on the basis of their physique.

The fall knocked the wind out of the man who gasped for air as Vito straddled him, Glock in hand.

"All safe," Vito yelled.

Lydia came rushing into the kitchen. "Oh my God, Tom? What on earth? It's my brother, Tom. Remember? You met him in Paris." Kneeling on the floor, she patted Tom's face. "Tom, are you okay? What happened? What are you doing here?"

Vito now looked at the man beneath him who was struggling to catch his breath, gasping and trying to speak.

"…came to…see if …you…okay…saw man outside…knife in…his hand…got my Beretta…in car…long story…shot him…oh shit…please… get off me."

Lydia and Vito helped Tom to his feet and into a chair.

"I can't believe you're here," Lydia said. "I thought you were still in Beijing. Were you the one shooting the gun? What was going on out there? Wait, don't talk. Let me get you something." She ran to the fridge and poured him a glass of iced tea.

"Before you do anything," Tom said haltingly to Vito, "I think it would be best…to see if that mound of flesh…on the porch… is alive. God, I hope so. I never shot a man… before. I only wanted to nick him. He was carrying a knife and looked like he was up to no good." Tom put a hand to his head and took the glass of iced tea. "I think I'm going to… pass out." Turning to Lydia, he moaned, "Sis, I love your iced tea, but do you have anything stronger?"

The ambulance arrived along with every patrol car from miles around. Tourists from around the lake began to converge on the cabin, as well. Officer Paul Mancini was first to arrive, having driven past the cabin just fifteen minutes earlier. He took the information from the three witnesses, including Tom O'Connor, the brother of Lydia Myers. He was the one who fired the shots and hit the intruder. His story was that he was only trying to warn the man off because he was carrying a knife and looked to be trying to break into the cabin. Lucky break. He could have killed the guy. That would have made things messy.

"I had no intention of hitting the poor fellow, honestly," Tom said. "I know I should have listened to Becky when she insisted I have shooting lessons, given that I insisted on getting a pistol. As it is, I picked the smallest one I could find to placate her. I mean, look at it. They call it a Nano, for God's sake. A baby pistol. Could any weapon appear less innocuous than this? But then, in the hands of a feckless gunslinger, such as I, any weapon, even a Lilliputian one, can be dangerous."

To Tom's relief, the wound he inflicted on the intruder was only superficial. Apparently, the impact of the bullet, along with the man's state of drug intoxication, had the effect of causing him to pass out. As he fell, he hit his head on the wood stand and bloodied it. While the amount of blood was shocking to all but Vito, the bullet only tore through his jacket and seared his right upper arm. The paramedics mentioned something about a mild concussion. It was hard to tell whether it was that or the drugs.

As they lifted the man onto the gurney, he came to and began babbling about getting the job done and how Jack would not be happy. Lydia, Tom, and Vito stood on the porch and watched in silence as they wheeled him up to and loaded him into the ambulance. Vito approached one of the officers and they exchanged words. He learned that they identified the man from a card in his wallet. He was Erik Gormann, from Brooklyn.

Lydia told Officer Mancini she knew him. He'd come to the cabin before, at the behest of her husband, Jack Myers. Mancini assured her he'd pass the information on to the NYPD. For Jack to hire him again, Gormann must have given him a convincing story about his first visit. She was sure he'd left out the part about her handing him the DVD with her blessing.

After the police and onlookers left, the three of them sat in the living room and talked for another hour. Tom had been up over twenty-four hours and the effects of lack of sleep and Jack Daniels was making him nod off.

Tom narrated the story of how he happened to arrive on the scene. "Becky called me in China and told me you were in some kind of trouble and needed money. I got approved for leave and came here as soon as I could. I left Beijing yesterday and decided it'd be best to rent a car in Boston and drive here. I planned it to be a surprise. So much for planning. Well, actually, it did turn out to be a surprise, all things considered. I do have to say, this wasn't the way I envisioned it. Lydia, I'm so sorry for all this drama. Please keep this between us. Don't tell Becky."

"Sorry? Are you kidding? You saved our lives. And put yours in danger. I mean, any of us could have been killed."

Vito joined in. "I'm just glad you didn't walk in and see your sister doing her dead woman act right there in front of the fireplace."

Tom gasped. "Oh my God. That would have been curtains for my heart. I can't even imagine..."

Lydia put her arm around his shoulder. "Hey, look at it this way. You're a hero. You saved the day and stopped that guy from doing any real damage, except to himself, that is."

"Ha! If that isn't schadenfreude at its best. Probably gave him the scare of his life. Unless he was too high to notice. The important thing is, you're safe, we're all here, we have all our body parts, I hope." Tom patted his arms and legs.

"It's wonderful to see you, Tom. So much has happened since I last saw you."

"Yeah. I sort of got the gist of that. Tell me about it. Oh, and if it makes you feel any better, I have a blank check with your name on it. Just tell me how much to write on it. The sky's the limit, only please don't go over ten thousand. I'd have to move some funds." Tom let his head drop back on the couch. "Christ, I still can't believe Jack could stoop so low. I'll bet he's sitting back right now, gloating over what he did. Probably thinking he taught you a lesson. Maybe thinking you're dead, goodness me, I don't know. It goes beyond reason. You know, Jack would have been a real popular guy back in the Dark Ages. He'd have been the expert thumb screw tightener. Or rack stretcher. Catherine Wheels would have been his specialty. What a beast. No, that's insufficient. A mega beast. Still not good enough. How about, a mega beast torture master?"

Lydia chuckled. It was the first time she could laugh about what happened that evening. She hadn't even stopped to think about what Jack was capable of. Only now was it becoming more apparent. She understood for the first time how right Shawn was and how wary she needed to be.

Vito decided it was time for him to leave Lydia and her brother alone. "I'm going to hit the sack and let you two catch up on everything. Lydia, Tom, just holler if you need anything, okay? Remember, I'm on duty twenty-four hours, so don't hesitate."

Tom gestured to Vito to come closer. "Before you go, let me see that play gun you're packing." Vito handed him his Glock. Tom stared at it and then held it in shooting position.

"Uh, I wouldn't do that if I were you," Vito warned. "It's loaded and there's no safety on a Glock."

Tom almost dropped the gun. Handing it back to him, he said, "Thanks, but I think I'll stick with my Nano. It's nowhere near as badass as this."

After Vito went to bed, Lydia told Tom everything that had happened since she came back from France and moved into the cabin. Tired as he was, he encouraged her to keep talking. He didn't want to miss anything.

"So the trial went bad when they found out Jack was inept, or was it because of the article in the paper?"

"Well, the article was one factor, but the fact that the woman he slept with in Paris, who shared a lot of information about the case, was a witness for the plaintiff's side. According to my attorney, Shawn O'Malley, she clinched it for the judge."

"No shit. You just said a name that rings a distant bell. That wouldn't be little Shawn O'Malley from Catholic High, would it?"

"The very one, only he isn't little anymore. He's about six three and he looks like an athlete. A very nice looking one, at that."

"Wait a minute. Didn't you also know him in college? You had the hots for him, right? Until Jack Sprat, or maybe now it's a propos to call him Jack the Ripper, came along."

"Yes, that's my divorce attorney. He's been wonderful so far. He bailed me out of the shelter, sent me money, and he's paying Vito to protect me. I'll reimburse him after the settlement, of course, but right now I have to say having a sugar daddy is pretty nice."

"How much sugar, might I ask?"

"If you're asking are we intimate, no."

"Lydia, you are so Catholic. Come on, spill."

"No. It's not by my choice, though. Shawn is being most ethical in his attorney/client relationship. I'm not exactly wanting to continue playing the role of a married woman being faithful till after the divorce, but he's a stickler for propriety."

"Translation being, you haven't jumped his bones yet."

"Nor he mine." Lydia got up to get a plate of cookies she'd made for Vito and was holding in reserve. "Sorry, but in all the madness tonight, I didn't even ask if you were hungry. I have spinach lasagna, garlic bread, salad, and a veggie antipasto. Also, there may be a couple cannolis left. Interested?"

"Does the pope wear gilded underwear?"

"Come on out to the kitchen. I'll get it ready in a jiffy."

Tom ate his supper while Lydia continued telling him the rest of the news. When she came up to the present, she said, "But that's enough about me. I want to hear about you and Beijing and how you managed to slip away. I guess the Chinese have adopted the concept of emergency family leave like us."

"Oh, yes, only they take it to the extreme compared to the good ol' U.S. If a chicken dies out of the ordinary, meaning not in the course of dinner preparation, they hold a funeral. My students take time off the watch road construction and to have their dogs shampooed."

"So your leaving didn't cause you any trouble with the university?"

"Fudan is very forgiving, and very concerned if any of their American faculty have a problem. I think they're afraid we'll go back home and spread propaganda." Tom paused to have a second helping of lasagna. "This is good, by the way. I love the chunks of beef. Oh sorry, those are mushrooms. Never had lasagna without hamburger before. It almost tastes better, but you never heard me say that."

"I'm glad there won't be any repercussions for leaving early. I know they always hate to see you leave. Thank you, Tom. This means a lot to me."

Not wanting to wax sentimental, Tom said, "Oh, the Chinese as a nation were sorry to see me leave, but I promised I would return. You see, I was their token fat person and they held me up as an example of what can happen when a person lives on an American diet. I've been credited with having deterred many a Chinese youth from eating fast food and for helping them retain the historically slim Asian figure. You know, some of those kids can eat circles around me and never gain a pound. It's unfair. There should be a law against that, or at least some severe sanctions. Something to even the playing field. Actually, there is. The American diet has infiltrated most of urban China and obese little kids are showing up everywhere. Good thing, too, or else they'd really have everything over American kids."

After his last sentence, Tom fell asleep sitting up. Lydia roused him and showed him to his bedroom and left clean towels in his bathroom. She smiled to herself. She now had a full house and two men to take care of, or at least one. Vito was supposed to be taking care of her.

She wished Shawn would come up for a visit, but the chances of that happening were slim. Besides, she wouldn't want to be dividing her time up among three men. If he did come, she wanted him all to herself.

Chapter 27

The days that followed were refreshingly uneventful. Each morning, Lydia got up early, did her run along the lake trail, accomplished some reading and research for her latest course on Case Management and had breakfast awaiting both men when they got up. She preferred it that way. No one to get in her way and no commentary on what food she was preparing till after it was served. It'd been some time since she had two men to cook for. She couldn't remember the last time she made a meal where Jack and Leo were both present, except for last Thanksgiving. She heard sounds of stirring coming from the two bedrooms.

Vito entered the kitchen first and protested when he saw her setting the table and putting out food. "Look Lydia, I'm here to protect you, not be waited on hand and foot. You've been cooking for us non-stop. Let us cook some of the time, okay?"

Tom ambled to the kitchen, yawning. "Forget it, DeFranco. It's a losing battle. My sister lives to feed others and loves to cook. She won't tolerate anyone taking over her kitchen for fear they might slip a little bacon or lard into the food." He yawned again, stretched, gave Lydia a good morning hug and poured himself a cup of coffee. "Which reminds me, I do have a complaint to lodge. Where are all the real sausages and eggs? I know you think you have us fooled, but you're wrong. Do you really expect strapping men like us to subsist on tofu disguised as eggs and fake sausages made from some dubious plant parts? It's not normal."

"Unfortunately, yes. And the sausages are made with textured protein. It won't harm you to have a respite from animal flesh. In fact, you may be surprised how good you feel."

"Ah, textured protein. I feel better now. Are you sure the textured protein didn't suffer in the process of becoming textured? I mean, was it free-range or kept in a cage? It better be organic or it won't cross my lips." Tom never missed an opportunity to tease his sister about her vegan lifestyle. "Alas, I guess we'll have to do with homemade muffins, vegan French toast, those rudely disguised sausages and scrambled egg look-alike, but not taste-alike. Lydia, one question. Are all vegans so devious in their culinary subterfuge?"

Lydia shrugged. "I'm hoping I'll get more devious as I go along, but I still have a long way to go. I once got the kids to eat spinach, which they both hated. I blended it in the spaghetti sauce. They never knew."

"There you have it. We are witness to the deceitful machinations of my sister, the crazed zealot who would go so far as to dupe her own innocent offspring and force them to eat tomato sauce laced with spinach. It's a blessing she'd not a doper and putting weed in their brownies. Then again, Becky used to con the girls into taking their vitamins by crushing them up in applesauce. Must be a female thing. Dosing the kids surreptitiously."

Lydia waved her spatula at her brother. "Tom, you always said you liked my meatless dishes. What happened?"

Tom gave her a quizzical look. "Didn't you know I pretended only to placate you? I thought if I went along with your delusion, you'd come around sooner or later and start gnawing on steaks with blood dripping down your chin like the rest of us carnivores."

Vito was enjoying the banter, but felt it was time to step in. "I honestly think she deserves a medal for making every meatless meal taste so good. If Nicole could cook like this, I mean, if we ever got together, I could almost see myself going vegetarian. If she wanted to, of course. There'd have to be an occasional pepperoni pizza thrown in when I'm with the nephews and, of course, my mother's meatballs whenever we had Sunday dinner, just to ward off World War III, but I think we could pull it off."

Something Vito said caught Tom's attention. "So what's this about the little French bakery girl? Are you two an item? I really liked her buns, er,

I mean, her brioche. Her croissants were good, too. Buttery. She's a very nice girl. Colorful. Her body art was...well, beyond compare."

Vito rolled his eyes and proceeded to tell Tom as much of the story as he wanted to share. Tom could tell he was leaving out some major parts and wasn't satisfied.

"So you left her abruptly and she got mad, but she has been in touch with you, and you're not sure if this thing—this affair of the heart—will continue? I must say, you don't sound like a man ready to give up the fight. Or perhaps pursuit is a better word. The fight will come later, and more often what you would expect. Trust me."

Vito hesitated. "I'm not ready to give up, no. I'd really like her to come here, but she doesn't want to."

"So, must I assume that you're not ready to do the expatriate thing and start saying, 'oui,' instead of 'yes?' or 'merci,' instead of 'mercy.' Or is it 'thanks?'"

Vito turned to look out the window. "Let's just say it'd be better if she wanted to live here. I know that sounds selfish, but I can't see myself living over there. I mean, who would hire a detective who didn't know his way around and couldn't speak the language?"

"Well, look at it this way. With Nicole, you could be hired by some English speaking men who wanted you to trail their wives, just like Jack did with Lydia. Nicole could be your sidekick. Your Mata Hari."

"I actually thought about that. Not with Nicole, though. Getting enough business to live on would be tough, especially with a family."

Tom set his mug down. "A family you say? Are you just speculating on the future or should I assume the deed is done and a conception has taken place? A bun is in the oven, or in this case, a brioche? That across the seas there is a fetus calling you daddy, or père, or at least preparing to when it can verbalize?"

Vito looked at Lydia as if for a cue. She smiled and said, "Tell him. It's okay. He can keep a secret."

"Yes. Nicole is pregnant and she's not happy about it or with me. She's living with Witherspoon now. At least I don't have to worry about them being out in the cold."

"On the contrary," Lydia said, "I'm sure he's spoiling her, knowing Ellie. Probably shopping for her daily. He loves to shop. I just hope she doesn't get angry with him and leave. He does have a tendency to be a bit controlling."

"And she has tendency to fly off the handle pretty easily," Vito added.

Tom was surprised with the news. "What are the odds? A young bakery girl gets in the family way by an American detective and ends up living with an aging flamboyant British gentleman. It could be a B-movie or at least a TV series. I should be writing down notes. This could be my future retirement."

"I wouldn't mind trying to work in Paris, but I don't want to end up like our visitor the other night," Vito said. "I want to know where I am and what I'm doing all the time, and at least be able to communicate a little."

"Oh, I do believe our friend could talk. I heard him curse before he hit the deck and uttered some gurgling sounds. Speaking of whom, I wonder what happened when they got him back to the Big Apple. And to his employer, for that matter."

Vito was glad the subject changed. "According to my brother, Gino, who works in Albany but keeps up with friends in the city, Gormann's in jail awaiting sentencing. Nothing's happened to Jack so far. He thinks Jack will get off scot-free because all he has to do is deny hiring him. I'm sure he left no trail, nothing that would incriminate him. Judging by Gormann's record of drug-related offenses, nobody's going to take him seriously. Jack sure picked the right man for the job."

Lydia passed the plate of whole grain toast to Tom. "That's Jack's forte. He has a preternatural ability to cover his trail and keep a few steps ahead of everyone else. I wonder if there'll be any repercussions from the article and the Montclair trial. I mean, beyond his demotion. I suppose we'll never know unless it comes out in the paper." Lydia put down her fork. "I'll call my contact at *New York Now*. I think he owes me for what he did."

She explained to Tom how Simon Vanderlaan had deceived her and used her story to embellish his article about the Montclair trial.

Tom guffawed. "I do have to give the ingenious young reporter credit. How he pulled that off and managed to convince you he was a hard-core intravenous drug user, a heroin addict at that, is a pretty amazing accomplishment. I mean we have to support entrepreneurship in all its forms. Most of my students would be lucky to be so enterprising."

"I can only forgive him because he really did a good job of exposing Montclair and pegging Jack. The article was well-done and scathing. I just didn't like that I hadn't been forewarned about it. Well, in a way, I had. He did send me the article prior. Mostly, though, I was upset because he fooled me so completely right up to the end."

Again, Tom laughed. "For my dear brother-in-law, I'm sure that bit of reportage was tantamount to being rendered a castrato. You know they used to do that in the 1600's, Vito. Turned choir boys who were reaching puberty back to sopranos by whacking off their..."

"Tom," Lydia scolded, "That's an awful thing to talk about at breakfast."

"I was about to say, 'their Vienna Sausages.' Ouch. As much as I like a young male soprano, I think that's taking it a bit too far. I always advise young boys to steer clear of choirs till their voices change to tenor or bass."

Vito stood up shaking his head. "I'll take KP for you, Lydia." He began to clear the dishes. "It was all great. Thanks. Maybe someday you can teach Nicole to cook."

"I'd love that." Lydia got up to take the food to the kitchen.

Tom continued sipping his coffee. "No need for me to get in the way when such an efficient staff has the operation under control. I think I'll go out and sit by the lake and indulge in some contemplation. Start writing that movie script. Catch up on my reading about this marvelous thirty-two mile long pond called Lake George. Tootles."

While Tom sat on the shore reading the pile of literature on Lake George he found in the cabin, Lydia and Vito decided to take the kayaks out.

"So, what do you know about boating disaster survival?" Vito asked.

Lydia cocked her head, wondering if it was a trick question. "Actually, nothing except to scream for help."

That was enough to convince Vito she needed some amphibious training.

Tom watched them set off, chuckling to see Vito ramming Lydia's kayak and the two fencing with their paddles. It was good to see his sister laughing after all she'd been through.

Once they were at a distance halfway between both east and west shores, they began a kind of gladiator game, standing up in the kayaks and swinging their paddles at each other while trying, but not succeeding, to stand erect. Lydia was the first to go toppling over the side, overturning her kayak as she fell. Tom knew there was no danger. If anyone could swim, it was his sister. She used to beat him in every race they attempted until he conceded the title of swimming champ to her and promised to beat her in every game of chess from then on. A feat he accomplished with no sweat.

From time to time he looked up to see them on top of the underside of the kayaks, flipping and climbing back into them, then overturning them again. Once, he missed sight of them altogether and was about to become alarmed until he heard Lydia's laughter.

He found something in the literature that caught his eye. Sightseeing cruises, buffet-style lunch included. It gave him an idea for the day's itinerary.

When Lydia and Vito returned, laughing as they dragged their kayaks onto the lawn, he called out, "How about a day of sight-seeing?"

"Why not?" Lydia answered. "There are some great hiking trails around here."

She and Vito joined Tom, taking the other two Adirondack chairs.

"Not quite what I had in mind. Listen to this. 'You can relax outside on the top deck of a cruise boat and enjoy the view of the Queen of American Lakes.' Now, wait just a minute. Why they don't say King? How many queens do you know with the name, George? Oh no, what's this spoiler? Oh thank goodness, I misread. I thought it said *no* alcoholic beverages available for purchase. I was about to organize an insurrection to dethrone the queen." Tom fanned himself with the brochure, then continued reading. "We could see Bolton Landing, elegant resorts, millionaire's summer mansions, blah, blah, blah... Then there's a big mother of all ships called the *Lac du Saint Sacrement*, which, correct me if I'm wrong, means Lake of the Saint Sacrament? What the hell? Come on. I went to Catholic School. I never heard of a Saint by the name of Sacrament. What deranged clergyman made that up? Probably some Anglican minister. I swear."

Lydia smiled and pulled her sun hat down low over her face. "I wondered about that name, too, till I read it was named by a French Jesuit in the 1600's. Translated, it means Lake of the Blessed Sacrament. There's also the Minne Ha Ha Paddlewheel Cruise of the lake's southern part."

"I like the sound of that better. Less religious. Sounds funny. Ha ha. Minnie must have laughed a lot. Oh, Lydia, you'll love this. There's one vegetarian option on the lunch menu of the Blessed Sacrament ship. Probably a communion host. Oh, and get this. Lunch is cooked fresh in the ship's galley. Ha! I should hope it's not catered by Burger King or cooked right there on the deck. Okay, now we're talking. Lunch includes a carving station with ham, turkey, and roast beef, with dessert thrown in. I know you're excited about that, Lyd. You could bring a protest sign and picket the carving station while Vito and I make our twelve-inch hoagies."

"I ate their vegetarian lunch option once. It was an iceberg lettuce salad. Wildly creative."

"Okay, kids, this is the clincher. You can even see nesting eagles along the way. Nesting? Frankly, I'd rather see flying eagles, or at least standing up eagles, but nesting? I mean, what's so thrilling about seeing a big bird lying around being a sloth in its nest? I see enough of that with my students in class. That's what I'll call it from now on. Students nesting."

"I used to do quite a bit of that when I was in school," Vito said.

"So, what do you say, guys? Up for a little rubbing elbows with the tourists and getting on our Bermuda shorts and cameras to see the Queen of Lakes, which should, in all fairness, be called the King, or at least the duke, or baron. George, remember?"

Lydia tipped the brim of her hat up. "I'll do anything you want to. At some point I want to drop something off at the shelter. I finished a drawing for Ron, the director. He wanted one done of the outside of the building to use for advertising purposes. It was the least I could do for him."

"Nice of you. I'm sure you miss the gourmet food and accommodations there."

"I actually do miss it, but not for those reasons. I love the people I met there."

"That's my sis. I think I'll name you Queen of the Homeless Shelters. Of course, you'll have to change your name to George."

Lydia thought of another idea. "You know we could hike up Prospect Mountain. It has spectacular views. There's also Pilot Knob. It's only a six and a half mile roundtrip with amazing views at the summit and lots of rocks to sit on at the top and enjoy a snack while you rehydrate."

"And defibrillate, you mean. You know how much I enjoy the thrill of cardiac resuscitation. Did you know you can drive up Prospect Mountain? But, I'll go along with popular choice. What say you, Mr. Vito of French

Money, aka DeFranco? Are you of the sweaty, arduous and heart stressing hiking bent or the relaxing, sip a Mai Tai on the top deck of a cruise boat enjoying the view bent? I think you both may have guessed my preference."

Vito shot Tom a sideways glance. "I think I better say the cruise boat."

Later in the afternoon, after they got back from a walk along the lake trail, Lydia got a call from Shawn. After a few minutes of asking how she was doing and if things were settling down, he told her the reason for his call. He'd gotten some unexpected news from the court. They moved the divorce trial date up by three weeks. The reason was that Jack had upcoming court dates based on allegations brought against him by Montclair, Inc. and the judge in question thought it best to speed up the divorce proceedings, rather than delay them.

It was unusual and unexpected, but Lydia knew it was something Shawn had no control over. He informed her that she and Jack would receive their summons to appear in court tomorrow. The trial was the day after.

Judging by the tremor in his voice, she could tell he was upset by the news. "It's okay, Shawn. We can do this. I have faith in you, and you have to have faith in me."

"Thank you for that, but I wanted to have time to do this right. I wanted witnesses lined up. Now I don't know if any of them will be able to make it."

"Jack will have the same problem, I'm sure."

"Lydia, I really hoped I'd have time to prepare you. These things can be very nerve-wracking, even for the toughest of witnesses. There are things I need to prep you for. Could we talk tonight? We need at least a couple hours, maybe longer."

"Of course. I'll be home all evening. Call whenever you can. I'll send the boys out for pizza or something."

"Uh, I'd suggest sending one boy out, but keep your bodyguard with you. I still don't trust Jack. I don't think the danger's over yet."

Lydia paused for a moment. Shawn's voice had an ominous tone to it. He really sounded concerned. Was he overreacting and being paranoid, or was she being overly confident?

"Okay. I'll keep Vito by my side. Oh, by the way, my brother Tom says hello. He wanted to know if you were still wearing your shamrock briefs. I didn't bother to ask what he meant by that."

Shawn laughed. "Oh man. Tell him I don't have them anymore. They went to the highest bidder."

With that, they hung up with a plan to talk later that evening.

Shawn called after supper and they talked for over three hours. Lydia learned more about divorce law in the State of New York than she ever thought possible. Shawn impressed her with his knowledge and his concern that hers would be up to par. The message was that she had to be prepared for whatever Jack, rather, his attorney, might throw at her. She had to stay cool and collected. She also had to hold her ground and not for one minute feel intimidated.

Before they hung up, he had one more bit of news. His tone changed completely, which came as a relief after hearing only the serious side for hours.

"The beauty part of this is that the judge will be Odell Weddington. He's another nemesis of Jack's. I got to know him pretty well when I was in Alabama, his home state. He also presided over that big case Jack lost. I overheard Jack talking about him after the trial, referring to him as the 'baboon from the bayou.' The reason Jim Crow laws should be reinstated. Jack would be behind bars if Odell heard his racist slurs. He's quite the character, bud. I think you'll like him. He's also one of the sharpest and fairest judges I've ever known."

That night Lydia dreamed of gliding along on a flat boat in the bayou, using a long pole to push herself along. Alligators were on all sides as Jack sat back taunting them and throwing marshmallows at them. He suddenly stood up, lost his balance and fell in the water. Lydia kept moving along, wondering where he disappeared to as she watched eddies ripple away from the circle the alligators had made.

Chapter 28

Odell Weddington saw the name on the case file he was reviewing and thought for a moment. It sounded familiar. Jack Myers. Hm. Oh yes. The People vs. Boyd Enterprises case. As he recalled, Myers had been quite the ungracious loser. He almost had him removed from the courtroom when the man hurled his briefcase and almost hit one of the bailiffs. He chose not to, only because it would have prolonged matters. He didn't want to see Myer's face again.

"Well, well, well, Mr. Myers. You are about to be divorced by your wife of twenty-two years," he said aloud to no one. He already had sympathy for the plaintiff, Lydia Myers.

The court was called to order at 9:00. Shawn began with the opening statement presenting Lydia Myer's petition for a divorce and the reasons underlying it. Lydia, being the first to file the divorce petition, was called to the stand to give her testimony.

She was nervous, especially when she saw Terrence Warshawsky and Serena Castelloes in the courtroom. She'd expected to see the others, too, because Shawn told her he was going to ask them to come if they could. There was Ron Davis, Janice Jewel, and Lunetta Loves the Lord from the Lake View Rescue Ministry. Also, Officer Paul Mancini, Simon Vanderlaan and, of course, Vito and Tom. Her children weren't present, as she had requested.

As Shawn instructed her, she took a deep breath and began her testimony. She tried not to look at Jack, knowing whatever looks he'd give her would be for the sole purpose of intimidating and distracting her. Twice during her testimony, he called out, "I object," only to be silenced by the judge.

Judge Weddington was not pleased with the interruptions. "Ms. Gunderman. Would you please inform your client that he is the defendant in this trial, not the attorney for the defense? Thank you." Turning to Jack, he said, "Mr. Myers, one more outburst of this kind and you'll be held in contempt. Continue, please, Mrs. Myers."

When Lydia completed her testimony, Jack went to the stand and delivered his testimony. It was almost verbatim what Shawn had prepared her for. His concern for her mental instability, her rash and irrational decision-making, her lying and impulsive spending, and her tendency to exaggerate her symptoms to get what she wanted. It sounding damning, the way it was presented, but then, hers hadn't exactly made Jack out to be a Boy Scout. The judge jotted notes during both testimonies.

Lydia was brought back to the stand to be cross-examined. Maxinne Gunderman approached. She was a formidable woman, wearing a severe black suit, white blouse, and orthopedic shoes that reminded Lydia of ones her grandmother used to wear. She had her charcoal gray hair pulled back in a tight bun and wore black rimmed glasses that reminded her of what they used to call "birth-control" glasses in college. The woman had all the style and femininity of an English bulldog. No wonder Jack had chosen her.

"Mrs. Myers, you've been married to your husband, Jack Myers, for twenty-two years, is that correct?"

"Yes."

"And during that twenty-two years, he supported you and your family in his capacity as an attorney. Was he a good supporter of you and your family?"

"Yes."

"And were you supported by him even during times when you decided to leave the home and travel, such as during your last trip to Paris which lasted twenty-three days, during which you enjoyed numerous occasions of, shall we say, living the high life, such as, on one occasion, running up a bill of nine-hundred dollars at a restaurant?"

"Yes. Actually it was nine-hundred twenty dollars. It was one expensive meal I shared with friends."

"A simple 'yes' or 'no' answer is sufficient. And your reason for going to Paris on this last trip was to get away because you were bored with life and needed a diversion, or was there more to it? In other words, were you needing to get away for another reason, such as one suggested by your psychiatrist?"

"Actually, I didn't have a psychiatrist, but I attempted to see one and was not able to because he was called away."

"Again, a simple 'yes' or 'no' answer is all we need."

"I find it difficult to do that when you ask several questions all at one."

Lydia glanced at the judge and saw the corners of his mouth twitch in amusement.

"Let me restate the question. Did you go to Paris at the suggestion of your psychiatrist?"

"No."

"And yet that was what you told your husband."

"Yes."

"So you lied to your husband about your reason for going to Paris."

Lydia glanced at Shawn who gave the slightest nod of his head. "Yes."

"And is it true that before you left the psychiatrist's office, you stayed behind and pretended to be a psychiatrist so that the next patient who arrived to find you in Dr. Aronson's office thought you were a psychiatrist?"

"No, and yes. I stayed behind to get paper to leave a note on the door. Mr. Warshawsky, the next patient, walked in and thought I was a psychiatrist, yes."

"And you continued talking with this patient without informing him that you were not a psychiatrist?"

"Yes."

"Do you find that deceptive and somewhat harmful to lead a patient on who is seeking psychiatric help?"

"I never thought of it as harmful, although it was deceptive, yes."

"So, you are saying you're unable to see the difference between deception and how it might harm a patient seeking psychiatric services."

Lydia stopped. Her face was heating up and she could feel heart thumping in her chest. She remembered what Shawn said and took a deep breath.

"I'm not sure I understand the question, if that was, in fact, a question."

Maxinne coughed. "Let me try to explain this in a way you can understand. You admit you deceived the patient, Mr. Terrence Warshawsky, by letting him believe you were a psychiatrist. So, my question is, are you able to appreciate the fact that deceiving a psychiatric patient by leading him to believe you were a psychiatrist could have been harmful to him?"

"I would suggest that Mr. Warshawsky would be the best determiner of whether our conversation was harmful to him."

"Please answer the question, yes or no."

"You leave me no choice but to say no, it did no harm to him. In fact, we had a very nice conversation which we continued down the street at a shop where we both enjoyed smoothies together. I found Mr. Warshawsky to be an interesting conversationalist and a very nice man. He liked his smoothie and thanked me for the experience." She glanced over to Terrence Warshawsky who was now looking down, smiling and blushing. The courtroom broke out in laughter and had to be silenced. The color of Maxinne's face deepened from gray to crimson.

"Mrs. Myers. You claim that your husband was never at home, always working, and yet you thought nothing about leaving him and going to Paris for almost four weeks without so much as asking him to accompany you. Is it fair, in your estimation, for a spouse to run off to a foreign country and enjoy a vacation fully paid for by the spouse who stays home working to be able to provide such a luxury?"

"Jack could have come, but then he would have to leave not only his job but his mistress behind. He chose to do neither. And there is no simple 'yes' or 'no' answer to that question."

"I detect some contempt toward your husband, the man who supported you and allowed you to travel at will, at his expense."

"Yes, you are correct in your detection of contempt. I don't think a husband should have an affair all the while he claims to be working long hours. Do you?"

More laughter in the courtroom.

"Please refrain from asking the questions." Maxinne leveled a glance over the tops of her glasses that was meant to be intimidating. Instead, it brought a smile to Lydia's face. "And you see nothing wrong with living off your husband's largesse as you gallivant around the world, not working, but enjoying the fruits of his labor?"

This time Shawn stood up. "Your honor, I object. Not only is the defense leading the witness, but she is interjecting her own archaic viewpoint, leading the court to believe that the issue here is that a wife's place is in the home and cannot be otherwise as long as she is being supported by her husband."

"Objection sustained." Judge Weddington turned to the questioner. "Ms. Gunderman. I see where you are trying to get to with your questioning, but would you please refrain from leading the witness and perhaps, at some point in your interrogation, get at what you think is the real problem Mrs. Myers needs to be held accountable for. So far, I don't see how her trip to Paris, agreed upon by her husband, is a worthwhile bone to chew on and the hounds are getting restless. How about we introduce some witnesses who might help your argument."

Titters were heard throughout the courtroom. This was the Judge Odell Weddington at his best and what Shawn admired most about him. Lydia stepped down and Shawn called Officer Paul Mancini to the stand. In five minutes he told the story of how he had picked Lydia up hitchhiking on Highway 9 North and why. Murmurs were heard throughout the room. Janice Jewel had a look of fury on her face. Lunetta was patting her arm to calm her down. Ron Davis merely sat, nodding his head.

Next, Vito DeFranco was called. He told the story of being hired by Jack Myers to track Lydia in Paris, to find out if she was having an affair. He interjected that, not only was she not having an affair, she was helping an aging friend get around and drawing people's portraits. He was allowed to step down.

One by one, the rest of the witnesses were called, all of whom had favorable things to say about Lydia. Ron Davis talked about how she helped others at the shelter and even gave what little money she had after selling her belongings to repay him for her stay. Lunetta told the story of her name, Lydia Chapel, and how much they enjoyed her company. "She fit in with all of us, just like a real down-and-out homeless person and I love her for that. And she was there thanks to that man over there." She pointed a finger at Jack and shot him a glance that could have seared flesh.

Janice talked about how Lydia had taken her under her wing and talked her into going back to college. With a scowl aimed at Jack, she said, "For that man over there to say she's the crazy one is, well, it's the biggest crock of shit I've ever heard." She was duly warned about her language even as she received an ovation.

Her brother Tom was last and perhaps the most elegant of all.

"For the past twenty-two years I have watched my sister, Lydia, struggle to raise her two children and play the role of a dutiful, loving and giving wife. No one is perfect, but I have to say that my sister came pretty close to that standard and raised the bar far higher than most of us could reach. She didn't complain and even made excuses for Jack, who was never around, always working, ostensibly, and never there for any of the family. I always suspected that Jack was seeing other women, but he was careful to hide it."

At this point Jack stood up again, shouting his objection and calling Tom a horse's ass. He was pulled back down by his attorney and warned again by Judge Weddington.

Tom continued. "Jack was a selfish man, a narcissistic man, a neglectful husband, a hypercritical father, but a very good attorney. I give him that. He fit well into the world of corporate law, defending bullies like himself, always looking out for his own gain and how he could rise up by infringing on the rights and dignities of others. Jack never acknowledged the worth of his spouse, always belittling and diminishing her in so many ways. She never objected because she is a peacemaker and a conciliator. I am so proud of her for initiating this divorce. It has been long in coming."

The courtroom broke into applause as Tom stepped down.

Next, it was time to call the witnesses for the defense. Terrence Warshawsky was first on the stand.

Maxinne licked her lips as she approached him. "Mr. Warshawsky. We understand that on April 2nd, you went to the office of Dr. Manuel Aronson and were greeted instead by Mrs. Lydia Myers, the plaintiff. Is that true?"

"Why, uh, yes, she was in Dr. Aronson's office getting a piece of paper to put a note on the door. She told me Dr. Aronson had been called away."

"And when you walked in, and I presume sat down, did she then begin talking to you in a manner that led you to believe she was a psychiatrist taking Dr. Aronson's place?"

Terrence looked down at his hands which were shaking. "Why no, she said she wanted to put a note on the door. Then I started talking and she listened. We put the note on the door and she asked me if I wanted to continue the conversation down the street at a juice bar called Greenies.

I said, yes, because, well, as a matter of fact, I'd never go into a place like that alone. But, I felt safe with her and so we did. I got a really good green shake. I believe it was called a Green Monster."

"And during this time, did you believe that Mrs. Myers was a psychiatrist and that you were talking to a psychiatrist?"

"Oh no. She wanted to talk about my cat and my hamster. No psychiatrist would ever let me talk about them."

Maxinne was now getting near her limit of tolerance. "Mr. Warshawsky, were you not summoned here today as a witness to testify that Mrs. Myers impersonated a psychiatrist and led you to believe she was one, and even assumed the role of psychiatrist with you?"

Terrence looked around the courtroom as if he was surveying the possible escape routes.

"I...I don't appreciate your tone. You sound angry. Mrs. Myers and I talked about my interests and my pets. At no time did she say she was a psychiatrist. I'm sorry if you got that impression."

Judge Weddington stepped in. "I think that's enough questioning of Mr. Warshawsky. You may step down, sir."

As Terrence Warshawsky went back to his seat, he flashed Lydia a broad grin and raised his hand in a tiny wave. She returned the smile with a thumbs up.

The next witness practically ran to the stand. Lydia looked at Shawn and both their eyebrows went up. What on earth would she possibly have to say in Jack's defense? The last thing Lydia knew, she'd broken dishes and defaced Jack's entire wardrobe of suits. What was going on here?

Maxinne had regained her composure. "Ms. Castelloes. You have been a friend to Jack Myers for the past two years, is that correct?"

"Yes."

"And during that time, you became friends and got to know more about him and his relationship with his wife, Lydia. How would you describe that relationship, according to what Mr. Myers told you?"

"He said he was lonely and didn't get the sex he needed from her. He said she was a prude and he needed more excitement in his life because he was a virile man with a large appetite for sex."

Jack stood up and pointed at her. "Not another word from you, you...."

"Order in the court," Judge Weddington brought the gavel down. "One more outburst out of you, Mr. Myers, and I'll have you bodily removed from court and make the final decision on this case. Do I make myself clear?"

Jack sat down, arms folded across his chest, scowling.

Serena continued. "I thought Jack loved me. He told me he was leaving his wife and we would get married. He said he wanted children with me. He told me he was bored and sick of his marriage and I was the only good and exciting thing in his life. He led me on. He lied to me. He lied all the time. He's nothing but a..."

Maxinne Gunderman wiped her brow with a tissue she pulled from her sleeve. "Thank you, Ms. Castelloes. That's enough. I have no further questions."

Shawn approached the bench. "Please, Ms. Castelloes, tell us more about your relationship with the defendant. Tell us everything."

The floodgates opened. Jack's face was purple. His attorney shielded her eyes with her hand. Serena told all. There were murmurs and exclamations from the courtroom. Twice the judge had to call for silence. Serena Castelloes was bearing her soul.

"And so, all I have to say is, when Jack offered me ten thousand dollars to testify on his behalf in his divorce trial, I said fine. I agreed. So here it is, Jack. Here's what your money is buying. The truth about you. I wouldn't touch you again if you were the last man on earth, you lying, stinking, piece of filth. So there!" Serena stood up from her seat in the witness stand and hurled a wad of bills secured with a rubber band directly at Jack. It hit him square in the forehead as pandemonium broke out and Judge Weddington almost broke his gavel.

Recess was called. Lydia filed out of the room with the others and they congregated outside. Hugs were exchanged while excited chatter abounded. Lunetta told her she wanted her to do her portrait next. Simon came up sheepishly and they embraced.

"Lydia, I'm so sorry I deceived you, on one hand. But, on the other, I'm not. I just want to thank you and assure you, I never used heroin. I'm clean, in fact, except for maybe an occasional bowl, so you don't have to rehab me. But it was nice knowing you cared."

Lydia hugged him again and swatted his behind. "I thought I was good at disguising myself, but I have to say, you take the prize."

Shawn came over and everyone wanted to shake his hand. Janice gave him a good long elevator look and said with a sigh, "Why is it that all the best looking men are either in law or law enforcement. Mm-mm. This one sure don't hurt the eyes."

Lydia was overwhelmed by the show of support. She wanted Shawn to put his arms around and hold her, knowing it was impossible under the circumstances. Tom did instead and she held onto him tightly.

"I never thought it would be this tense. I dread to think what the rest of the trial will be like. I fear they'll make me out to be a witch because I'm vegan."

"Oh, that's old news," Tom said. "I was hoping more for a sentence of having to eat red meat every day for one whole week." He ruffed up her hair.

They all found a deli nearby and Tom bought lunch for the group. As they were eating, Lydia looked up to see Terrence Warshawsky outside, staring in the window. She jumped up and ran out the door.

"Terrence. It's so good to see you again. Please, come in and join us. I want to hear all about Delilah and Hammie. You're looking well."

A red-faced man followed her back into the deli. "Let me buy you lunch. Are you a meat eater or vegetarian?"

Terrence shrugged his shoulders. "Anything you're having would be fine with me."

She ordered him a veggie club and a fruit smoothie. When he searched in his pocket, she put her hand up. "This is on me. You were brilliant in court. I owe you."

The recess passed quickly. When they returned to the courtroom, there was an atmosphere of gaiety that hadn't been there before. Judge Odell Weddington stepped out of his chambers and all stood up. Once he seated them, he thanked them for their presence.

"It is not often that a decision on a divorce is made with such alacrity and such rapidity, but I have to say, history is being made today, at least for me. This is largely due to all the evidence provided by you good people and the handling of this case by the attorney for the plaintiff, Mr. O'Malley." He nodded in Shawn's direction. "Rapid though it may be, I have come to the disposition of this case following careful and considerable judgment. I see no reason to hear from any more witnesses. There has been a multitude of evidence provided to substantiate and support my conclusion. There is an allegation of bribery on the part of the defendant that must be looked into further. Given the evidence and all the testimony we have heard today, I hereby grant a divorce to Mrs. Lydia Myers based on proof of adultery and mental cruelty exacted against her by the defendant, her husband, Mr. Jack Myers. The evidence is plentiful, unimpeachable, and irrefutable. We will finalize the distribution of the marital property in my chambers, as I think we do not need or want a media circus nor another standing ovation in the courtroom. This trial is over, adjourned, go in peace, and let the hound dogs rest. Mrs. Myers, Mr. Myers, and their attorneys. We will now meet with me in my chambers. Court is adjourned. You all have a nice day."

The courtroom broke out in applause. Lunetta, Janice and Ron all stood up, whooping and hugging each other. Vito threw his black fedora in the air. Officer Paul Mancini looked around nervously, hoping nothing more than a celebration would break out. Shawn clapped his hands and gave his client a perfunctory hug, while Lydia bowed her head and wept.

An hour later, Lydia and Shawn walked out of the chambers in silence. Hugs were exchanged outside on the esplanade, along with more tears and laughter. Tom picked Lydia up off the ground and spun her around, then wiped his eyes.

"Guess I better head home and see the wife and kids," he said. "Gotta return to the land of rice and pagodas next week. They're floundering without me. The regime may have toppled by now."

Janice and Lunetta gave Lydia warm hugs and threats that, if she didn't visit soon, they'd make her homeless again so she could stay with them. Ron told them to stop and gave Lydia a proper handshake and a promise that, if she ever needed his help, he was there for her. Vito first shook her hand, then took her in a huge embrace and kissed her on both cheeks.

"The French way," he said laughingly.

Officer Mancini came up and shook her hand. "Hurry back to the Lake. It's boring there without you."

At one point she saw Jack in the distance, talking to a man she assumed was a colleague who'd attended on his behalf. Both were looking grave and shaking their heads.

When everyone was gone, Lydia looked up at Shawn. "How can I thank you? You were...masterful. There aren't words. I never saw you at work before and honestly, I'm simply awestruck. Shawn, I now know why you have the reputation you do. You're damn good."

Shawn pulled her toward him and held her in a long embrace, kissing the top of her head as she nestled her face against his shoulder. Quoting an old cartoon character from their childhood, he said in a different voice, "I yam what I yam, and that's all what I yam." Then, more seriously, "I do admit it was different with you. I did it for us. I needed this divorce as much as you and I was bound to do it right. In all honesty, I never dreamed it'd go as well as it did. Lucky for us, the defense was pitifully weak and unsubstantial. Jack really thought he'd built a case to have you carted away to a mental hospital. Unbelievable."

When they got to his Jeep, he opened the door and helped her step in. Once inside, he didn't start the engine. They looked at each other for a full minute, then he pulled her close and their lips met.

The kiss lasted several minutes. Both had tears in their eyes when it was over. The only words spoken were, "We did it, little buddy." and "Oh, did we ever, Skipper."

Lydia pulled back slightly to look into his eyes. "I say we adjourn to a private, intimate setting and discuss this case further over a glass of wine. What say you?"

Shawn smoothed a few loose strands of hair back from her face. "You're still my client. You call the shots."

Lydia's eyes were sparkling. "Oh, I think you're more than just my attorney. So much more."

"I think you have the burden of proving that statement. Let's go."

Chapter 29

Their table couldn't have been more perfect, tucked away in a back corner of the dimly lit Bohemian-chic restaurant in the Village. They may have been anywhere in the Middle East, surrounded by waiters wearing bedroom slippers who moved soundlessly to and fro as they spoke in whispers, the soft music of sitars creating an atmosphere both exotic and mesmerizing. Torches on the wall with burnt umber mica shades bathed everything in a golden glow of firelight.

Shawn sat across from Lydia and held her hands. "You look beautiful, by the way. I didn't get a chance to tell you. I was having a hard time taking my eyes off you in court. Of course, Jack's attorney was some competition, but... Sorry, that was mean."

Lydia flushed. "Thank you. You do, too. And I loved watching you in action. You can be pretty formidable when you want to. Janice told me to not let go of you because, in her words, 'That is one fine-looking fish. And smart.' So, how did I do for my first time on the stand in the Supreme Court of New York City? It was an experience I truly never want to have again. I was so nervous. I felt like I was babbling half the time. I just couldn't keep my thoughts straight and remember everything you told me. Now, I really am babbling."

Her sincere self-effacing manner made him ache. "You were as calm as a cucumber, or so it appeared, and as articulate as the judge himself. I don't know how much you got to see, but he was really enjoying it. A couple times I saw him holding back from laughing. His shoulders were literally shaking. He got a real kick out of Janice and Lunetta. Every time Jack spoke, you could almost see his lips curl back in a snarl. I've never seen him quite like this. The southern drawl just added to the texture of it all."

"You're serious? I had no idea." Lydia was momentarily baffled. "It was all I could do to keep myself calm and halfway focused. I missed the whole show. Guess I was too worried about getting my part right. So I did okay?"

He wanted to take her up in his arms right then and crush her to his chest. "Award winning. Even Judge Weddington looked like he wanted to give you a hug. Especially later, in his chambers, when he awarded you half of all the marital assets, including the house, the bank accounts, IRAs, 401k's, and Jack's offshore accounts, which I noticed came as a surprise to you."

"I had no idea. But then, I didn't really know Jack very well at all. I'm just glad the kids are taken care of and covered through college. Plus, the alimony is more than adequate. I suppose we'll have to sell the house and divide up the assets."

"All that can be decided later. I'll continue to represent you. I know Jack won't give anything up without a fight, even though it's court-ordered. You made out quite well, my dear. In most people's estimation, you're going to be a well-heeled divorcée."

"You know I never wanted all that. I wasn't going for the money. I only wanted to be free of Jack and to get what was fair. I really only expected alimony and my share of the house. You don't know this, but all of my savings, including a small inheritance from Aunt Matilda, went toward the down payment. I didn't even want the place. It was far too expensive, but Jack insisted."

The whole thing seemed like a dream to her. She thought for a moment what it would be like to have her own money again. "I can finally pay you back, with interest, for all your generosity and kindness, and whatever you paid the others who testified. I saw you handing them envelopes. They were pretty pleased. Don't you dare skimp on my bill, promise?"

"I gave them a small stipend for their trouble, plus travel expenses. You know, they really like you. Lunetta told me she knew you weren't a hooker the first time she laid eyes on you. Janice disagreed with her, though."

"Yes, I know Janice thought she had me pegged. She wanted to know all my tricks of the trade and how I managed to buy such nice things."

"I'd like to know your tricks, too. Maybe you could demonstrate."

"Uh, you know I'm high-priced. It'll cost you."

"Don't forget, you owe me. But, seriously, if it hadn't turned out as well as it did, I wouldn't have charged you anything. I'd have done it for you free, any day. I hope you know that."

Lydia's eyes welled up with tears. She picked up Shawn's hand and kissed the back of it. "I know. And I so appreciate that. Thank you, Shawn. You've been wonderful. You are by far the kindest man I know."

He leaned across the small table and kissed her softly on the lips. She returned the kiss with a little more fervor. When they both sat back, there was an electric current pulsating between them.

"So what was that term Judge Weddington used? Economic misconduct? Did he make that up?"

Shawn noticed the shift in energy immediately. She was right to change the subject. This wasn't the time or the place. But that would change. Soon.

"Economic misconduct is often brought to bear in divorce cases. It usually refers to a wasteful disposition of assets, such as when a spouse squanders the family money on things like gambling, drugs, or extramarital affairs. In this case, our dear Jack, in keeping up a mistress and stripping you of everything when he took away all your money and access to it, was deemed guilty of economic misconduct. That's why I like Weddington so much. He doesn't let anything slip by. I don't think Jack ever took that into consideration. He went pale when he heard the words. Did you see his face?"

"I did. It was a shade somewhere between dull green and ash gray. I thought he was going to be sick. I'd only seen him look that way once before when he got seasick on a deep sea boating trip. I noticed something else, too. There was that look on his face again, only this time it was feral. It scared me. I thought for a moment he might go ballistic and try to kill all of us in the judge's chambers. Even his lovely attorney seemed to be keeping her distance, as if she was afraid of him."

"Wasn't she something? I'm sure Jack chose her, first for the female factor, which was dubious at best, and for her reputation as a bitch on wheels. A real woman hater, I'm told. I suppose it's because she never identified with being a woman. She surely did nothing to help his case. When she started down their one and only defensive track to prove you incompetent, you could tell pretty quickly she knew it was a lost cause. You were great, by the way. Judge Weddington couldn't stop nodding his head throughout your testimony. He was really enjoying it."

Lydia took a sip of wine and almost spit it out with a laugh. "I was so impressed with dear Terrence Warshawsky. I have to take him out for a smoothie again. He was priceless."

"And invaluable. From now on, I will refer to this as the 'smoothie defense.' He certainly disappointed them and helped you, even though they were counting on him to incriminate you. Poor guy. He was so nervous, yet so sincere. Even the judge's eyes were twinkling."

Lydia thought she'd do something special for Terrence the next time she planned to spend any time in the city. There was someone else in the courtroom who impressed her even more. "Serena. Oh my word. Wasn't she a pisser? Jack actually paid for her defense and she went and turned the tables on him. I have a whole new respect for her. I thought Jack would have taken charges out against her for what she did to his suits."

"Ah, yes. He failed to take into account the 'scorned woman' factor. I'll bet he threatened her with charges in exchange for her cooperation. He still may go after her for damages. He could, but I don't think it would do any good. She looks like she could take him on any day of the week."

"If he does, I'll help her," Lydia said firmly. "She did put up with him for two years, after all."

Shawn couldn't believe what he was hearing. "You're too much, Lydia. You'd go out of your way to help the mistress that contributed to the breakup of your marriage. I don't even know what to call that. Maybe you really are non-compos mentis."

"You finally figured me out." She sipped her wine. "I've been hiding it all this time. Seriously, I feel only gratitude. Serena helped set me free."

Shawn raised his glass. "I'll drink to that."

A waiter approached and stealthily laid down a feast, then moved away as quietly as he'd arrived. Over a lunch of couscous, hummus and pita points, tabbouleh, an assortment of flavorful olives, curried vegetables and pan-seared naan, they talked and laughed about the rest of the trial and all their observations. Lydia was astounded at how much Shawn took note of and she was fully enjoying his hilarious rendition.

"I almost lost it when Janice took the stand with her low-cut top and more than ample cleavage. Then, when she flashed her eyes at the judge, puckered up her lips and said, 'You know what I'm talkin' about, brother,' he and I both nearly burst out laughing. He was trying so hard to keep a straight face, but he gave it away when he tipped over his glass of water and pretended to duck behind the bench for a while. Then Tom, in all his seriousness, still managed to get a laugh out of everybody when he said, 'the alleged seducer of the alleged mistress, and their alleged affair, which, of course, is all hearsay, except for the not-so-alleged photos, not to mention the unabridged movie of another brief affair in Paris.' I thought I was going to have to excuse myself."

"Tom does have a way with words. He wanted so much to tell it his way. He did a great job, even though I was afraid he might be thrown out."

They lingered over a final glass of wine, sharing a dessert of gulab jamans and coconut pudding.

"You know, I think I could possibly consider being a part-time vegetarian," Shawn said. "This food is phenomenal."

Lydia cocked her head and looked into his eyes. The man was articulate, intelligent, affectionate, and oh so good to look at. He had a sense of humor, as well. Was it any wonder her heart gave a sudden lurch when he took her hand?

"Want to go somewhere else now?" he said.

"Yes."

"How about my place?"

"I thought you'd never ask."

Inside the apartment, he took her purse and jacket and placed them on a chair in the vestibule. Placing both hands on her shoulders, he stood gazing at her, half-smiling, half wondering how they had finally arrived at this moment. It was something he wanted to hold onto and treasure for at least a minute, because he didn't know how much longer he could control himself.

"Do you want me, Shawn?"

The words had the effect of fanning the embers that had been glowing throughout their meal into flames that were going to consume both of them.

His desire for her was so overpowering, he had no words to offer. Instead, he reached for her, pulled her to his chest, tangled his fingers in her hair, and covered her mouth with his. It wasn't a voracious kiss, but a tasteful enjoyment of tender lips caressing, full of flavor and passion. He'd dreamed of this moment for so many years. This wasn't the time to rush it. There was no need to. He'd waited so long for her and now she was here, in his apartment, in his arms. He intended to sip, savor, touch and caress every inch of her.

She responded by pressing in closer and wrapping her arms around his shoulders, then his back, then lower to his buttocks and thighs. Her hands were moving over him like a skillful masseuse intent on giving as well as drawing as much pleasure as she could.

"Take me, Shawn."

He picked her up in his arms and strode to the bedroom, laying her gently on the bed and covering her body with his, careful not to crush her under his weight. Her body was so warm, so light, so fragrant. What was that intoxicating scent? Gardenia? Jasmine? He had no idea and didn't care to know. It was Lydia. That was all that mattered.

How long they kissed and caressed, he couldn't say. It might as well have been an eternity, or a couple of minutes. Nothing else existed. The world, time, and everything else melted into a dream of sense pleasure. He was finally with Lydia in the way he wanted to be ever since they'd met. Even in high school, he'd entertained fantasies of making love to her. At that time, he figured there was no chance. It truly was all fantasy. Lydia O'Connor never saw him as anything but a pal.

Lydia mused that she'd never been carried to bed before, other than as a child, which she couldn't remember. It had a dizzying effect. Shawn's strength and the solidity of his body, along with the delicious masculine musky scent he emanated had her senses reeling. Her heart was beating much faster than normal, faster even than when she ran her full six miles. But she wasn't exerting herself in any way, other than to respond to his touch, his lips on her throat, neck and shoulders. The feel of his lips through her blouse, his tongue grazing her breasts, produced an erotic sensation that made her want to cry out and beg to be stripped naked and taken fully and completely that instant.

But he had other ideas. He sat up and gave her a lingering look. "You're here, in my bed. I can't..."

"Shut up," she said, pulling him down. "We can talk later."

His mouth closed over hers as he felt her body melt in surrender. Then he helped her sit up and lifted her blouse over her head. She, in turn, unbuttoned his shirt and slid it off his shoulders. Seeing his naked chest, she made a sound of moaning approval as she slipped out of the rest of her clothes. Dropping his pants on the floor, he climbed over her and began nibbling on her lips and neck. She moaned and pulled him down, running her hands over his back, feeling the rippling muscles she'd known were there but never had a chance to explore.

He was so strong. So solidly built. His shoulders were broad and sturdy, like he did hard labor, or just worked out diligently at the gym. His chest was covered with just enough hair to be wildly masculine but not apish. It was so enticing. But his legs...they were like pillars of granite pressing against hers on either side, holding her tightly between them in a trap she had no desire to free herself from.

He could feel her heart racing as he stroked her skin softly, smoothly, delighting in deepening her desire, encouraged by her response. He thrilled to feel her tremble beneath his touch, moving his lips and hands to parts of her crying for attention, all nerves and synapses firing as an electric current shot through and between them, everything coalescing into a flood of physical yearning. He could feel his blood coursing through his veins, his own heart pounding, desire burning deep inside him as his lips moved down her throat, over her lightly tanned freckled shoulders. Her shoulders shivered and her moans of pleasure drove him on, whipping his ardor to higher heights than he'd ever experienced before.

He was having her, at last. Lydia O'Connor, the woman of his dreams, the maid of his fantasies. Having her in his bed, making love to her was no longer the stuff of dreams from which he used to awaken alone and disappointed. Even when he made love to his wife, as much as it shamed him, he used to imagine she was Lydia, so great was his longing for her. Stephynia had never been ardent in their lovemaking. He always felt it was an act of mercy on her part, self-sacrificial, when she allowed him to take her. He, in turn, felt like he'd overstepped some invisible boundary and had violated her, leaving him feeling more alone and frustrated after the act was completed.

Come back to the moment, he told himself. But how could he have known this moment, this first encounter with someone he'd lusted after and wanted for so long, could possibly live up to his hopes and expectations? Yet, it was. She was. The feeling was so overpowering he thought it might consume him completely. Be careful, he warned. If he let all his emotions come to the surface he'd end up in a puddle and wouldn't that be pathetic?

No, there would only be passion, lust, desire and the need to please her. He would take all he could and give to her all he could. His animal side was being unleashed, allowed to come out of the cage and play now. The sentimental side could stand aside and wait its turn. He was making love to Lydia O'Connor at last.

Damn Jack Myers forever for coming between them. But maybe he should be thanking him. He may not have appreciated her as much back then, nor she him, in his awkwardness and retarded approach to lovemaking. This was better. He knew himself now and was a confident lover. He felt it had to be the same for Lydia. How else could she have chosen a man like Jack back then? He hoped this meant as much to her as it did to him.

She was almost in a dream-state, floating on the waves of his touch, the warmth of his body, the feeling of his flesh pressed against hers. When she found his lips on hers, she melted into them, lost herself, felt her body dissolving into his. It seemed they were melding into one and no separation existed between them any longer. How was it possible that she'd never experienced such a sensation before? Was this what making love really was? How could she have missed this over all the years of her marriage?

She didn't want to sink into the realm of pain or regret over that thought. Leave it behind. Rather, she wanted to think this was a special kind of magic that happened between two people who were completely and utterly right for each other, completely committed to giving and receiving love. Jack gave only insofar as it guaranteed he'd get what he wanted. Even in his lovemaking he was stingy and self-serving. But here, with Shawn, she was experiencing lovemaking at its best and most fulfilling. It was so far above and beyond what she could have expected. Transcendent was the only word she could think of.

When his hands cupped her breasts, she gasped and uttered a low moan. He teased her with his fingers, then his lips, touching, massaging, nipping gently, then kissing and sucking her softly. Her pleasure could not be contained. She writhed beneath him, grasping at his firm backside, pulling him closer, spreading her legs apart to make room for him. Her moans were becoming more guttural.

She was vibrating with sensation, not sure she could take any more in. The she closed her eyes. "Shawn."

"Lydia, little buddy." He brought her back with a laugh. "Come back, look at me."

She looked into his eyes. The sea glass blue waters of the Caribbean sparkled and shimmered. They were full of hope and promise. Angelic. What kind of man was this? And why hadn't she seen this in him before? Why hadn't she encouraged him more, or gone after him years ago, before Jack came barging into the picture and changed everything. It wasn't the time for such reflections. She was here now, with him, and the moment was beyond what she ever could have imagined. The sweet sensations rippling through her were unbearable. She wanted him with a lust that enveloped her. She was drowning in it.

"Shawn, now."

"Lydia, I love you."

When he joined with her completely she gasped with pleasure that came from the depths of her being. It caused everything around her to cease to exist. It was just the two of them, floating in space, detached from the world. They were in their own secret place, a place of total joy and consummate pleasure. She was beneath him, in him, around him and they were consumed in their heat and the moisture of their bodies, moving together in a dance of ultimate sensulaity.

It was beyond what he had ever imagined. There was no describing it. He'd jumped off the cliff into the sea of ecstasy and was swimming in an ocean of bliss. He wanted it to last forever. He wanted to pleasure her forever. He knew she wanted the same for him. This moment could never end.

They held each other in silence for a timeless period, neither wanting to speak or change the effect of what had just happened. Words would only have diminished the magic, detracted from the surrealistic feeling of it.

Lydia was first to move. The weight of Shawn on top of her was preventing her from taking a deep breath.

"Sorry, sorry, I'm crushing you. Are you okay?"

She took in a long full breath. "Absolutely. You?"

"Incredibly."

They lay with their heads on the pillows, staring at each other. Both smiling. Neither moving.

Lydia laughed. "God bless that Serena."

Shawn propped himself on his elbow. "God bless her and God bless Jack. I never thought I'd appreciate anyone for being such a colossal asshole. Or her for being so vindictive."

"You know, we owe it to them, really. If it weren't for them, I wouldn't have called you to be my attorney and we wouldn't be together right now."

Amazed at her summation of events, Shawn reached out his hand and tweaked her nose. "Hey, little buddy. If you hadn't gone to France and been followed by Vito and come back to find Serena in your home, not to mention the photos and DVD, you might still be married to Jack Sprat."

For some reason, the thought tickled her. "Jack Sprat could eat no fat. His wife, being vegan, could eat no lean. And so betwixt them both, you see, she cleaned his clock and got...well, free." She giggled. "I know, bad rhyming."

"How about, and so betwixt her lawyer and she, they wiped Jackie's clock clean?"

Lydia pounced on Shawn and knelt over him, ruffling his hair with her fingers. "That's what I love about you. You're not only a great lawyer, you're also an amazing poet. Okay, so here's another one. Humpty Jack sat on a wall. Humpty Jack had a great fall..."

"Wait, wait. Let me finish...all of Jack's money and all of Jack's fame, couldn't put Jack together again."

"Okay, nice, but how about this? All Maxinne's work and all of Jack's scheming, still made Jack come away screaming."

Shawn scratched his head. "Nice sentiment, better rhyming. I'll give it a nine and a half. No, a ten. It's brilliant." He moved to turn Lydia around and onto her side so he could spoon with her. "I like this. Peas in a pod. Or spoons in a drawer, although mine are all thrown together hodgepodge."

"Spoons are meant to be hodgepodge. At least if you're a man living alone." She wondered about Shawn's living situation. He'd been divorced several years now. Had it ever been otherwise? Maybe it wasn't the time, but she asked anyway. "Have you lived with anyone else since your divorce?"

"Nope. Only dated, occasionally. Once in a while, I had an overnight guest, but it just didn't feel right. I was always too busy to get really involved with anyone. I'm sure there are some women out there who think I'm a hopelessly non-committal bastard."

"Are you?"

"Well, maybe not hopelessly. Definitely not a bastard. I had a mother and a father."

"I hope not. I could accept a hopelessly committal legitimate kind of guy."

"That's me. And I could accept a woman not in her right mind who goes around impersonating psychiatrists."

"Hey, I was pretty convincing. Give me some credit."

"I give you all the credit. You can psychoanalyze me anytime. But only when you're naked."

"Now that could really get me into some ethical situations."

"Not if I don't report you."

"We've got a deal."

Chapter 30

It wasn't easy saying good-bye the next morning. Lydia awoke early, leaned over and kissed Shawn on the cheek, then slipped out of bed to make coffee. She had to meet Tori and Leo at 9:00, then, whenever they were done, drive back up to Lake George. Although she'd kept both her children informed of current events, she didn't think it would be right not to meet with them in person, if they were willing to take the time, that is. Besides, she wanted to be sure they were dealing with all the news of late and still able to maintain relations with their father. She wanted to impress on them that whatever happened between their parents, it had nothing to do with them and they should both feel free to be on good speaking terms, at least, with their father.

Shawn awoke and found the bed empty and let out a long wailing sound. Lydia heard it from the kitchen and came running.

"What's wrong? Are you okay?"

"No. I was dreaming I had an angel next to me in bed and she said she was never going to leave me, then I woke up and she was gone. Why did she leave me? Wait, before you answer, is that coffee I smell?"

"Yes, Prince Charmless. Would you like your angel to bring you a cup?"

"You'd be an angel if you did. And what's this about charmless? Come on in here and I just might change your mind." She climbed back in bed and they made love, this time in a drowsy, early morning sort of way.

Still glowing, they sat on the bed after, sipping their coffee as Lydia told him her plans for the day. He wasn't happy, even though he had a full day scheduled and wasn't going to have any free until much later in the day.

"So you're going to abandon me for George, is it? Well, I'm jealous. I just might have to pay him a visit and put him in his place. Why did you have to move so far away? Couldn't you stay in the city a while? Do you have to go back?"

Lydia had asked herself the same question earlier. "I promised some people at the shelter I would draw them, and I have to finish my course and take my final this week. I still have one more paper to write. Also, I didn't make any preparations to leave the cabin unattended for more than a couple days. So, it looks like I have to go back to George."

"I hate him."

"He's got nothing over you."

"No, just thirty-some miles of sheer unadulterated beauty. It's hard to compete with that."

"There's no competition. Just come up whenever you're free and we'll enjoy George together."

"A ménage à trois?"

"Something like that. Come on, Skipper. Get up. You have work to do and it's time for me to shove off."

Shawn moaned. "Do I have to, little buddy? I was hoping you'd stay and be my sugar mama so I wouldn't have to go to work."

"What? And deprive all those dissatisfied housewives of their divorces? No sir. You have a duty to perform. You must carry on liberating the huddled masses yearning to breathe free."

"Uh, I think you're getting me confused with the Statue of Liberty. But, okay. You're right. I do have a job and I guess I can't depend on you to make me your love slave and take care of me."

Lydia smirked. "Love slave? Now that I might be able to handle."

They hugged and kissed and hugged some more before Lydia had to break away and catch the taxi that wouldn't wait any longer and was letting her know by blaring his horn. The kids agreed to meet her downtown at a café they both liked that catered to college students. When she arrived and walked in, the noise almost knocked her back. She saw Tori waving to her from a booth in the back. She forced her way through the crowd, recalling her college days when being squeezed like sardines in a can in the name of social bonding was commonplace. Now she felt like a newborn being pushed down the birth canal. Both kids got up and hugged her.

"Where'd you stay last night? With Uncle Tom and Becky?" Tori asked. First question, first lie. She wasn't ready to tell the kids about Shawn. Not just yet. She'd just divorced their father, after all.

"No. Actually I stayed with a friend, recently separated. She wanted some adult company. She has small kids and needed some intelligible conversation. It was nice seeing her."

Leo gave her a look that made her wonder if his intuition allowed him to see right through her. "So, tell us all about it. Did it go okay? Is dad happy? Are you?"

Lydia gave them the sanitized version she'd rehearsed in her mind during the cab ride over. She told them it went well, they agreed on everything, the settlement was fair, and they parted on somewhat amicable terms. She was happy it went as well as it did.

Both kids stared at her in disbelief. Tori was the first to protest. "Mom, listen. We know what a shit dad has been. We know what he's put you through. We know about the affair and we know he cut you off and you ended up in a shelter for the homeless. God! How fucked is that? Would you please, for once, treat us like adults and tell us the truth, for shit's sake?"

Leo put his hand up to silence his sister. "Let her tell it her way. We know there's more to the story. The main thing is, you're divorced and that's good. We're happy for you, mom. We're not thrilled with dad, or the publicity about the other trial, or the fact that almost every day someone comes up to us and asks if the Jack Myers in the *New York Now* article and now the *New York Times* and the *Daily Herald* and the *Washington Post* and probably even *Mad Magazine*, for all we know, is any relation to us. I mean, it's pretty humiliating when you have to lie about who your dad is."

There was nothing Lydia could say to remove that burden from her children. They already knew some of the truth. She didn't need to embellish it or add fuel to the fire. He was and would always be their father, even if he was no longer her husband.

"Look, in time I hope we can be a family and be on civil terms with each other. I know you're adults and you have to make your own decisions, but I suggest, no, I beg you to please consider being on good terms with your father. He can be a much better help to you as an ally than an enemy. Just think about it, okay?"

"I hate him, mom," Tori said. "No matter how hard I try not to, I do. I hate him."

"Please, Tori. Don't. I don't hate him. I hate some of the things he's done, but there's a lot of good in your father. He had taken very good care of us, all of us."

"Yeah, and his mistress, too. But it's not just about us. He's a conservative, anti-human rights, anti-environment, inhumane capitalist. He's disgusting. His politics and beliefs are fascist. He represents all that's wrong with today's world. I can't help it. It's the way I feel."

Leo was nodding his head in agreement. "For him to even take on a case like Montclair and defend them is a referendum against human rights and environmental protection. Montclair is a monster. You read the article. It sums it all up. We're not like Dad. We don't want to be like him or live that way. It's all about greed and personal gain. Nothing's good or noble about it. It's all bullshit."

It was at times like this that Lydia was most proud of her offspring. They really did think and they had scruples. She loved that their values were more in line with hers than their father's. What could she say? Her children were coming into their own as adults and had a right to their own beliefs and feelings, whether toward her or their father. Perhaps it was time to tell them about Shawn.

"I won't argue with you. But, I just hope that someday there may be a reconciliation. Maybe you'll find something in your father to love and admire. I won't push the issue because I admire you for your beliefs." She hesitated. "There is one more thing I think it only fair to tell you."

Coffees arrived and they busied themselves with creamers, sugar, cinnamon, and other additives. Tori loved to doctor up her drinks, while Leo was a half n' half man only.

"So, don't keep us in suspense. Who's the BF?" Tori asked.

Lydia sat back, astounded. Once again, they saw right through her. Where had they gotten this ability? Was it always there?

"His name is Shawn O'Connor. He was an old friend from high school, then college. We went to Columbia together."

"Did he know dad?"

"Yes."

"Not a fucking lawyer, I hope."

"Yes, a lawyer. He's my divorce lawyer."

Tori dropped her spoon. "No shit, mom, you're really seeing your divorce attorney? How totally radical. What, did you hit it off from the start when he said, 'I'm going to *voir dire* you now,' or 'Come to the boudoir and I'll file your affidavit?' Does dad know? Well, of course he knows him, but does he know about the two of you?"

"I don't think so. He may suspect something. He knew we were friends in college."

"Oh. So, it wasn't just like you struck up an old acquaintance. You hired this guy to represent you. To free you from your train wreck of a marriage." Tori gave her mom a long hard look. "Okay, so please don't tell me you were seeing this guy when dad came along, and you could have chosen him but you chose dad instead? Like, this guy could have been my father? Leo's father? God no. Life is so fucked sometimes."

Lydia wasn't about to bare her soul in such a crowded environment, in an airtight booth, talking over music so loud it was necessary to shout to be heard. And at 10:00 in the morning, no less. "That's a story for another time."

Without warning, Tori stood up, slung her bag over her shoulder and said, "I gotta run. Got a 12:00 class and don't want to be late again." She gave her mother a cursory hug and peck on the cheek. "Glad you did it, mom. Good luck with your attorney friend. Hope he's not another asshole."

With Tori gone, Leo leaned across the table, cupped his hands megaphone style around his mouth, and said, "I'm really happy for you, mom. Dad deserved this. I hope this new guy makes you happy. I know you're a happy person, but you know what I mean. You won't have to worry about dad anymore."

She took both his hands in hers. "This won't affect you kids at all. He's taking care of all your college expenses. It's in the divorce settlement. But, whenever you need help now, you can come to me. I have money now. Well, not right now, but I will soon. We'll still have family get-togethers if your father agrees. I have no hard feelings and I really hope someday we can be friends. If not, then at least be civil to one another."

Leo's eyes welled up. He stopped talking and looked down. Lydia's heart took a dive when she saw his upset. "Oh, honey, I'm so sorry this had been so hard on you and you haven't really haven't had any time to process it all. Are you okay?"

Leo nodded, still looking down, and wiped his tears. When he looked up, she saw the tear-stained face of her little boy who fell off his bike and came running to her for solace. It was a look of both hurt and defeat. "What is it, Leo?"

He looked around, then leaned in closer. "Mom, I have to tell you something. I hope you'll take it okay. I think you'll be cool about it. I know dad won't. Mom, I...I'm not who you and dad think I am. I'm...different. I guess you would call it my sexual identity. I hate that term. Sounds so clinical. I don't like the word gay, either, because, well, who's ever gay when they have to hide in a closet and not let people know who they really are. As for homosexual, that falls right there on the couch in the psychiatrist's office. An aberration. Someone with a problem that needs to be ..."

"Leo, stop for a minute. Look at me. I'm your mother, I love you, and I...well, I always had an inkling. I love you for who you are. I love you however you are and however you choose to live your life..."

"It's not a choice..."

"I know that. What I mean is, if you choose to come out and shout it to the world and tell everyone, even your grandparents, I'm with you. If you decide to keep it private among just a few of us, that's fine, too. Does Tori know?"

"She pretty much guessed and I confirmed. She's okay. Thinks it's cool. She likes some of my cooler friends."

"Do you have a special friend? I don't mean to pry, but I'd like to think you had a friend who understood."

Leo nodded. "His name's Artemio. He likes to call me Leonardo. He's an art major, from Argentina."

"That's wonderful. Maybe you two can come visit me at the cabin."

Leo burst into tears and put his arms around her. She let him cry and patted his back. He was still her baby boy, sweet and vulnerable as ever. Several minutes later, he blew his nose, dabbed his eyes and cheeks and stood up. This time he gave her a quick, happy embrace.

"I love you, mom. Thanks. You may not be perfect but you're pretty damn awesome and way cooler than most mothers. Most people, actually."

At the cash register, he hugged her one more time, kissed her cheek and waved goodbye as he went out the door. She paid the bill and stuffed a generous tip in the jar. It was time to head home. Time to heal. Time to be alone to sit and meditate in the peace and quiet and figure out just what new shape her life was going to take from here on.

And there was that paper and final to finish.

Chapter 31

I'm divorced. I have my life back. I'm Lydia O'Connor again. I'm falling in love with a wonderful man and an incredible lover. My old pal. My buddy. My lover. I'm no longer Mrs. Jack Myers. Not Mrs. Lydia Myers, either. I'm me. Hey world, meet Ms. Lydia O'Connor.

Lydia rolled over in bed, plumped up her pillow and let out a shriek of joy.

I'm happy. I'm loved. Shawn is brilliant. Everything about him shines, even his teeth. He's strong, muscular. He has great thick, wavy Black Irish hair. And his eyes. Cornflower blue eyes like the ones I pick along the roadside. Oh, and his body. I can't go there. Wow. What is it about that body? It sends bolts of lightning through me. Okay, stop. Stop! He's a man, a male, a human. He has his flaws. We all do. He can be a bit pedantic. He eats meat. So what? He talks to me. He makes me laugh. He loves being with me. He loves touching me. He loves me!

His hands. Oh my, what masterful hands. What a soft and tender touch, but with ardor behind them. Oh come on, girl. You're thinking like some horny teenager. Stop being so superficial. Stop focusing on his body.

Oh, but what about his lips? Those kisses. Now there's somebody who could give lessons. Most men can't kiss, at least not anywhere near the way he does. Not that I'm any expert, but Jack, who'll I now call, the "ex," couldn't kiss to save his life. He smothered my mouth with his and then went to work like he was unclogging a drain, plunging with his tongue, dislodging molars. I got more satisfaction from my dentist when he probed my gums. How terrible of me to think such a thing. Or am I just being honest for once?

Shawn is a purveyor of the sweetest soul-melting kisses. The feel of those luscious, full, soft, hungry lips all over my body... oh good Lord, stop. I'm getting hot just thinking about it.

Geez, girl! Get over yourself! You've been divorced only, what? Four days? And you're already crazily into another relationship with a man? Take your foot off the gas. Put on the brakes. Ratchet it down. You're a mother of two grown kids. You're not diving in for the first time into the pool of romantic love. Okay, maybe you are, but look at it this way. There's a name for this. It's called rebounding. You're in a rebound romance. Shawn, for all intents and purposes, is your target. Keep it in perspective, girl. Besides, you need to rest. Take it easy for a while.

Lydia lay her head against the pillow, eyes closed, smiling at her morning lecture. It felt good or, at least it would have felt good, had she not had such a throbbing headache and even some slight nausea.

She thought about her mother. Never go out without a head covering. You'll catch your death of cold. Well, maybe she was right. It was chilly in New York and she hadn't worn a head covering. It had rained a little. Shawn seemed to be sneezing quite a bit. Had she picked up something from him? Great. How romantic is that? Romeo sharing his snotty cold.

It was probably just a combination of lack of sleep, nerves, anxiety over the trial, huge emotional shifts ranging from dread to regret to bliss, then boomeranging back to reality when she had to come home to the cabin. Not the other home. That was the house now. The house that was waiting to be sold.

A body couldn't sustain such a roller coaster ride for too long and she wasn't a fan of roller coasters to begin with. The kids used to beg her to ride with them, but she'd stand her ground and stay rooted. Some things she could do. Fly through the air on two little rails, screaming her lungs out as she whipped around nerve shattering hairpin turns or careened down tracks at forty-five degree angles was not one of them.

She got up and went to the bathroom to splash cold water on her face. The mirror not only mocked her, it frightened her. For goodness sake, did she really look that bad? She looked like she'd aged ten years. There were bags under her eyes that looked more like wrinkled little scrotums. Her color was off, too. There wasn't a name for it, but it would have worked well in some horror flick about zombies. Thank goodness Shawn wasn't here to see this. Besides looking so bad, she felt chilled to the bone. She checked the thermostat in the bedroom. It was set on 66. She turned it up to 72.

This had to be the start of a spring cold. Seasonal changes usually brought on sniffles, which she got over quickly. Her immune system had always been strong, thank goodness. There were times when she had to play nursemaid to two children and a husband who were all throwing up and fighting fevers at the same time. Hot tea, warm blankets, and dry toast were the order of the day. And rest. She could afford one whole day down, doing nothing. Besides, all she felt like doing was sleep. Even if she had a doctor in Lake George, which she didn't, she wouldn't have had the energy to drive herself. No, it was best to stay home and not go out. It was probably a touch of the flu. Since she'd never had it before, it was about time she had her first taste of what everybody was always telling her about.

This really was the pits. She felt exhausted. Sleep was the best thing. Her mother always believed in its curative powers and, for that reason, spent an inordinate amount of time in bed. It was probably why she never liked lounging around in bed or sleeping late. She tried to instill the same in her kids, but to no avail. Leo usually didn't surface until 9:00. Tori was worse. She could stay in bed till noon. Neither of them could ever take 8:00 classes.

Lydia smiled as she reflected on their life. Her kids had it so different. Unlike her, they didn't have to take all their classes early in the morning so they could rush from school to go to a job that lasted until 8 or 9 at night. She had no regrets. It was good training. It instilled in her a strong work ethic. Of course, all that fell by the wayside when she stayed home to raise the kids, at Jack's insistence. If it was still there, and she hoped it was, she'd look forward to going back to work once she finished her master's degree.

Maybe she could work at the shelter. But was she going to stay at the Lake? New York City was a long drive. There would be little to no work for Shawn up here and she'd never expect him to give up his lucrative position and relocate just to be with her. It would only make sense for her to go back. No. She couldn't do that. Not to the city, at least. She never wanted to live in Manhattan again. Maybe close by, like New Paltz, or somewhere in the Catskills. A short train ride away.

She hadn't thought much about the future. As she sipped her mint tea and nibbled a piece of dry toast, her mind suddenly plummeted into a well of despair. Shawn and she couldn't be together. At least not for any length of time. He'd probably only be able to visit occasionally. Once a month, at the most. She wouldn't want to drive to the city more than once or twice a month. They were going to have a long-distance relationship whether they liked it or not. The thought was almost unbearable.

The toast didn't go down well and she had to make a quick dash to the bathroom. When she got back to the bedroom, she fell back onto the bed. Was it really a fall or just a lazy way of getting prone? She couldn't tell, but it felt good to snuggle under the covers as she tried to regain some warmth. The temperature outside must have been fluctuating. Spring was doing it best to push winter out and take dominance, though the breezes off the lake were still chilly, even in the heat of summer. Today they seemed particularly brisk. She could hear the trees swaying and the wind whistling through them.

In minutes, she was asleep and would not have awoken in the afternoon except that the phone next to the bed rang. It was Shawn. She groggily fumbled to pick up the receiver.

"How's the newly divorced Miss O'Connor doing today? Feeling like a liberated woman yet?"

She only wished. Her head was not having its best day, judging by the pounding in her temples. Feigning wellness, she said, "I'm great, feeling quite liberated. Just a bit washed out at the moment. I've been in bed all day. I guess that's normal after everything that's happened."

"Sorry to hear it. How did the visit with the kids go?"

She had to stop and think. When was that? Oh, yes, three days ago, after she'd left Shawn's bed. Her lover's bed. It seemed like a dream now. "Fine. It went fine. They were both very accepting. Not happy with their dad, of course. Tori especially. Very supportive of me."

"Were they surprised at the settlement?"

"I really didn't go into much detail. Just told them to come to me when they…if they needed anything. They were fine, I think…" She drifted off for a moment.

"Lyd, you sound drunk, or hung over. Have you been celebrating a bit too much?"

"Celebrating? No. I did have a glass of wine with supper last night. Just one."

"You sure don't sound like yourself. Are you sure you're okay?"

Lydia didn't want their first post-coitus phone conversation to focus on her feeling like garbage. "Yes, I'm okay…fine, really. Just tired. I was napping when you called. How are you? You were sneezing quite a bit."

"Oh yeah, allergies. I hate to admit it, but I have an allergy to some perfumes."

Lydia wondered if she'd worn perfume. She had sprayed on a bit of musk. Yes, that had to be it.

"I'll refrain from using any from now on." She paused and tried to quell a surge of nausea. "Shawn, it might not be a good idea to come up this weekend. I may be coming down with something. I'd hate to pass it on to you. Maybe next weekend would be better."

"Let's see how you feel toward the end of the week. The earliest I could break away would be Saturday. You'll have plenty of time to catch up on your sleep by then."

"Yes…that sounds good. Okay, then. Good-bye, darling. I love you." Lydia dropped the phone into its cradle. She'd never called him 'darling' before. She was smiling as she fell back to sleep.

Shawn heard the phone click off. What an abrupt ending that was. She didn't sound like herself at all, unless this was a side of Lydia he didn't know. Was she brushing him off or was she just that tired? She did call him darling. Maybe a couple day's rest would get her back on an even keel.

He told himself not to overreact. They were, after all, only four days into their relationship—the new updated version, that is. He had to assume there was a breaking in period. Getting used to being in love and making love with someone he really loved. They were getting their bearings, so to speak.

He wished he was with her in bed right this moment, pressing his body to hers. But there were other things to occupy his time right now. Things like the stack of manila folders sitting on his desk and an endless wave of lawsuits and divorce cases.

He had to smile, though. As much as he enjoyed his work, it still baffled him how marriages could go so wrong. Her marriage was right up there in the top tenth percentile of shitty ones. Her divorce had gone better than most. He'd give it five-stars. She came out so far ahead and poor little Jackie's head was probably still spinning. He had no pity for the man. He got what he deserved.

There was only thing that concerned him. Jack had been burned badly, to the third degree. What would that do to him? How would he react once he fully realized the extent of the damages and the price he had to pay? Jack wasn't a man to take anything lying down and such a blow to his ego, not to mention his wallet, would be monumental.

He wondered if he'd been premature withdrawing Vito DeFranco's security and leaving Lydia on her own in the cabin. The phone rang. His next client had arrived. He'd try calling later to see if she was feeling any better.

Chapter 32

Another day in bed and she was seriously going to think about calling a doctor. Of course, that would be futile because they'd only tell her it would be three or more weeks before she could get an appointment. She'd suffer a few more days, gradually feel better, and be completely over whatever this was before her appointment date, so what would be the point? Nothing was staying down, not even tea or water. She had no appetite. Even the aspirin she took for the headache did nothing because it immediately came up with another volcanic eruption from her stomach.

Shawn called several times, but she was either asleep or too tired to put the phone up to her ear. All those times she'd downplayed the flu symptoms of other people and thought they were exaggerating now returned to haunt her. She begged forgiveness for having been so insensitive. As for prayers, hers were repeating a similar theme. *Lord, if you spare me and make me feel just a little better, I promise I'll never disbelieve another person's flu complaints. I'll be totally sympathetic.*

She got up and went out on the back deck, bundled in a comforter, looking at the water glisten as the evening breeze brushed over it. Tiny wavelets raced to the shore, shimmering in the late afternoon sun. The fresh air felt good. She took in deep draughts of it. It made her feel a tiny bit better. But it was so cold. Two pairs of socks and fuzzy slippers weren't doing the job. She needed a heating pad, but there wasn't one in the cabin. She would add it to her list of emergency supplies, once she had the strength to start one.

Enough of this, she scolded herself. This is ridiculous and unnecessary. She was fine. Just tired. She needed to push herself. Get dressed. Go for a walk. Go grocery shopping. She needed to get ingredients for a lovely meal for Shawn when he came up. Flowers, too. And a good bottle of wine. The thought of it made her want to retch.

She retreated back into the cabin and stretched out on the couch. It was nighttime before she awoke. She thought she heard a car pulling into the driveway. Had Shawn slipped away early? Oh, how wonderful. No, not wonderful. She didn't want him to see her like this. No. Surely it wasn't...

She heard footsteps and a key turn in the lock. The door opened.

"Shawn?" she called out.

She sat up just as the footsteps approached the living room. The dark figure stopped in front of her. She gasped.

"What are you doing here?"

Jack looked down at her with a smile on his face. It was the smile she used to see after he'd successfully worked a case to his satisfaction. A look of smug satisfaction. A gloating, sinister look.

"Hello Lydia. I came to see how you were doing." He continued standing and staring, as if studying a paramecium under a microscope. "You don't look so good."

"I'm fine, Jack. Just tired out from everything. I think I may have caught a bug." She averted her eyes, no longer able to hold her head tilted up so she could see his face. "Why are you here?"

"Like I said, I wanted to see how you were doing. Not so well, I'm afraid. That's too bad. Maybe I can help you."

She shook her head slowly, back and forth. "No, Jack, it's not necessary. You don't have to help me. I'll be fine. Really." Her heart began to pound. "Why don't you leave now? I'm sorry you made the trip for nothing."

"Oh, don't worry. It wasn't for nothing. I have a client up here, in Bolton Landing. I have to meet with him tomorrow. I thought it'd be a good opportunity to check in on you. You know, talk about the house and the cabin. Get some things straightened out."

"My attorney is going to handle all that. I have nothing to say about it."

"Oh, but you do, Lydia. Don't feel like the matter is taken out of your hands. You have a lot to say. And I want you to know, I have no hard feelings. You got all you deserved. I was wrong. I finally came to my senses when I heard the judge's closing statement. He was right. I do own...I mean, owe you for the twenty-two years you devoted your life to me and the kids. All you did...the management of the house, our vacations, my money. You took care of it all, Lydia. I'm here to tell you how grateful I am."

Lydia's brain was caught in a tornado. She wondered if she was dreaming or was this unfamiliar facsimile of her ex-husband really standing here in front of her. He looked like Jack. He was wearing Jack's clothes. The ones he wore when he wasn't working. But, he didn't sound at all like Jack. Should she just close her eyes and rest her head back and sleep, or try to wake up?

"I appreciate what you're saying, Jack. I had no intention of hurting you. I wanted only an uncontested divorce...you remember that..."

"Hush, hush, let's not talk about that now. Let me get you something. Are you thirsty? Hungry?"

Now she knew this wasn't her ex-husband. Jack Myers never once in their years of married life ever offered to wait on her, or even get her a glass of water when he went to get one for himself, especially not when she was feeling under the weather. At those times he avoided her completely as if she had leprosy. He never could tolerate a state of weakness in anyone, not even the children. When they cried or needed their diapers changed, he would leave the room.

Sher lifted her hand to her forehead. "No. Thank you. I'm fine."

Jack sat down in the recliner and turned it so he was facing her. "You'd be warmer if you were in your own bed. Why don't I help you there?"

Bed. What was he thinking? Surely not. No. She'd never be able to fight him off if he forced her into bed.

She wanted to wail, but kept her composure. "I'm okay here. You could build a fire, if you want." Be nice. Just stay calm. Maybe he'll get tired and leave.

Jack got up and began preparing the fire. As he fumbled with the wood and fire starter, she sat back and closed her eyes. What could she do? How could she make him go? She couldn't even reach for her phone. It was in the bedroom, on the bedstand.

In minutes, a small fire was smoking and making a sputtering attempt to establish itself behind the chainmail curtain. Jack was never good at making fires.

She thought about Shawn. What would he think if he knew Jack was here with her, paying her a visit? Would she even tell him? Should she tell Jack he was coming to visit her? It would probably be best not to. It might instigate something in him that could be dangerous. She knew how he felt about Shawn long before the divorce. Now, it would surely launch a full-scale war if either side provoked the other. She trusted Shawn would maintain his composure and not do anything foolish, but Jack. He was unpredictable. He once took a swing at a fellow attorney who said something belittling to him, in jest. She once heard him make a priest curse. She saw him push people, even the kids, to the limit, just so he could enjoy watching them struggle to maintain composure. She'd called him on his behavior at those times. He laughed it off and told her she was making more of it than necessary. In his logic, she made it worse by her protesting.

He sat back down in the recliner and intertwined his fingers in a thoughtful pose.

"You know, Lydia, there was a lot I never had a chance to tell you. The trial went so fast and so much was overlooked. The judge was obviously biased toward your side. He usually does have inordinate sympathy for female plaintiffs. Must be that southern gentleman upbringing. An engrained Deep South matriarchal propensity. That, and being black, he tends to identify with the underdog and the scum of society. It makes for a poor judge, but, you know how it is. Affirmative Action. They had to meet their quota even in law school."

Here was the real Jack at his best. Lydia knew better than to contradict him or say anything to the contrary, not that she had the energy to do either. She'd lie back, let him ramble, do her best not to listen and give him the impression she was taking in every word he said.

Think of something else. Shawn. The kids. The lake. The shelter. Yes, she could think about being back at the shelter, among friends. Safe.

Jack sat up and leaned forward. "I think it's time we set the record straight, so to speak. You had your day in court. You had your little triumph. It was all stacked in your favor. I'm sure Shawn thought he'd done some amazing feat of representation, but, the truth is, a law student could have done the same. I accept that. My attorney was worse. A hopeless fuck up—a disillusioned lesbian who doesn't have the slightest chance of ever attracting a member of her species. She deluded herself into thinking she could be a hard hitter. A first-rate player. She should have stayed in college and taught law."

He paused, threw his head back and laughed.

"Before you go thinking I have anything against lesbians, might I remind you that I've worked with some, even hired one myself. A secretary. She was competent. She knew when to speak and when to keep her mouth shut. She was attractive, too. Not some mustached prison matron with a special dispensation from the pope to wear her legs upside down. Some of the guys in the office even hit on her before they realized. I admit my attorney fell short of being either competent or convincing. More's the pity, otherwise we'd be having a whole different kind of conversation, wouldn't we?"

Lydia refused to let her facial expression belie her feelings. All she could do was nod. This was Jack's idea of a conversation. He did all the talking, everyone else listened. Anything beyond that typically resulted in an argument during which Jack would argue relentlessly until the other party relinquished their stand or walked away. At every party they attended together, she noticed how people gravitated away instead of toward him. She used to tell herself it was his superior intellect. That it was intimidating. She was such a fool.

He got up and went to the kitchen. She heard cabinet doors opening and slamming, then the sound of something being poured. He returned to the room carrying a half-full tumbler in one hand and a bottle of Jameson's Irish whiskey in the other. It was the bottle Tom had bought and drank only a couple shots the last night of his visit. Jack did not do well with liquor. She knew from experience how it affected him.

"I see you're still hitting the bottle," he said. "Doesn't surprise me, out here all alone with nothing else to do but drink. I suppose when you get really lonely you bring home some local buck, some tree cutter or road worker. You like fucking with that class of people, don't you, Lydia?"

She looked down but said nothing, eyes blurring as she stared at her hands.

"So, I'm here to tell you my side of the story. I think it's important for you to know. All the years I worked to support you and the kids, all the hours I put in, all the times I had to tolerate, even kowtow to stupid, ignorant people. All the times I had to swallow my pride and eat shit and do what others wanted. You never heard me complain or bemoan my situation. Why? Because I was doing it for you. If I sought a little solace, a little physical comfort on the side, who could deny me that? I certainly wasn't getting it at home. You were always too busy with the kids, too involved with your charity work and fundraisers, too busy taking classes, too busy trying to make something of yourself."

Lydia knew what was coming next. She'd heard it before. The story of how he raised her up from poverty and mediocrity. The story of his elevation of her status in the world. She wanted to vomit, not only because of feeling nauseous all day, but because of the knot tying itself in her gut over what was coming.

"You were nothing when I met you at Columbia. A student on scholarship who barely had lunch money and had to borrow from friends till her financial aid check came in. Remember the time I bought two new tires for that heap of junk you called a car. An embarrassment is what it was." He took a long drink of the whiskey. "You were so grateful back then for everything I did for you. Little did you know it was the only way to get you to pry those intractable Catholic legs of yours apart." He laughed again, his tone derisive. "Remember the time I called a taxi to take you home when your car wouldn't start? You were so appreciative, you let me fuck you for the first time. Oh, and how you liked it when I lavished money on you. You know, that's where I made my mistake. I see it now. I baited you with money and you took the bait and hook and the whole goddamn line and ran with it. I bought you so easily. But then, the others were all the same way."

Lydia coughed and almost choked on her vomit. She stood up, barely able to maintain her balance. Reaching for the arm of the couch, she said, "I have to use the bathroom."

"I'll wait." Jack got up and put a couple logs on the fire which was barely showing any live embers.

When she returned and sat back down, she noticed he had turned the recliner and was now staring at the fireplace.

"You know my folks never approved of our marriage. They knew from the start I was marrying beneath me. They warned me. Mud doesn't mix with prime topsoil. Inferior metal doesn't turn into gold. And they were right, of course. But, being young, I had a mind of my own. I thought I could mold you, improve you, bring you up to standard. Not up to par, but just to an acceptable level so I wouldn't be embarrassed to be seen with you. Your friend, your attorney, Shawn O'Malley, knew he was no match, so he did the only thing he could do. He conceded. He withdrew from the game. Did he ever tell you what I used to call him? The ball-less wonder. I never liked him, you know. He was always a wimp. No matter what I threw at him, he never fought back, coward that he was. I guess that's why it's so fitting you two were drawn together. Like attracts like."

Lydia could take no more. "Jack, I'm really not feeling well. I need to go to bed."

In a soft, controlled voice, devoid of concern, Jack said, "No. Sit for a while. I'm not done. When I am, I'll let you go."

She sat back down and closed her eyes. *Shawn, please, Shawn. I need you right now. I want you with me, now. I can't do this alone.*

His voice changed now. It was sterner. More threatening. "You tried to take everything from me. My children. Did you know Tori sent me a long email telling me how much she hated my guts? My colleagues won't even talk to me except to discuss cases we're working on. You turned Serena against me, somehow, I don't know how, but I know you did. You had me followed in Paris, even to my hotel room. Did you ever stop to think what a violation of privacy that was? You set me up, videotaped me without my permission. You tried to bring me down. You even tried to ruin my career. But, you know, dear ex-wife, you never once succeeded. You only proved beyond a shadow of doubt how base and petty, how insidious you really are. You always hid behind that façade of being so wholesome—a vegetarian, a good mother, a lover of nature, an environmentalist, a humanitarian. Oh yes, you were generous, alright. With my money. It didn't hurt you at all to throw it at the beggars and low-lifes, the perverts and queers. You know it disgusted me that you paraded around Paris with that disgusting queen, Weatherstone, or whatever the hell his name is. The pathetic pansy. I often wondered if you weren't of a homosexual bent yourself, you seemed to enjoy being in their company so much. You and your gay entourage are just caricatures of people. People with no substance. All hedonists, narcissists. You always found pleasure in the most perverse of things and always passed yourself off as someone you're not."

Jack's face was dark now. Ominous. Lydia had all she could do to stand up and stay upright. Her head was swimming, eyes felt fuzzy and blurred. Even her breath was coming in shorter and shorter gasps. She really did need medical attention, and she knew she wasn't going to get it. It was pitch dark outside now. She heard a coyote cry in the distance. An owl gave a low mournful series of hoots just outside the window. She started to walk toward the bedroom, but had to hold onto the back of the sofa.

Jack took another drink and continued. "You can do whatever you want now. You have all the means. All the money I worked so hard for. It's a pity there really is no justice in this world. But, you know, Lydia. It will catch up with you. You won't enjoy it for long. You're getting old. Your youth and beauty are slipping away every day. Have you taken a good look at yourself lately? You're washed up already. Dissipated."

She thought back to her image in the mirror this morning and shuddered. No. She was not going to let him get to her. She had to get away from him. Her head was splitting.

"Jack, just please tell me, what do you want? If it's money, you have it. If it's the cabin, or the house, you have it. Just tell me what you want from me and I'll give it to you. Then leave. Please, leave me in peace. I'm sick. I have to rest."

Jack stood up. "I'll leave when I'm damned good and ready."

She felt herself losing her grip on the couch as her knees buckled. She leaned across it, trying to balance herself. Her head was swimming.

"I have to go to bed now." She heard herself speaking the words as they reverberated in her mind. "You can leave anytime. I can't listen to this anymore."

The next thing she knew, she was on the floor. The wood was cool against her cheek. Had he hit her and knocked her down or had she fallen on her own? Her head was throbbing. She thought she heard a knock at the door. Voices. One was Jack's. The other sounded familiar, but whose was it? She heard bits of the conversation.

"Alright then, Mr. O'Connor. I'm glad to hear she has family with her. Enjoy your stay."

That voice…it was someone she knew. Not a neighbor, but someone… someone from here, someone from the area.

The door slammed and she heard the click of the lock. Car tires crunched on the gravel of the driveway.

Jack walked into the living room and stood over her.

"Nice to know you're being looked after. Some dumbass cop checking to see if the lady of the house is snug and safe inside. I assured him you were. Halfwit locals."

Lydia tried to push herself up onto her elbows. If she could get to her knees, there was a chance she could stand up. Jack was busy pouring the rest of the whiskey into his tumbler. He took a gulp, swallowed, and let out a belch.

"Come on, girl, you can do it." He laughed as she pulled herself to her knees. "Atta girl, keep going. Maybe you'll make it, maybe you won't."

Sobs were strangling her throat as Jack grabbed her by the wrists and forced her up.

"Stand on your own two feet, me bucko. You never did before. Might as well start now. You won't be needing me to hold you up and carry you along as always, pathetic gold digger that you are." He braced her with his hands and brought his face close to hers. "We're going for a boat ride. How does that sound?"

Chapter 33

Lydia stumbled down the path, propelled by one arm that had a tight grip on her waist while the other kept her upright and shoved her along.

"Just think how romantic it'll be, just you and me on the water under the twinkling stars and...look, a new moon." He stopped when they reached the rowboat overturned on the lawn.

"Jack, no. Don't. Please don't." She tried to shout, but the words sounded like whispers in her ears. "No....no...Jack....please....don't do this....please...let me go."

He pushed the boat into the water and lifted her in. "Wouldn't want to get those pretty feet of yours wet, now would we?"

She gripped both sides of the boat as he shoved off. The air was having an interesting effect on her senses. She felt she could breathe better, more deeply, and her headache was lessening to a dull ache. Though still trembling inside, she felt less nauseous and was noticing for the first time how thirsty she was. There was nothing left in her to throw up. She would have sold her soul for a bottle of water right now.

"Where are we going?"

Jack sang out loudly. "Where oh where has my Lydia gone? Where oh where can she be?"

"Jack, stop this now. I want you to turn around. Bring me back to shore. You can take the boat anywhere you want. I have to get back."

Jack was slurring his words now. He had consumed the entire bottle of Jameson's because she saw it lying empty on the floor as he dragged her out of the cabin.

"Next stop, all aboard, prepare to disembark. Hope you remembered to wear your floaties."

Lydia felt some strength returning, at least to her lungs. As loudly as she could, she shouted, "Jack, no. Turn around. Don't do this. Stop. Jack. Stop. Help!"

She heard distant music wafting across the water, probably from a beach south of them. She saw lights in the distance from shore side restaurants, but couldn't tell where in the water they were or how far from shore. She could try to swim, only she knew she didn't have the strength.

"Help," she screamed as loudly as she could. "Help, someone. Help."

"Shut the fuck up," Jack bellowed, his voice echoing across the mountains. "Shut your goddamn fucking peasant mouth. Shut your lying whore mouth, you cunt!" He stood up and reached for her.

The next thing Lydia knew, she was in the water. Her bathrobe opened wide and spread out, sucking up water, becoming like an anchor around her. Her slippers and socks filled with water and pulled her down. She kicked them off. The water was frigid, the coldest she'd ever felt it. Her body was beginning to fold into an unbendable lump of cold metal.

Something Vito told her came to mind. *When the water's freezing, think warm, breathe warm...and move. Move as much as you can.* She saw Jack standing up in the boat, oar in hand, yelling.

"I'm king! King of the goddamn lake. King of the deep. King George of fucking Lake George!"

Lydia summoned all her strength, reached up and grabbed the side of the boat with both hands and pulled. Jack let out a scream as he toppled headfirst into the water, then came up sputtering. She knew it wasn't to her advantage to be in the water with him. He could easily take her under and hold her there with one hand. She had to think fast, do something, anything to disable him, and quickly. She dove under, unhooked his trousers and pulled them down to his knees.

The next sounds that came from him were guttural, animal-like, and incomprehensible. She found the oar he'd released and grabbed it with both hands. Raising it over her head she brought it down hard.

Crack. The sound meant she'd hit her mark. Jack didn't cry out, but he wasn't going down either. He was uttering curses as she kept her grip on the boat. The next thing she knew, he had her by the ankles and was pulling her toward him. She tried to kick, but his grip was too tight.

"Get away. Help! Help!" She heard her words repeat in the distance.

She could see lights nearby. Were they coming closer or just on the shore? She couldn't tell. He grabbed again and yanked her hard. She tried with all her might not to lose her grip on the boat, to no avail. She let go. Vito's voice shouted in her mind. *Use everything you got. You don't play fair when your life is on the line.*

The oar bumped her face. She grabbed it, shortened up on the handle, rolled onto her back as Jack pulled her away from the boat, then rammed it down past his arms with all her might. Whatever part of him she hit, she couldn't tell, but it mattered. His hand released her, he screamed once, then she saw him disappear under the water. For a few moments he was gone. Then she felt his hands on her ankles. Before she went completely under, she heard him scream, "Now, dearest wife, you're going to...."

He pulled her down between his legs and straddled her.

Lydia didn't know how long she was under. She didn't remember anything until she spewed water from her lungs and drew in a gasp of air, choking and sputtering, struggling to breathe again. Someone was wrapping a towel around her, lifting her.

Warmth. Heat. Lovely, delicious body heat. She melted into it as she gasped.

"You're safe now. You're alright. It's over."

She didn't want to open her eyes. It didn't matter anymore. She was out of the water, breathing air, her body responding to a warm touch that was now kneading her skin.

"We're almost there."

She recognized the voice but didn't believe it. It couldn't be. It sounded like Shawn, but how? No. She was dreaming. Hallucinating. Maybe she was dead. Was this what death was like? All wet and shivering, trembling and gasping for air? Her mind drifted away. Everything turned dark and soundless.

A sound like ticking, followed by beeping noises awakened her. She ached, her head hurt, but she felt oddly warm and dry. If she hadn't been so groggy, she might have recognized the man sitting beside her bed, fast asleep, head resting back, mouth slightly open. She stared for several minutes before he twitched and his mouth closed. Next, his eyes opened and peered back at her. Blue sapphire orbs.

"Hey, little buddy." He took her hand and squeezed it.

"Hey, Skipper." She smiled and beamed at him. "First question, where are we? Second question, how did we get here?"

He leaned over and kissed her forehead. "First answer. We're in the Land of Oz, not to be confused with Ozzie and Harriet, a decent sitcom, granted, except that we'd never fit the stereotypes. Second answer, we got here by magic carpet."

"I see. And do you have three wishes to grant me?"

"I think you're getting your fairy tales confused. I'll take you for a ride on my carpet and maybe we'll find a lamp to rub. If we're lucky, a genie will pop out and grant us three wishes. How does that sound?"

"One more question. Is this a dream?"

Shawn smiled broadly, then gathered her up in his arms, careful not to upset her IV. "Yes, you're dreaming, my love. I'm your dream angel, you're my dream fairy, and we're on a dream adventure. Once I get you out of here, that is."

"Oh, I don't know about that. This is a pretty awesome palace."

Someone knocked at the door. She recognized the familiar face.

"Just checking to see how my most interesting Lake George resident is doing. Feeling any better?"

Lydia realized that she no longer felt nauseous, her headache was gone and she was voraciously hungry. "Officer Mancini. I'm fine. How are you?"

"Well, all things considered, now that I'm in dry clothes, I'd say I'm doing pretty good."

Lydia tried to lift her head off the pillow. "If I wasn't vegan, I'd say I could eat a horse. "How about a tofu horse?" Shawn offered.

Officer Mancini and Shawn exchanged glances. Mancini spoke first. "Which one wants to tell her the story and which one's going on a food run?"

Shawn stood up. "I'll take food reconnaissance. You can brief her. After all, you were there before I arrived on the scene."

Officer Paul Mancini held his hat in his hands as he straddled a chair close to the bed.

"I'm glad you're okay, Lydia. I had a feeling when I came to the house and saw who was there, something was up. Obviously, he didn't remember seeing me at the trial. Guess my expert testimony wasn't that impressive. At any rate, when he wouldn't let me in, and I didn't see you, my hackles went up so I called for backup. We got back just as you were about fifty yards from the shore. My partner and I took possession of the two kayaks, after we called an ambulance." He hesitated, coughed, and continued. "I got to you just as your husband, sorry, your ex-husband, was dragging you under."

"How did you stop him?"

"Hm. Good question. Let's just say it took a little pistol persuasion." He put a finger to his lips. "The butt end of my gun across the temple. Works like a charm." My partner and I got you up into the boat and he rowed you back to shore, after pumping quite a bit of the lake out of you. I dragged your ex back, as much as I wished I could have left him there."

"What about Shawn?"

"He arrived just in time to lift you out of the boat and carry you up to the paramedics. They took over from there. He's a good man. I like him."

Lydia paused, not sure she wanted to know the next answer. "And Jack? Where is he?"

"There's no need to worry about him. Suffice it to say, he has a nice suite in the county jail. He'll sleep it off and wake up to a host of criminal charges tomorrow. He smelled like he'd been hitting the bottle pretty heavily."

She looked away for a moment, seeing the room around her for the first time. A nurse came in to check her vitals.

"You're looking so much better, Mrs..." She looked at her chart. "O'Connor. Any longer in that house and you might not be in such good shape." The nurse patted her shoulder. "Carbon monoxide poisoning is nothing to sneeze about."

Lydia looked up, confused. "What did you say?"

For the briefest moment, the nurse looked puzzled, as though she might have had the wrong patient chart. "You came in suffering from carbon monoxide poisoning. Did you notice any flu-like symptoms? Headache, nausea, chills, fatigue? Those propane heaters people use in their cabins this time of year bring a lot of business our way."

"I wasn't using a propane heater. I turned on the furnace."

The nurse exchanged glances with the officer, then left the room. She stopped at the door to say. "I'm glad you're feeling better. You should be going home tomorrow. Sleep well."

Chapter 34

Nothing is as it always was
Nothing ever stays the same
Nothing ever turns out as planned
Nothing was, it simply is

The words of the song replayed in her mind like an old scratched record album, bringing her mood lower than it had been for the past few days. She finished slamming the supper dishes into the drainer, tidied the kitchen by throwing things in the cupboard, and prepared to take her final exam in Methods and Practices in Counseling. It was her last exam, the final that would mark the culmination of years of study and endless papers, projects, and practicums. The end of her program. She was neither anxious nor eager to begin it. It wasn't that she wasn't ready or hadn't prepared adequately. She was furious.

She'd devoted hours to studying, completed all the readings, kept up with the message boards and written all the papers. Her final research paper earned an A minus. Minus because her damned professor had to exercise his scholarly prerogative to nail her on some misplaced quotation mark in the APA formatting. As if it mattered. Academic arrogance was all it was. Another pompous professor attempting to exert inauthentic power. She was sick of it.

As far as she was concerned, it was all meaningless. She wrote about the importance of genuineness in a counseling relationship. As if anyone really knew what genuineness was or what it looked like. She liked to think she was genuine, but then, didn't she, like everyone else, present a façade to others? A persona to disguise and hide all her private misgivings, her fears and insecurities, and all her unacceptable thoughts, such as the ones she was having right now about Jack. If her thoughts were made known, she'd probably be regarded as dangerous or, at best, unhinged. A counselor with homicidal ideation. She once thought of him as genuine and look what he turned out to be. A flaming narcissistic sociopath.

Such were the thoughts feeding the fire of her rage when the phone chimed and she saw it was Shawn. She let it go to voicemail. She was in no mood.

Once again, she found herself at Jack's mercy, needing protection, being cautioned by everyone—the police, her kids, her doctor, Vito, and especially Shawn. "Take special measures to ensure your safety. Don't leave any doors or windows unlocked. Let people know where you are at all times. Don't go out after dark, get a weapon." The last one was from Vito who promised he'd teach her how to use it. At least she'd convinced Shawn she didn't need his bodyguard services around the clock, which he tried to press on her. "Always have your cell phone with you. Watch where you park, be sure to look under the car and in the back seat before you get in. Carry a whistle." The advice never ceased.

For all intents and purposes, she was a walking target. She might as well go to the hardware store and buy one to wear on her back.

She didn't want a weapon. She didn't want to live in fear. She wanted her life back. Divorce was supposed to have freed her from Jack, but now he was a bigger menace than ever. And how could such a person, such a maniac, be allowed to walk free after menacing, threatening, assaulting and coming damn close to taking her life? Money was the answer. Money was his ticket to freedom. And misguided family support. His parents would never allow their golden boy to spend more than a few hours behind bars. He was out of jail before he even warmed the bench.

Sure, the protective order was in place, and she knew enough from other people's experiences, from her own counseling training, and from Shawn's warning, that it was not a protective shield or a bullet-proof vest. It was no guarantee of safety. Just a piece of paper. Except that, in Jack's case, it was the proverbial red flag waved tauntingly in the bull's face.

Damn it all to hell, it wasn't fair.

There was no holding back the angry tears that welled up. None of this was fair. Just on the brink of finishing her master's program, just in the early stages of a new and promising relationship, just beginning to nurture the fragile bud of a relationship that wasn't quite ready to unfold and she felt no joy. Not even a spark of enthusiasm for any of it.

She couldn't feel happy. Jack was sucking the joy out of her life like an incubus, draining her of energy and hope. Would she ever feel differently? What made it worse was the thought that she was allowing him to do this to her. She was still letting him exert a Svengali-like influence on her because there was only one way to stop him, which was illegal, not to mention insane. She was intact enough to know she had to stop ruminating about it. If she acted on impulse, she could see herself spending the remaining years of her life working, as Shawn once said jokingly, in a prison mail room. Being a woman, she'd probably get kitchen duty and have to make mystery meat dishes for the other inmates.

She had to think of other things. Shawn. Dear, sweet, wonderful, loving, sexy, humorous, hard-working, though a bit obsessed with work, Shawn. He saved her life, with some help from the police officers, of course. He carried her to safety, stayed with her at the hospital and brought her home. He helped her get settled, saw to the repair of the hijacked furnace (obvious to the repairer that it was an intentional rerouting of the duct to flood exhaust into the bedroom). He was there for her every minute for two whole days.

He fielded phone calls from reporters, law enforcers, neighbors, even a priest from the Church of all Saints a few miles down the road. He made her meals, shopped for groceries, and cleaned up the cabin. Though he tried to conceal it, she caught a glimpse of the Jameson's bottle that had been on the living room floor as he carried it out to the trash. The streak of blood on it was her own. He stocked the wood pile and made lovely fires for both of them and they enjoyed them, snuggled together on the couch.

When she tried to do things, he ushered her to a chair or the couch, telling her she could keep him company but not lift a finger. She spent the time reading and studying. Her final exam was coming up. When she awoke in the middle of the night in a panic, believing she was being pulled to the bottom of the lake by a giant squid, he comforted her and rocked her in his arms till she fell back to sleep.

Then he went back to work leaving her with a list of admonitions and cautions. He had to go back. His life was in the city. Hers was here in the cabin. Life was cruel. To get really cliché about it, she recalled the words of another song. *Love hurts.* Her life was turning into a daytime TV drama. A Country-Western song.

How ironic that Shawn said how he admired the way she handled everything. If only he knew. She had been quaking inside. The thought of what happened still caused her to feel nauseous. Never in her life had she felt so weak and helpless. She thought she'd be better off taking up with Terrence Warshawsky. They could spend their time flinching at sounds and talking about what frightened them the most. She was becoming neurotic. Jack had finally succeeded in pushing her off the ledge and the thought of that made her even madder. But it did something else to her. It was the impetus behind her resolve not to let herself wallow and feel sorry for herself. Not dwell on what had happened and be drawn into the mire.

She would fight back by being stronger, tougher, and more resilient that she ever believed possible. After all, he hadn't killed her, as much as he tried. And if there was justice, he would suffer the consequences. It didn't make her feel any better when Shawn made some remark about him being placed in some exclusive prison resort where he'd be in the company of celebrities and corporate criminals enjoying golfing privileges and being waited on during an obscenely brief incarceration.

Shawn assured her things would get better and everything would work out. They had each other. But they didn't. He wasn't here, and she wasn't going back to the city. She couldn't think about that right now. Everything was too tumultuous, too unsettled. She was too raw and nowhere near stable enough to think reasonably about anything, much less a romantic relationship. It was enough to have Shawn as her friend. A very loving friend, but a friendship, nonetheless. Shawn was perfect. She couldn't ask for any one better. It simply wasn't the time. She wasn't ready.

She assured him her heart was linked with his and always would be. To promise any more wasn't possible. They didn't talk about the future of the relationship or even joke about the possibility of marriage. Shawn was intuitive enough to know she wasn't ready and for that she was grateful.

Her twisted and subjective views on the subject would surely have injured him. She knew from their early years together that he venerated marriage as a sacrament, as any good Catholic boy was taught to do. Right now, in her mind, marriage was a trap, a sentence, a poisonous binding contract that had the potential of being lethal. She hoped she wouldn't always feel this way, but right now she did and she wasn't about to let go of her disillusionment.

She finished the exam in two hours and submitted it online with little sense of relief and more a heaviness in her heart. Exams and papers aside, she'd miss the contacts she'd made on the message board, especially some of her friends in foreign countries and one in Hawaii whom she made plans already to visit sometime in the coming year and to whom she extended an invitation to visit her in New York.

The next days passed in a blur. She spent time working at the shelter, helping in the kitchen and doing filing for Ron in the office. When they were available, she sketched some of the residents. Ron said he'd try to find funding to hire her, but it was always a sketchy proposition and he never knew when or from where his funding would come. The shelter needed work and he was always looking for some source of undesignated funds to handle the repairs. He had enough money for day-to-day operations, but beyond that, the grants were small and usually particular about how the money was to be spent.

The roof needed repair and the plumbing issues had gone from serious to crying in agony for attention. Lydia offered to give him the money he needed to replace the roof and install all new plumbing as soon as her settlement money came in. He thanked her for the offer, but said he'd look for funding first before he considered draining her resources. It would cost a small fortune to keep the building in halfway decent shape and no one needed to carry that burden alone. Still, knowing it was a possibility that emergency help was available put his mind at ease. He wanted her to work for him, but, for the time being, having her as a volunteer was the next best thing.

In between running and walking around the lake, Lydia spent time on the phone answering people's calls of concern, assuring them she was fine, fully recovered, with no residual damage. Then she had to listen to their outcries and declarations of animosity against Jack. It didn't make her feel any better for others to take her side. The call that surprised her the most came from Serena. She wept over the phone and apologized for being the "other woman" who came between her and Jack and ruined their marriage. As for Jack, she summed him up as a slimy slithering snake who deserved to be crushed under people's feet and eaten by vultures. Lydia liked her graphic disposal of him. Serena told her she was repenting by doing novenas on her knees and lighting candles every day, praying not only for God's, but Lydia's forgiveness, as well.

Lydia said she forgave her, adding that she needn't worry. She didn't hold a grudge. She also said her novenas and candles had to count for something, not that she could speak for God. Whether it helped or not, she wanted Serena to know she hadn't been the cause of the divorce, nor the cause of the rift between her and Jack. That chasm had formed long before Serena arrived on the scene in her stiletto heels and low-cut sweaters.

The real challenge was her parents. When she finally gave in and called them, she sat back, laid the phone down on the table, and listened as her mother, Mary Anne O'Connor, wailed and moaned for a good twenty minutes. She used the time to finish a sketch of the lake she'd started days ago.

"I was so worried when I heard the news. Of course, I had no idea. No one calls me anymore. I never know what's going on with my children. I don't know where I went wrong. What I did to deserve this? I just can't imagine Jack behaving that way. Did you do or say anything to upset him?"

"Probably so, ma." Her mother hated to be called ma, saying it was the name of a mother goat. "I'm sure I must have done something to make him want to kill me."

He mother gasped. She could see her clutching her breast.

"Please, don't say that. I can't listen to that. My heart can't take it."

"Okay, then. I'll try harder to soften it for you." Lydia picked up her kneaded eraser and went to work on an errant tree limb. "When Jack tried to teach me a lesson by attempting to drown me."

"And you went and got divorced before telling me. Before I could even have Father Noonan talk to you. Bless us and save us. You know it's against the church. You were raised Catholic. You went to Catholic school. I don't dare ask if you go to mass anymore."

"Actually I did attend mass in Paris not too long ago."

"Oh, thank the Lord for small blessings. But you probably are excommunicated by now, anyway, whether you went or not. After all, you married outside the church, and a protestant at that. I did my best to stop you. I don't know where I went wrong, but you never listened to me as a child or an adult. You probably aren't listening to me now."

"Oh, I am. You're coming through loud and clear." Fortunately, she knew when her mother was in one of her self-pitying rants, she didn't hear anything anyone else was saying. It helped.

"You were such a willful child. Just like your sister. No, Theresa's even worse. You know I haven't heard from her in over a year."

"A demon from hell, I'm sure, ma."

Lydia knew for a fact that Theresa called their mother a week ago because they talked for three hours only yesterday. Every so often, in between erasing, smudging, and shading, she would interject, "I know, ma." "Yes, it's a tragedy." "It's been so hard on you."

When her mother ran out of steam, her father, Liam O'Connor, came on the line. That caused her to get up and bring a bottle of wine and a glass back to the table. It was only four in the afternoon but she was going to participate in someone's happy hour, no matter where in the world it was. She poured herself a glass while her father started in.

"What I just don't get is how the two of you, with all Jack's money and his good job, and the beautiful house you have, and all the things he's done for you…what I just don't get it, why wasn't that enough? I mean, you were living the dream. You had it all. What went wrong?"

If it wasn't so close to the truth, such a ludicrous question might have made her burst out laughing, which she knew would only annoy her father.

"You're right, dad. We did have it all. We were living the dream. In fact, we had more than *it all*. Jack had mistresses and a secret life. He had money in offshore accounts I knew nothing about. He had control of everything. He had me followed by a detective because he hoped he could catch me cheating to ease his own conscience, not that he has one. Oh, and did I mention he tried to kill me? Twice? Yep, I'd say that, as far as most American families go, we really did have it all."

She waited as her father took time to process what she said.

"He had mistresses?"

"Yep, at least two I know of, but there were others. I just didn't try to find out about them all."

"And he tried to kill you?"

"Yep, again, dad. You can read the hospital report if you want. It's also in the newspapers. He first sent someone to cut me up with a knife. When that failed, he tried doing the job himself, first, with carbon monoxide poisoning, then by drowning me. Oh, and that was after he smashed a bottle of Jameson's over my head."

"What? Jameson's? A full bottle?"

She knew that would get his attention. Her father considered Jameson's the Holy Grail of whiskeys. Only the Irish could do it right.

"No. Empty. He'd polished it off before he swung it at my head."

She knew that came as a relief to her father. How anyone could assault someone with a bottle of Jameson's and waste a drop of it was beyond belief. She waited, imagining the cogs turning in his brain, trying to line up and put everything he heard into some meaningful context. Just as she expected, he managed to.

"You know this has been hard on your mother and me. We've had trouble sleeping ever since we heard the news from Tom."

Knowing Tom, he'd given them a colorful and annotated version of the facts.

"Yes, I'd imagine it would have disturbed your sleep. It did mine, too."
Try having a squid pulling you down the bottom of the lake every night. Or a madman dragging you down a path in a pitch dark forest, or pushing you headfirst into a vat of boiling black oil.

"I never really liked Jack. He didn't go to church. He didn't like to come to family dinners. He tried to tell me once how to repair a truck engine, like he ever got grease on his hands."

She had to catch herself before she tried to defend Jack's not needing to know about things mechanical. Old script. Strike through it.

The conversation was giving her a headache so she decided to apply one of the skills she'd just learned in her program about establishing boundaries.

"Okay, dad, mom. I know you've been through a lot and this has been very upsetting for you both. You must be tired out from this conversation and all the worry I've caused you. So, let's call it a day. I'm going to let you go. Take care now, both of you. Love you."

As usual at the end of their conversations, her mother would deliver her last platitudes.

"Lydia, before you go, there's something I have to say. It's time you came back to the church. I don't know if you can be accepted back, but you should try. Find a good Catholic church near you. And say your beads every day. The Blue Army will be praying for you, too."

Her mother was referring to their latest Catholic movement—an attempt to apply militancy to the praying of the rosary. Lydia and Tom used to joke about their parents marching in uniform, goose-stepping and wearing armbands with crucifixes on them.

"Return to your faith, Lydia. We'll be praying for you every day."

"Thank you, mother and dad. You two are the best. Good luck with the Blue Army."

Before hanging up, she heard her mother slipping in one last invective. "…and be sure to ask God for forgiveness for your divorce."

Chapter 35

A long trek around the lake and a plunge into icy water followed by a shivering toweling down left Lydia feeling a modicum of sanity returning. She wanted to keep running, but five miles was all she could manage, given that she was recuperating. She still felt moments of weakness throughout the day and wondered if any permanent brain damage had occurred from the carbon monoxide. She probably could stand some psychotherapy at some point for posttraumatic stress. At least now she could diagnose herself.

Walking back to the cabin, she began to feel more cheerful. It was about time. After getting dressed in her most comfortable, over-sized sweat pants and a fleece top, she was ready to respond to Shawn's third call of the day. The other two she'd let go to voicemail.

He sounded concerned, starting the conversation with, "Are you okay, bud? You had me worried. Look, do you think you could send me text messages during the day? I don't mean every hour, but just a few to let me know how you're doing...and, you know. I'm not trying to be controlling. I just..."

She interrupted. "I know Shawn, and I'm sorry. I've just been a bit overwhelmed with the outpouring of caring and concern I'm getting." She told him about her conversation with her parents last night, after which she was in no mood to talk with anyone. She spared him most of the details of that train wreck.

"So you're excommunicated, eh? Well, I must be, too. We should start a club. Maybe we should take a trip to Rome and tell her we had a private audience with the pope. We could tell your mother he said we were still in good standing as long as our dues were paid up."

"I think she'd have her doubts. My mother is so firm in her belief that even the pope wouldn't be able to convince her we were forgiven. She'd argue with God over that."

"Well, we could go the Southern route and be baptized in a river. Washed in the blood of the lamb, cleansed of our iniquities. You know, we never got to enjoy our own baptisms, babes that we were. It might be kind of cool to wear the white robes and be dunked backwards into the water."

Lydia forced a chuckle. "I think I got my baptizing a week ago." It was time to change the subject. "Hey, I have some good news. I finished my program. Sent my final in. I'm done. I'm a counselor now. Well, not licensed yet, but almost. Gotta put some time in the trenches first."

Shawn gave a cheer. "That's awesome, Lyd. Wow. You completed a final after recovering from…well, never mind. I think your professor should slap a purple heart on your diploma. I hope you get an A for Absolutely Awesome on your performance."

"That would be AA, which I'd take as a subliminal suggestion that I need to quit the bottle. He's more likely to reprimand me for using the wrong pronoun because I referred to the client as 'she,' not 'he,' which is something I always found offensive and exclusive."

"Ever the liberated woman. You go get 'em, buddy. If anybody deserves to kick chauvinistic butt, it's you." He paused, realizing what he said, inwardly cursing himself when he'd been trying hard not to bring up recent events. "Sorry, I'm really trying to steer clear but, well, you know…I'm an asshole."

"No. Don't say that. It's hard to not let the elephant in the room go out for a leak once in a while."

"Buddy, did you just make that up? Huh? I'm borrowing that one."

"Yeah, well, I do charge royalties for my pithy sayings."

"Speaking of pithy, not that what you said has any connection whatsoever to what I'm about to say, unless you think of the word pits, which reminded me of black olives, which triggered a memory of a pizza I had recently. Sorry. So, what I'm leading up to in a very convoluted way is, how about dinner next weekend here in the city? It may entail having to spend the weekend at my place. What do you say?"

"I find that shamelessly coercive and witness leading."

"Uh, coercive, yes, but witness leading, not hardly. Well, maybe if you stretched it a lot. More like obfuscation of the facts. At any rate, I stand accused. Can you do it? I have a special eatery I want to take you to."

She had an immediate flash of a woman sitting across the table from Shawn in a restaurant, nibbling something he was feeding to her with his fork. Jealousy? Surely not.

"Meaning an eatery you experienced with someone else and you want to see how it compares when you're with me?"

"Kind of like that. I went with Jeff Lipschitz from the office. Guess what his nickname is?"

Lydia let out a groan. "I'd rather not."

"Bugsy. Ha! See, we're not all nitwits here. Anyway, Lipschitz, aka Bugsy, said he'd been there before and really liked it, so he talked me into going. It's a Thai, Indonesian, Indian, Middle East fusion kind of place with great high-backed chairs and thick Turkish rugs. The waiters wear those long pajama tops with baggy pants and turbans. Jeff was an okay date, by the way, but he didn't care for the wine I chose and he refused to kiss me good-night. Thought maybe I'd have better luck with you."

There was a moment of sudden, painful longing for everything to be the way it used to be with Shawn. Because it wasn't possible, she would have settled for halfway back to normal, for life to be nearly the same, only better than it was before now because they were together. Almost.

A sudden cascade of emotion had her fumbling to find words. She didn't want to leave the lake, she couldn't bear the thought of going back to the city, and it hurt to think she and Shawn would be separated by her own fears and insecurities.

The pause was awkward and long enough that Shawn had to break the silence.

"Hey, buddy. Did I lose you? I understand if you can't do it, Lyd. I just wanted to …well, to see you again. Quite honestly. I'm having quite a time just trying to chase thoughts of you out of my mind for more than a few minutes at a time. I'm afraid I'm going to start interjecting 'Lydia,' or 'buddy,' into all my sentences. You know how embarrassing that would be in court?" He lowered his voice to a serious tone. "Your honor, in this current *Lydia*, er, litigation, I would ask that the *buddy*, er, the brother of the defendant would please refrain from discussing the *sex*, excuse me, the six different times he... Are you getting the picture?"

When she stopped laughing, Lydia wiped her eyes and said, "I get it. A real hazard to your profession."

She so wanted to be with him. Her heart was aching to be there, sitting on his couch, sharing a bowl of popcorn with him, laughing till her face hurt and she was burping her wine. Going to the city was a bigger mountain than she was ready to climb.

"Let's take a raincheck on that, Shawn." She bit her lip. "It sounds great and I promise I'd kiss you good night and maybe even hold your hand, and I'd surely love your choice of wine, if it wasn't too sweet, but... I'm just not ready. The very thought of going back, to being anywhere even remotely in proximity to... Well, you know. I just can't do it right now."

In the past, whenever she caught herself in a mood of self-pity, or negativity, she rallied against it. Now, she had no defenses. The solid stone fortress she'd built around her was impenetrable and she had no desire to break it down. Not even for Shawn.

"Buddy, I get it. I know you'll be over this soon. I don't want to pressure you. Just let me know when you're ready. I'd come up there if I could, but it's just not going to happen right now. Work is a cruel and demanding..." He almost said mistress, but changed his mind. "Taskmaster."

They talked for a few minutes longer until they were both reassured that everything would be okay. They were still together, no matter the distance between them. After they hung up, Lydia decided to check her email to see if she had a return message from her professor acknowledging the receipt of her exam. Technology, especially when it came to your future career and livelihood, wasn't to be trusted implicitly. She saw the message. It was terse as usual. She'd never met the professor, but she had a picture in her mind of a short, homely man with a perpetual scowl on his face and a broomstick handle up his behind. At least she was done with him and the program was over. She thought she'd feel elated. What a letdown.

But wait. There was another message.

After reading the email twice, Lydia walked out on the back deck and down to the water's edge. The sound of soft dance music, something from the fifties, one of those *Baby, oh Baby* songs, floated on the breeze. Before she knew it, her hips were swaying slightly back and forth.

She thought of Shawn, the two of them dancing together, perhaps on a cruise boat, the lights of the city sparkling on the water, the Eiffel Tower in the distance, illuminating the night sky. She thought of all the places she'd love to take him, all the food she'd introduce him to. All the lovely places lovers went to feel their souls soar and their passion ignite.

She looked at the ring on her finger, now catching a glint from the full moon. The shiny fourteen-carat gold Claddagh smiled back at her. She hadn't wanted to accept it, but he assured her it wasn't an engagement ring or even a promise ring. It was just a gift. A token of his admiration and something to let her know how he felt about her. A long overdue gift. It brought a tear to her eye that spilled over and inched down her cheek.

Jack's face loomed before her eyes and her mood changed.

She no longer wanted to be afraid. She refused to let herself live a life of looking back over her shoulder, wondering if and when he might be stalking her, waiting for another chance to get her. This wasn't her idea of living, cowering in a dark cave of fear and dread, outside of which a world of beauty, joy and adventure existed. How could she live from day to day never knowing what to expect or what to prepare for? How could she go on always having to look back over her shoulder, obsessed with setting all the new locks on the doors and windows and never forgetting to activate the alarm system Shawn insisted on having installed?

No. She wasn't going to live this way. She was going to begin a fresh new script of her unmarried life. She refused to let Jack plague her mind. She was going to prove how infinitely stronger than this she was.

Which was why she went back inside the cabin and called the number.

"Hello, Ellie? It's me, Lydia O'Connor. Oui, c'est vrai. I'm divorced now."

She heard loud exclamations, then listened as he spoke to someone else in the room, evoking sounds of cheering and clapping in the background. It was Nicole. Witherspoon put her on the phone.

"Lydia! Bonjour! I am so happy for you. Oh my god, the baby is happy, too! She's jumping for joy! We are both so happy."

They talked for a few minutes until Witherspoon insisted on taking back the phone. Vito's name did not come up.

"Now listen here, you unmarried hussy. There's no better place to celebrate your independence than here and you know it. So what do you say? Nicole and I are waiting for an answer. When will you come to your senses and get your pretty little derrière back on French soil?"

Lydia found herself shedding tears of joy. They were the words she needed to hear but hadn't known it until this moment.

"As soon as I can get a ticket and pack my bags. Please tell Jacqueline I'm coming and tell her not to put me in my old room. Anywhere else in the Hotel St. Claire would be fine, as long as I can see the Eiffel Tower."

That night, standing at the shoreline, she watched the lights from the distant village sparkle and dance on the rippling water. At the same time, across the ocean, the shimmering lights of the Eiffel Tower grew dim in the early morning light. Lydia O'Connor went back inside, smiling at the thought. She made her plans, booked her flight and went to sleep, comforted by the thought that her worries would soon be over.

Sometime in the night, she found herself seated on a magic carpet, her arms wrapped around the waist of a skipper who was really a prince in disguise. He was laughing as he steered the flying carpet with great precision, taking them over sea and land until they finally arrived at their destination. There, as the carpet dipped so low she could lean over and see her reflection, she trailed her fingers in the waters of the River Seine.